Dear Yootha... The Life of Yootha Joyce

Paul Curran

First Published by Mossy Books
mossybooks@gmail.com
Copyright © Paul Curran, 2014

A CIP catalogue record for this book is
available from the British Library.

ISBN-13: 978-1494911645
ISBN-10: 1494911647

For Mum & Dad.

Also for John, a great help in getting me going!

Preface and Acknowledgements

Dear Yootha...

That's how people would start. They would write to Yootha about their most intimate problems, so convinced were they of her performance as Mildred in the sitcom *George and Mildred*. This sexually frustrated, vulnerable yet predatory character had reached such levels of believability, that some were convinced that Yootha would be the one to sort out their worries. "I'm no Marjie Proops darling, but I try to help in my simple way," she admitted.
She was enormously popular; her fame still echoes now, almost thirty five years after her death in 1980, fed by numerous TV repeats of *George and Mildred* and the earlier *Man About The House*.

Her appearance was captivating and distinct. She was blonde with high cheekbones, and had an excellent figure. She demanded one's eyeballs. "The razor smile, the biting tongue, the accusing eyes," all added to people's amazement at what nature could create.

Yootha was aware of her distinctive face and was able to laugh at her own looks. "I look like Dracula's daughter," she would quip. "My face was made by somebody who just didn't care that much - it was thrown together." Barbara Windsor, who worked alongside her early in her career, remembers that Yootha "had what I could only respectfully describe as an ugly beauty." Interviewed in 1979 by the famous columnist Jean Rook, Yootha received a full anatomical analysis. It justifies Yootha's chosen career. She was clearly born to be looked at in film, television and on stage. Rook's description certainly left nothing out: "The ever moving predatory hands, are softly lit with topaz and gold rings. Her boobs are as pointed as her teeth, and she is deathly sexy. She has eyelashes like poisonous spiders. Her mouth is vast and luscious, like a gaping sea anemone. Or Jaws, or a mail box. Or the red hole. Or a cave filled with what looks like 132 jagged pearl teeth. To men, the mouth, which could kiss or tell, or even kill you, is irresistible. To realise the true size and power of it, you have to see it in the gleaming pink flesh. Even without a tape, I'd work it out at a third again as wide as Sophia Loren's and twice Farrah Fawcett Major's. It's more than a gap in her face, it is a geological marvel."

Looking at Yootha's long career, you wonder where she'd been before her phenomenal success. *George and Mildred*, in which she played alongside Brian Murphy, was one of the most successful TV sitcoms of the Seventies. TV success also saw both actors branching out, achieving record audiences on stage, at summer seasons in the UK, Australia, and New Zealand.

Where had Yootha come from? What training had she had? What kind of person was she? Most importantly, what went wrong when her success became a problem? Fear of failure, nerves, the strain on relationships, depression, alcoholism, and ultimately withdrawal and self-destruction, all seemed to follow. "She was so famous, people pestered her wherever she went," recalls Brian Murphy. "You just remember we were reaching 18 million viewers and her face was really well known."

The tragedy was that the Mildred role became too fixed. "She had so much to give and should have had more time to show the public what a great actress she was," says co-actor Jeremy Bulloch.

Socially, Yootha would always appear friendly and approachable; her sense of fun was often on display. People loved her wherever she went. Joy Jameson, her agent, said to me: "I can't think of anyone who had a bad word to say about her." To her family, friends and fans, and particularly to those who worked with her, her death was an untimely loss. The actor Dudley Sutton remembers "She was an absolute joy to be on stage with."

Charities and in particular, animal welfare causes had become a central part of her life. The Dogs' Trust [then The National Canine Defence League] and the Durrell Wildlife Conservation Trust benefited immensely from her enthusiastic support. She would be sadly missed.

Much about Yootha is unknown: we're not helped by the fact that "She never talked about herself." "I knew nothing of her background", Theatre Workshop actress Toni Palmer said to me.

Yootha refused to confide, or be helped, but she was always ready to help others. We're left with a sense of sadness and curiosity whenever we see her performances. There is no full-scale biography, and what accounts of her life exist tend to be plagued by uncertainties and discrepancies, some repeated even by Yootha herself.

Yootha has always captivated me, maybe for the same reasons as every other person who saw, or had experience of her. Why? Over the years, I have collected photos, interviews and career details. Eventually, twenty years ago, I started the *Yootha Joyce Memorial Society*, with contributions from Brian Murphy and Joan Littlewood. I always assumed that a biography of her would have been attempted, but nothing ever has. As time went on, my own collection expanded into a mini-archive: in particular, to my great pleasure, some time ago I was given a box with some of Yootha's own memorabilia. I began to feel a sense of duty to write this book, as a lasting tribute to her.

As part of my research into Yootha's past, I had a meeting with the actor and current archivist Murray Melvin at the Theatre Royal, Stratford East, which was very encouraging. Murray had worked with Yootha in her early days as an actress.

Talking to him, at the home of Joan Littlewood's Theatre Workshop; The Theatre Royal Stratford East, a place which brought out some of the best artistic talents of the 20th century, was exhilarating: it was buzzing with atmosphere and reeking of history. Murray was pleased that at last, someone was doing something about Yootha: "She was so special," he told me. His parting words to me were, "Everything I have to offer is all for Yootha." He inspired me to get the project moving, as did the invaluable help from all those acknowledged in this introduction.

My search for information required much patience. I followed leads wherever and whenever I could.

I was delighted to interview Toni Palmer, who had worked with Yootha in the early Sixties. Complimenting her on her part in the film *Smashing Time*, from 1967, she said "you must be an old fashioned soul," but on telling her of the length of time it had taken me to gather information on Yootha, she replied "Well you'd better hurry up with it!"

In my brief correspondence with Eileen Atkins, she said "It's a pity you didn't start the biography before she died. It's quite a job for you to find out what would have been a very interesting life." What Yootha would have made of a study of her life we will never know, and as I was only eight when she died in 1980, I never had the opportunity to ask her. Christine Pilgrim, Yootha's close friend, who featured with her in the film *Burke and Hare,* told me "Yootha would probably have said, 'What a hoot, Darling!' But she'd have been really chuffed."

I would like to thank those who have been so generous in offering their time and help for this project and also to those I may have overlooked. I would also like to thank Rex Features, *The Daily Telegraph*. Alistair Smith at *The Stage*, Trinity Mirror, Lin Newell, Ellen Newton and Jane Foster at Fremantle Media. Michelle Briant at *TV Times* & Tom Smith at *Woman's Own* (Time Inc.) Guardian News & Media Ltd. North One Television, Robin Bray at ITV, Tom Green at The Writers Guild of Great Britain, Dr Eva del Ray at The British Libray, Alan Chudley at www.arthurlloyd.co.uk. Claire Wetherhead at Bloomsbury Publishing Plc, Robert Ross at Umbrella Entertainment, Australia, for use of copyright material. Every effort was made to trace those holding additional copyright material, and to those I omitted, I would happily add appropriate credit in any further editions of this book.

In particular I'd like to give special thanks to the following people. Glynn Edwards, Valerie Edwards, Fabian Hamilton M.P, Rosy Hamilton and the late Adrianne Uziell-Hamilton. Also Joy Jameson, Christine Pilgrim, Tom Edwards, Brian Murphy [for his help with the *Yootha Joyce Memorial Society*], the hugely entertaining Dudley Sutton, Karen Fisher, Murray Melvin and the archive at Theatre Royal Stratford East, who have been so generous. Barbara Windsor O.B.E, for her brilliant encyclopedic knowledge and advice, Scott Mitchell, Toni Palmer, Dame Eileen Atkins D.B.E, David Barry, Ian Burford, Denis Norden C.B.E., April Glaze, Nicholas (Bond) Owen, Sir Roger Moore, Gareth Owen, Sally Thomsett, Liz Smith M.B.E, and her agent Kat Oliver, Antony Booth for kind permission to use extracts from the Pat Phoenix book *All My Burning Bridges*. Steph Booth, Cherie Blair C.B.E. Q.C, Tessa Cunningham, Jude Aquilina, Katie Briggs, Lyn Harvey, Zelie (Smith) Armstrong, Andy

Armstrong, Neil Sinyard, David Bret, Patricia Zline, Tony Bilbow, Tex Fisher, the late Joan Littlewood, Jean Gaffin O.B.E, Rachael Fiddler, Robert Gillespie, Melanie Crabb, Valerie Revitt, Jean Newlove, Joan Bakewell D.B.E, Philip and David at 'HOYD Publishing.' Alan Davidson, Penny Parry Williams, Tessa Le Bars, Ray Galton, Alan Simpson, Susanah Corbett, Jeremy Bulloch, Sally Harrison, Florence Jones, Jytte Mortimer, Brian Cooke for his inspiration, the late Peter Frazer Jones, Gordon Dickerson, Jean Marlow, Lee Durrell M.B.E and Tim Wright at Durrell Wildlife Conservation Tust, Clarissa Baldwin M.B.E at Dogs Trust, Peter Cellier, Rod MacNeil, Cliff and Eve Douthwaite, David Jeffery, Carl Gresham (The Gresh), Colin Essex, Carolyn Cowan, Paul Corin, Jonathan Gibbs and his dad. Emma Clarke, Michael Conefrey, Sarah Jones aka 'chatty Cathy', those on Twitter, Colin Howe, Sarah Louise Roscoe, Gavin Culloty & Victor Olliver. My apologies if I left anyone out; if I did, I apologise and I thank you.

Paul Curran
August 2014

CHAPTER 1

Yootha Joyce Needham was born into a family where entertainment was already in the blood. Her father, Percival Henry John Needham, or 'Hurst' as he was known; was, according to Yootha, a bass baritone singer with an "incredible" voice. Her mother, Jessica Maude Needham, née Revitt, [known as Maude] also sang, though she was mainly a pianist. Yootha said all her family sang: they were all musically talented, and "would play musical instruments." Yootha's grandmother, Jessica Rebecca Revitt [Rebecca] had, according to Yootha, also appeared on the stage. Unfortunately it has been impossible to verify this, because the records are spotty, and they were probably supporting artists rather the main act. A few curious facts, however, have come to light.

Maude was born on 20th November 1895, at 14 Henshaw Street in Southwark. Her parents were William, born in Lambeth, and Rebecca in Rotherhithe, and they had married on the 29th May of the same year, in Newington St Mary. They lived at 36 Rodney Place, in the Elephant and Castle. William was a greengrocer, and Rebecca a pub licensee – both jobs on the edge of respectability. Perhaps the pub gave Rebecca an outlet for her singing? Yootha said that just before she was born in 1927, Maude was just starting to become well known as a concert pianist. However, facts about Maude's childhood and performance career [if she had one] are very hard to come by. Yootha said her mother had been a student at the Guildhall School of Music. However, there is no record of her attendance there. None of the people I contacted who knew Yootha had any information on Maude either. All we know for certain is that she went to school near where she lived, at Putney Secondary Modern; in 1910 -11; when she was 15, she was in Form V.
In that year, according to the census, Maude was living with her three brothers, Williamson, Henry and Arthur, at 22 Fitzwilliam Road, Clapham. All three had jobs as clerks: Williamson in a cable telegraph company, Henry in photographer's shop, and Arthur at a general printing firm. By this time, Maude's father William had a job as an "artist colour man" and warehouseman; he was a manager specialising in stationers' sundries. Rebecca looked after the household, as many women did in those days. Perhaps they had moved up in the world.
Much of the information I have from this time comes from a small album/scrapbook that Maude kept from September 1910 onwards, which contains contributions, in the form of poems, songs, drawings and cuttings, from her friends and family. The opening page gives some idea of its contents:

"You may look at this album
But learn ere you look,
That all are requested to add to this book.

You may quiz as you please,
But the penalty is. :-

That you likewise leave something
for others to quiz.

Owner.
Sept 19th 1910."

In the nature of such old documents, the album is difficult to interpret; many of
the contributors are hard to identify, too. Maude continued it through the war
years, and in fact some of the items are from people who lost their lives in the
War.
Turning to Yootha's father, Hurst: he was born in September 1894 at 16 Frith
Street, Chelsea. His mother, Mary Jane Needham, worked as a daily help, and
his father Isaac was a painter, labourer and electrical fitter. They were obviously
poor – though as Yootha later said, they were "a close-knit Jewish family," –
and didn't live for long at the Chelsea address. In 1898, in fact, Isaac died, aged
only 39, when Hurst was only four. By 1911, we find the Needhams in Bristol,
at 15 Woodborough Street, where he was living with his 76-year-old
grandmother Harriet [who died that same year], his widowed mother, and
twelve-year-old sister Marjorie. By this time, Hurst's other two sisters, Eva and
Gladys, had already left the family home, Eva to find work as a domestic in
various parts of England. Gladys emigrated, and went to work in the US, later
settling in Canada.
By 1913, when Hurst was 18, he had left Bristol, and was living at 9
Gainsborough Road, Blackpool. He was registered as a carpenter. Given the
location, it seems very likely he performed there, though we have no record of
it:

By 1914, the Revitts were also setting out on their own. On 1st August of that
year Maude's eldest brother Williamson married Grace Lattimer; she was a
bridesmaid. All the family were there – obviously a happy memory to last
through the horrors of the First World War, declared only days before. The
couple settled in nearby Wandsworth. In the same year, Henry and Arthur left
home, headed for the Western Front.
On 18th May 1915, Hurst too enlisted for short service at the local recruiting
office, joining the 6th Battalion, though records do not say what regiment: at this
stage, he was registered as a watchmaker. It is hard to work out exactly where he
went: all we have to go on are a series of photographs from Maude's family
album. It seems likely that, like Maude's brother Arthur, he went to the Western
Front. Judging by a photo in the album, it seems, too, that for a while, Hurst was
also posted to Egypt with the Egyptian Expeditionary Force in 1917, returning
to France some time later.
We do know that Arthur Revitt and Hurst Needham became pals when they
were on leave. The soldiers, in fact, would spend only a little more than 3
months at the front per year. Visits home must have been vitally important. One
set of notes from the album records a trip out to Brighton, with Hurst, Arthur,
and Maude herself. They reveal a saucy sense of fun: perhaps this even found an

outlet at the front itself, where the bored troops were entertained by improvised music and theatre.

CHAPTER 2

During 1917, the Revitts moved house twice. At first, they lived in 29 Lydon Road, Clapham. Later that same year they moved to 57 Bennerley Road, Wandsworth, in a lower-middle-class suburb, built around the 1850s.
We can only imagine what thoughts Maude must have had about her brothers fighting miles away from home, in Soulstece France; certainly she must have been fearful for them.
Sadly, on 8 August 1918 Arthur died. The official notice was "Arthur Thomas Revitt Rifleman, 8th Battalion, London Regiment (Post Office Rifles). Died of wounds. Son of William and Jessie R. Revitt, of 57 Bennerley Road, Wandsworth Common, London. Native of London. Age 25." He was laid to rest 16 miles south west of the French town of Doullens. The cemetery opened towards the end of April 1918, during the final German advance.
In that same year, it appears that Yootha's father, Hurst, was injured. "He was gassed," remembers Glynn Edwards, Yootha's future husband. This was also confirmed by Yootha herself. There were many deaths from poison gas, and its after-effects blighted many lives. In Hurst's case, it brought on emphysema, a condition that slowly attacks and destroys the lungs. Many men were so badly incapacitated by the poison that they found it difficult to hold down a job.
When Hurst came back to England, he was hospitalised in a convalescent centre in Richmond-on-Thames. His mother Mary, who had been living alone in Bristol, moved into the Wandsworth area to be near her son. She took rooms in 114 Sugden Road. Even though Hurst's lungs got steadily worse as the years passed, there must have been something left for Yootha to call his voice "incredible."
Probably, it was after the war that Hurst and Maude became close. Maude had joined the women's volunteer reserve to help the injured; In all likelihood, she sang and played to them. She would have taken the time to visit Hurst during his recovery. Perhaps music brought them together. Hurst contributed song lyrics to Maude's album.

Yootha said that her father, when he came back from the war, began to adapt to singing in revue, which was less taxing on the voice. He would eventually receive a war pension of 7 shillings a week from the government as part of his compensation. According to Glynn: "Hurst was involved with the D'Oyly Carte," the famous company which specialised in the operas of Gilbert and Sullivan. "He went on tour with their productions, I think in between work as a chippie" he says. However, research on the very comprehensive website of the company revealed no indication of Hurst having performed with them. "I'm not sure if he would have had any billing. I can't be very helpful with the tracking of their careers and performances," he told me. Perhaps Hurst was working on an amateur basis as an entertainer as well as doing the occasional work as a chippie? The search goes on.

Hurst's song lyrics

We have little or no information about Maude and Hurst in the post-war years. Photographs do show them appearing to have some much needed fun after the war, holidaying in Ilfracombe and Herefordshire, where they stayed on a farm. Yootha offers us a clue about them as performers, as she said in an interview in 1976 that Hurst found Maude's piano playing was an "invaluable" support. What does seem clear from the photographs is that they were happy together. In 1922 Maude's brother Henry returned home to Bennerley Road, having won the Victory and British medals as a private in the Royal Fusiliers. He married Marjorie and they set up home in the basement of Bennerley Road. The following year, they had a son, James. In March 1924, it was the turn of Hurst's sister, also Marjorie; and then in September 1925, Hurst himself married Maude. Money must have been tight, especially considering the problems with Hurst's health. At some stage, they moved in with Maude's parents. We can only speculate as to what they did to make ends meet. Perhaps Hurst continued working as a carpenter.

Maude became pregnant in November or December 1926. In August 1927, Maude, now 32, and Hurst, 33, were still living with her parents. Henry and his family soon moved out and took a place in Chiswick, allowing the Needhams to set up home together in the basement flat.

Hurst and Maude had been married for some two years when Yootha, their only child, was born, on 24th August 1927. It's a curious name, by any stretch of the imagination; Yootha later admitted she "loathed and detested it." It has two or three possible origins. One ancient historical meaning comes from a Maori word meaning "joy". Another, less well known, is the Australian aboriginal meaning of "thirsty": appropriate enough, as Yootha was indeed "a very thirsty lady," said Brian Cooke, one of the writers of *George and Mildred*.

However, there is one quite different, and very possible explanation for the name. Yootha Rose, the famous singer, toy maker and trustee for National Toy Museum, began to sing during the war, at concert parties in the UK. Her father, the Australian singer Charles Rose, had toured with Nellie Melba, one of the most famous singers of her time. At the time of Yootha's birth, Yootha Rose would be performing at the same time as Hurst was, but the cast lists from her tours do not feature him: this seems a more likely explanation of the name. Delving deeper into the subject, it appears that Yootha in an interview for the book *This is Their Lives* by Jonathan Meades in 1980, claimed that Yootha Rose was "a dancer on the same bill in Clapham as her father." Yootha said, "She owes her name to her mother's indecision. She had no idea what to call the child, so the baby's grandmother suggested that she be called after the next woman to walk through the door of the nursing home ward. This turned out to be Yootha Rose."

In an interview with the *TV Times* in October 1976, Yootha told the story of her birth. According to her, Maude, heavily pregnant, "decided it was stuffy and wanted to walk on Wandsworth Common." This was, she said, during an interval of one of Hurst's performances at the Grand Theatre at Clapham Junction.

I made several attempts, by various means, to check on Hurst's presence that day at that theatre, but I could find nothing. The popular entertainer Bransby Williams, in *Mi Padre* headed the bill on that day. I contacted Williams's grandson Paul Corin, and asked him whether Hurst had appeared in the production of *Mi Padre*, which also toured the country. Unfortunately, Paul did not have any playbills or cast lists for these productions: I was left uncertain of how much truth there was in Yootha's claims.

Anyhow, Yootha maintained that while Maude was out for air, she began to experience contractions. The pain was alarming. She set off to find the nearest house to call an ambulance; but then she spotted a nursing home on Bolingbroke Grove, just off the Common, and promptly went in.

The Bolingbroke nursing home, where Yootha was born, had originally been

two buildings. Westwood Tower at No. 19 and Elmhurst at No. 20 were both used for a time in the 1910s as retreats for alcoholics; they were bought in 1920 by Battersea Borough Council for conversion into a maternity home.
Yootha claimed that she "should have been born in Hampstead," and that her mother had travelled down to visit Hurst at the Grand Theatre. As the birth was eight hours long, she said, her mother could have easily returned there for the birth. Since Maude and Hurst were living at Bennerley Road at the time, it seems much more likely that she had simply gone out for a walk near where she lived. Why would Yootha invent such a story?

At her birth, Yootha's appearance attracted commentary even then, she said: "My nose was as wide as my mouth. It actually touched my left ear. That straightened out, but the mouth didn't."

The Bolingbroke nursing home in which Yootha was born was damaged during the Second World War, and demolished. In 1948 Lane Court flats were built on the site; they are still there today. However, the house in Bennerley Road where she was brought up in for the first few years of her life is still standing: a house she later would claim she and her family were bombed out of during the war!

CHAPTER 3

Yootha spent her early years in the basement flat in Bennerley Road. One of the first pictures of her as a baby is part of a set that was used in the opening credits of the first series of *George and Mildred*, in 1976. In it, she seems to be sitting either on an occasional table, or a very unusual three-legged high chair. It looks a bit risky, for a two-month old baby! When I asked about the image at Fremantle media, who own the copyright for the series, I was told by Jane Foster, the person in charge of the image library, that "the opening titles would have specifically been put together by the graphics department at Thames TV at the time, and no hard copies would have survived." A couple of other images in the same group are from her childhood: one, of her sitting on large cuddly toy, was her personal favourite. But none match the exterior of the houses she lived in in those days.
Yootha's grandfather William died in St James' Hospital, Balham, on the 28th April 1929, aged 66, when she was only two: a blow for Rebecca. He left £476.1s.4d. Memories of Yootha as a child are very few: friends and colleagues seemed to know little or nothing about her early life, and there are very few photos or mementos. We do know, however, that her mother and grandmother would take her out on the train to Brighton as a treat. A particular favourite was a side-trip to Poynings, to the Royal Oak, where they would have tea, go for a little walk and enjoy the views of the Devil's Dyke. They went in June 1929, and there is a picture of Yootha, taken by her mother, aged 18 months, happy paddling and playing on Brighton beach.
On the back of one of the photographs, in Maude's handwriting, are a few

details of a trip to the dentist. Yootha was famously nicknamed "Tootha" in her childhood: perhaps her teeth were pronounced already at that young age. Later she would say that she was terrified of trips to the dentist. Once, in fact, she said that her teeth "should have been capped." Her other greatest fear, she said, was being photographed – she even claimed that catching sight of photos of herself would leave her quite scared – a strange phobia for a film actress. As a child, however, she looks comfortable enough.

During the early thirties, in the years of the great depression, Hurst and Maude must have struggled. Yootha remembered that Hurst, with his increasing problems with emphysema, moved from stage revue – a genre dependent on topical material – into variety. Although it was easier to do, he loathed it, so that Yootha remembers "it made him very unhappy." Quite likely, it was it because it was often vulgar and crude: Yootha often mentioned Maude's respectability, which she was very keen to maintain. No doubt she, too, found it hard to get bookings for her piano-playing.

Yootha's memories of life with her performing parents are telling – though she never said what Hurst did to earn the needful. She remembered "they had nothing one minute, then everything to eat and wear the next." All the money that came into the household was promptly spent, and there was little left over for a rainy day. This attitude to money, it seems, filtered through into the latter part of Yootha's life: she would be overdrawn even when she was most successful. "I'm sure [Hurst] would have done a moonlight flit if he could. And so would I," Yootha remembers, "but my mother would sooner have pawned me."

Hurst's mother, Mary Jane, died at Kingston-on-Thames on 25th October 1931, aged 73: she was buried in Kingston cemetery. We know very little about her – why was she living in Kingston, for instance? How did she fare as a pensioner in this time of economic depression? We simply don't know.

In 1933, with the proceeds from some carpentry work, and maybe some extra bookings, the Needhams moved out of the Bennerley Road basement, into 4 Lindore Road, just a few streets up from Rebecca. Yootha now began her education, at Battersea Central Co-educational School. She always remembered how vulnerable she was as a child, so no doubt this was a difficult time, with no older brothers or sisters to help her settle in. What this vulnerability stemmed from, she never said – perhaps she simply didn't know. What is clear, however, is that she ended up loving the school, calling it a "marvellous place." Cliff Douthwaite, who went there at around the same time, remembers that "whilst Battersea Central School was considered to be co-ed, it had separate floors to keep the sexes separated."

By 1934 the Needhams had moved to another address, 6 Gayville Road, Clapham, again only a short distance from Rebecca – perhaps this was the "moonlight flit" Yootha referred to? In any case, the stability of a fixed home seems have been lacking in her life, and she said that her grandmother was responsible for her upbringing most of the time. Her parents were "away so much," she said, that it was inevitable that she went to live with Rebecca. Most likely Hurst and Maude were touring, perhaps with Bransby Williams in another performance of *Mi Padre*, which is listed as being put on in Keighley, Yorkshire, at the Queen's Theatre and Opera House, for example, though I have found no records of their performances.

Being around parents in the entertainment business must have had a huge influence on Yootha's outlook on life. But her father was not always encouraging. Once, when she tried to sing like her mum and dad, Hurst commented that "she hasn't quite the tone her mother has." Yootha was clearly marked by this, and remembered that "When you're eleven or twelve that destroys you." She said, in fact, that she "wasn't desperately fond of him." But it didn't stop her trying, and she developed a tremolo that, she later said, she "never quite lost."

CHAPTER 4

When Yootha was twelve in 1939, the war brought enormous changes for her, as for many other city children. She was one of the many who were evacuated from London in early September of that year. To a lot of children, the evacuation was an adventure, a great challenge, and a new experience that would stay in their memories forever. Some, however, found it disorientating, and even terrifying. The speedy – some would say panicky – dispatch of large numbers of children from the cities to the assumed safety of the countryside can in hindsight seem rather naive. There are some cases of vulnerable children going though terrible experiences. Barbara Windsor tells the story of her evacuation to Blackpool in her autobiography *All Of Me*: the couple who were supposed to be looking after her were eventually taken away by the police.

The pupils of Battersea Central School were sent to Petersfield, a market town in Hampshire less than twenty miles north of Portsmouth. Yootha would have travelled with her fellow pupils all "armed with carrier bags and gas masks." From the station, they were taken to two separate buildings, boys to one, girls to the other. The boys were introduced to the town and shown the local sights, like the Savoy cinema, and the local shops. Then they were taken to Petersfield parish church, where they sat for some time "being entertained by a pupil of the church organist, who was practising the national anthem." Yootha and the other girls, after their long train journey, were taken to the Junior Council School, where they were "given refreshments, including half a pound of chocolate!"

One of the pupils, Cliff Douthwaite, remembers that "While the school was evacuated to Petersfield, the girls stayed there in civilisation, whilst the boys were billeted further afield - half of them based a few miles north at Hawkley and the other half a few miles south at Rowlands Castle, so none of us met." Yootha said she hated life at Petersfield. To give us an insight into what life was like there at that time, we luckily have a wonderfully vivid account by David Jeffery, in his book *Petersfield At War*. He tells us, for instance, that: "Some girls were 'selected' for billets by their hosts, who fetched them directly from the school hall, while others went in a crocodile through the town and waited for the Billeting Officer to knock on people's doors to see if they would or could be accepted." Given that Yootha was a vulnerable child, we can only imagine the effect this had on her. Glynn Edwards remembers, "Yootha certainly wasn't very happy about it."

Even though there were opportunities for parents to visit their children, homesickness was obviously a problem. For those who did fall prey to it, "there was one weekend exeat available each half term - all they had to do was to persuade their last teacher on a Friday afternoon to let them go early so that they could rush to the station for the 5.15 train to London."

Would Yootha have had someone to go home to? Admitting that during her childhood, her parents where "away a lot", maybe it was a case of "like it or lump it." Glynn Edwards told me that Yootha never told him what her parents were doing at that time, "I know Hurst would have been too old to fight again [he would have been about 45]. I think he was busy working as a chippie, but I just don't know any more."

It was not an easy transition: the school equipment and records took some three weeks to make their journey from one school to another. The allocation of classroom facilities became quite a challenge, too, with "visitors far outnumbering the 'home' pupils: 250 black and yellow uniforms of the Battersea girls easily outnumbered the hundred or so blue dresses of the Petersfield County High School for Girls." Classes were organised in various venues around the town. Mostly, the girls were based at the local high school, which at the time "had all but been condemned as unsuitable and insufficient." With the "influx of the Londoners, it began, almost literally, to groan." "Some of the girls experienced some wolf-whistling from the Royal Engineers, who were based in the Britnell and Crawters garage, as they passed on their way from school assembly to their main classroom in the Congregational church hall."

The evacuation brought some of the differences between rural and working-class city life into sharp focus. Some children found the changes too much to cope with at the most basic level. One evacuee said she "never got given fish and chips and buns, but only fresh vegetables from the garden!" Country life was foreign to them. "They couldn't understand why so much importance was attached to the closing of a field gate or the sin of breaking through a hedge. Of course, from the time of their arrival their conduct was viewed with suspicion and mistrust by those who have a natural antipathy towards townsmen and it was not long before all childish misdemeanours were attributed to the evacuees."

One particular incident recounted by David Jeffery illustrates the gap between the two cultures: "The RSPCA complained of evacuees interfering with animals on market days in the square." On one occasion, "when a stray pig made its way into the high street there were up to seventy or eighty children of all ages chasing after it, screaming, shouting and laughing, and for some time they impeded any practical efforts to catch the animal. The children were said to have behaved like 'thoughtless young barbarians'."

During the "phoney war," the period between September 1939 and April 1940, when the predicted bombing of London, and the feared use of poison gas, didn't materialise, many of the evacuees went back home.

Yootha may well have stayed in Petersfield. If she did, she would at least have had some entertainment. Some of it the children organised themselves, as David Jeffery tells us: "The Battersea girls would use the Methodist hall for their drama, dancing and singing". No doubt Yootha played her full part! Efforts were made to keep the children and soldiers billeted there stimulated: "Stafford Hipkins [one of the schoolmasters] arranged for a West End cast to come and perform Goldsmith's *She Stoops to Conquer* in the Town Hall." Films were regularly shown: "the Savoy cinema showed a *Charlie Chan* adventure, Boris Karloff in *Super Sleuth* and a romantic adventure, *Sword of Honour*."

The winter was very cold that year, so much so that the pond was frozen over and skating became possible. Over the Christmas period, special efforts were made to keep people entertained. There was "a cheery concert at the YMCA, with a baritone soloist and elocutionist providing the main attractions. 150 evacuee children were also taken to the Savoy cinema to see Shirley Temple in *Little Princess*, as well as being given a party at the Town Hall with Christmas tree, crackers and boisterous games!" In fact, it seems that the Savoy was the place for the evacuees to hang out; David Jeffery tells us that "Unbeknown to their teachers, the evacuated boys and girls from two Battersea schools occasionally went to the Savoy together." He also tells how one young cinema-goer, Roy Barrow, often went to the Savoy with his parents on a Sunday afternoon: "he recalls how the smoke was so thick inside that he used to throw orange peel up in the air so that it would be illuminated in the light from the projector!"

CHAPTER 5

By the end of summer 1940 many evacuees started to return to their homes in the cities. The Luftwaffe bombings had never materialised, and many thought it safe to go back. Of course, as is well known, they came back to the worst of the blitz, between September 1940 and May 1941.

It's not clear if Yootha went to live with Rebecca at Bennerley Road, or with her parents at Gayville Road. She later said that on her return to London they were "promptly bombed out." There was indeed one suggestion of such a bombing, though it hardly bears Yootha's story out: in this case, a resident of Bennerley Road found an incendiary bomb lodged in his roof rafters – it was later made safe. Yootha later said that her grandmother once said to her "If there's a fire, you have to grab what you can carry and no more." According to Yootha, the bombing meant that they had to find a completely new home, miles away in Croydon, at 35 Gladstone Road, where she lived after the war with her parents and grandmother. She in fact said that she was living in Hampstead at the time, but this seems very unlikely, and there is no record of it. It seems more likely that, bombing or no bombing, they moved from Clapham to Croydon, an area which had also suffered badly during the war: it got more 'doodlebug' hits than any other London Borough.

In 1941, Yootha started a new school in Croydon, which turned out to be a daunting experience, in contrast to her "marvellous" time at Battersea Central and away in Petersfield. "It was not something I could get used to," she admitted: she remembers that her fellow students were "awfully giggly." Croydon High was an all girls' school, which has produced its fair share of successful people over the years, such as the actress Judy Buxton, treasure hunter Anneka Rice, and the cellist Jacqueline du Pré. Yootha remembered the heavy workload she had there, with a lot of "unthinking homework."

At this time, her family were wondering what career she was going to pursue, and what talents she could develop. It seems that her aunts and her father thought she couldn't play the piano or sing like her mum and dad: in fact, they didn't think she was "much good at anything." One can imagine that these comments must have angered and upset her: the main impression, however, is that she had a permanent sense of her own inadequacy, and that this, in turn, made her anxious to prove herself. She felt determined to prove them wrong, to excel at something, anything, rather than be "not quite as good as the family." At this point in her life, Yootha said, she had "the fighting instinct to the fore."

Already aged 14, Yootha was keen to leave school as soon as possible. Maude told her she could, but only if she managed to matriculate. Yootha's determination to have gathered pace over the months, and her teenage rebelliousness produced a good deal of tension in the family. At one point, inspired no doubt by the Anglo-Polish Ballet, who had performed at the Grand Theatre and Opera House, Croydon, in September 1942, she announced her intention to be a ballet dancer, a curious choice if ever there was one, especially as in those days the ideal ballet-dancer was delicate and "feminine," and certainly not someone who gets scared looking at her own photographs! Yootha's expanding shoe size, too – she eventually reached a size 8 – put paid to that choice; as she said in an interview, that "blew her chances."

Yootha was determined to succeed at something. Her aim was to leave school and get into the world of work. She was all set to leave school, she remembered, when "I got on my little hind legs and said, 'I'm going to be a hairdresser.' I could as well have said I wanted to be a seaman. But they nearly fainted at high school."

It was a short time after, however, that she declared she was to be an actress: according to Yootha, no one could understand why she had chosen such a profession. Maybe her experience with the touring theatre company, or the drama at Petersfield had given her some inspiration? Yootha later claimed that her decision to become an actress was based on the fact that "nobody knew what to do with me."

In July 1942 she eventually matriculated, and left school. She recalled that to achieve that, she "almost worked herself into a nervous breakdown for a year." For the rest of 1942 and most of 1943 she began to immerse herself as much as she could in the acting profession: although if she was working as well, she never mentioned it to any of her friends. However with her fighting instinct inside her, she said she had the firm intention to "break the family tradition, to become a straight dramatic actress."

CHAPTER 6

In spring 1944, aged 16, Yootha sent off an application to the Royal Academy of Dramatic Art [RADA]. She chose to study there because, at the time, "a lot of people would have sent their children to finishing school in Switzerland." Because of the war, however, "they enlisted them at RADA instead!" She also said that her parents actually thought her choice to be an actress was a "disgrace!" Glynn Edwards, however, told me "they both approved of her acting," since they were both in the business: "I'm not sure they disapproved at all," he said.

She was auditioned on 26th May 1944. She never said what her audition pieces were – RADA guidelines at the time required two prepared pieces. Her fellow-actor Roger Moore (whom she didn't yet know), got through his by falling back on his "schoolboy recital of *The Revenge*" and a piece from *The Silver Box* by Galsworthy" – this gives us some idea of what sort of material RADA required. Roger Moore got into RADA by a piece of luck: director Brian Desmond Hurst offered to pay his fees – 17 guineas, a substantial sum at the time, plus one for the audition. "Opportunities like that are straight out of publicity handouts" as he said. Yootha's case was quite different – the more so if, as she said, her parents disapproved. Her grandmother Rebecca agreed to pay her fees when she was successful at audition, and she was guaranteed a place, to start in the autumn – she began on 3rd September 1944. It must have been daunting, but she would also have been proud of landing such an opportunity – she had a competitive streak, as she always said, and valued her career above all else. During the war the main RADA building in Gower Street had been badly damaged, and students had to make do with a smaller building in the same street. Later students remembered that while the rebuilding went on, "all the classes were accompanied by pneumatic drilling." The actor Robert Gillespie, best known as Dudley Rush in *Keep It In The Family* and hundreds of sitcom appearances, later worked with Yootha, and had studied at RADA a few years later; he remembers, "We didn't have a theatre to perform in except for a makeshift black box stuck in the basement."

We have very little in the way of anecdotes from this period, but we can get some idea of the atmosphere from the reminiscences of some of her fellow-actors. Roger Moore remembers her fondly. For him, these were "the happiest days of my life." He was the tallest in the class, which mostly consisted of girls – sixteen, to four boys, in fact – because of the war. One of the other girls in the class was Lois Hooker, a Canadian, later Lois Maxwell Marriot (1927-2007) who won the Golden Globe Award for Most Promising Newcomer for her performance in *That Hagen Girl* in 1947: she eventually found fame as Roger's assistant, Miss Moneypenny, in the Bond film series.

Recollections give a good insight into what life was like for Yootha at this time. Students were filtered into three streams, A, B, and C: Yootha was in Group A. In her first term, she got a grade 2, as did Roger. Her report said that she was "a good student": she was moved up to "middle A." They worked all day, every weekday, from 10 a.m. to 5.30 p.m., and 6.30 on Fridays, with an hour for

lunch. As for life outside the classes: Roger says "most of the students were pretty broke most of the time. The few who did have money were generous with it, buying the teas and meals and so on. There was a group of four of us at RADA, who worked out some marvellous systems of survival. One thing we used to do was go to a Chinese restaurant, each buying a full portion of something and then sharing. There was a teashop next to Goodge Street station where most of the students went after classes. Out of sheer concern for the other customers they used to shove the students into a room of our own at the top of the building. Up there we would often push the tables together as a makeshift stage and prance our way through an impromptu show. Anything for a laugh."
Classes began on Monday mornings, with acting and mime, taken by Miss Carrington and Miss Phillips. Roger Moore gives a good example of what it could involve, in this story from a 1972 *TV Times* interview: "The task one day was for us individually to go through the motions of decorating a room. Inevitably I decided to turn the whole thing into a comedy send-up. The chair we had as a prop was to become in my mime a set of steps used to paper the wall. The idea was to turn and get a pot of paint whereupon I fall off the steps, which I duly did.

I had failed to appreciate that the floor of the room in which we were doing this was rather badly nailed down. With exquisite timing I did a back flip off the chair and crashed on my back to the floor, whereupon a nail became impaled in the back of my skull.

'Well done. Very good,' they said, applauding. 'All right. You can get up now.' 'Thank you,' I said in some anguish from the floor. 'If someone will remove the nail in my head, I will.' Yes, I got on well in mime classes."

As well as acting and mime, there were classes in voice projection, movement, diction, fencing, dancing and verse-speaking. Usually on Fridays there was a talk by Dame Irene Vanburgh, one of the Academy's founders, and the sister of Sir Kenneth Barnes, who had been principal since 1909. Roger Moore remembers that he was called "Granny Barnes," and, according to him, was a wonderful Principal: "He always had a dog at his heels, who used to bite everyone with a kind of peppery venom. He would sit in the principal's box at the back of the stalls throughout every performance the students did at the theatre. He made a point of keeping his light on during the performance and you could not only see him but hear him chuntering away in a sort of quavering Cheltenham voice: 'What did he say? What did he say?' and 'Time for tea, Nancy' he'd say to his secretary."

Actor Robert Gillespie, told me "I was at RADA from 1951-53. Clearly after Yootha." However, he recalls on his website, janenightwork.com [of which he is artistic director] that Sir Kenneth was a "terrible old snob, who came alive on the days when the Queen Mother attended – or any other Royal relative." "The fast track into work, then, was to be either Jewish or homosexual, and there is a story of Sir Kenneth interviewing a prospective young actor and asking, among a number of other salient questions: 'Are you a homosexual?' 'I'm afraid not, Sir Kenneth', supposedly came the reply (it was reported)." "Each term would end with a class performance which would be assessed by Sir Kenneth in his

office, afterwards. One day we were summoned about a performance we'd given. Sir Kenneth invariably entered his viewing box at the back of the tiny auditorium with his little dog; nothing could happen till the dog was comfortably settled. (I can't remember the mutt's name, but let's call it Henry.) We were all aware that something had happened during the performance and there was a rumour that Sir Kenneth had left before the end.
We all gathered in Sir Kenneth's over-crowded office wondering what was up. Sir Kenneth was clearly outraged. Something had occurred in our production that he should have been warned about and he wanted to know who was responsible. He outlined the plot of our high drama concluding: '…and as the story reached a climax, the gun was picked up, aimed… and fired. And Henry fainted! Now who did this? And why wasn't I told?'

We were detained for some time while this investigation ground on – nothing about the quality of the drama came up – as no-one was prepared to come straightforwardly clean about it. 'It took Henry some minutes to recover. I want you all to apologise. I never, never want anything like this to happen again!'"
At RADA, Yootha progressed into upper middle A2 in her second term. The students were beginning to find their feet and settling into the life as actors. The lack of men we've already mentioned meant that Yootha, like the other girls "would often have to take on the male roles." It must have provided lots of fun. Roger Moore remembers "Yootha was always ready for a laugh, as was Lois, when we performed together." He recalls, "We'd dress up in the most extraordinary fashion and wear the most outrageous clothes. We must have been the ancestors of today's highly colourful hippies. Not necessarily academically, but it taught us how to laugh and how to live. It was a time for youth to burst out. And it was my joy to go pop with the best of them."
Surely Yootha must have benefited from this playful, carefree atmosphere. In early 1945 she took part in some rehearsals that led to performances later on in the year. Here are Sir Kenneth Barnes's comments on her performances:

Pride and Prejudice. Jane Austen – 28th March 1945.
Role - Lydia Bennet - Yootha Joyce Needham "A poor specimen."

Henry V. William Shakespeare – 9th July 1945.
Role 1 - Archbishop of Canterbury - Yootha Joyce Needham. "Improved, spoke well."
Role 2 - Private John Bates - Yootha Joyce Needham. "Yes."
*Sir Kenneth Barnes also writes "A good production."

This Happy Breed. Noel Coward – 12th July 1945 & 13th July 1945.
Role - Sylvia - Yootha Joyce Needham. "Sense of comedy - good."

The female students were also called on to play a number of male roles at The Old Vic [then a kind of National Theatre], as there was a shortage of men there too. Yootha never mentioned if she was among those called. She did however go after classes to The Old Vic, in the gods, to watch Laurence Olivier, Margaret Leighton and Joyce Redman "They were the best ones," she later remembered: "Once, Olivier and Leighton fell over on the stairs in *Henry IV, Part II*, and they just got up, laughed and went on. And I thought, 'that's what I have to know about: style. Not to pretend it hasn't happened.'"

Yootha's second term reports in July 1945, were not that favourable. She remembers that she was beginning to feel rather "restless" and anxious to get out and do the job of acting, and although she was still graded a "2", her punctuality was a problem: "Bad attendance" and "Late" were among the comments. Things reached a climax when the director told her at the end of the year that she "had absolutely nothing to offer the profession." Undeterred, and with the first year of studies under her belt, Yootha took work during the summer break at her local theatre, the Grand in Croydon.

CHAPTER 7

"The Grand in those days had been closed in the early part of the war when Croydon was extensively bombed, but reopened in the latter part of 1942." After the war, the theatre reopened for repertory companies and put on an annual pantomime, one of which starred Eileen Atkins in *The Legend of Mother Goose*. The Grand had an impressive history, like many "provincial" theatres in the 20th Century. Opened in 1896 by the famous theatrical impresario Herbert Beerbohm Tree, it premiered George Bernard Shaw's *Man of Destiny* in 1897. In the Edwardian era there was a mixture of popular melodrama and light plays; then, in the twenties, it became a receiving house for touring companies, and in the forties and fifties had featured famous artists like Michael Redgrave and Betty Marsden. It closed in April 1959 and was later demolished, though not without fierce opposition, supported by actors like Fenella Fielding, and a petition signed by nearly 100,000 people. Croydon Council had considered buying the site, but the proposal was narrowly rejected. Instead they gave planning permission for an eleven-storey block of shops and offices.

Yootha's brief time at the Grand proved difficult to track. She herself gave differing versions of when she was working there, saying it at one point it was "during her first summer break" at RADA in 1945, then again saying it was "after she completed her RADA studies in 1946; she was in fact there during her first break in 1945. Yootha was certainly restless and eager to perform: she remembered walking down Croydon High Street with her mother one day, and popping into the Grand to ask for an acting job. The Arthur Lane repertory company, who were based at the theatre, laughed at Yootha's request, saying "yeah, like you and 5,000 other people": nevertheless, Yootha said, they did offer her work as an assistant stage manager. As far as one can tell from the records, she was fact engaged from 27th June until late August 1945: just in time, then, to pick up on her studies in September. Yootha's billing in this first production was not, it seems, as an assistant stage manager, but as an actress. Yootha's first role was in the Margaret Kennedy play *Escape Me Never*, a sequel to *The Constant Nymph*, beginning on 23rd July 1945. Company director Arthur Lane took the main part, that of Sebastian Sanger. However, much of the attention went to Yootha and actors in other small parts. The review at the time commented on Arthur Lane's lack of enthusiasm in the role, but praised Yootha, billed as a 'Girl' in the production. The review in *The Croydon Advertiser* on 27th July 1945 comments "The ingenuity shown by the minor characters make this play not to be missed," and again: "it is very noticeable in this production that the small part actors have taken great pains; Jack Martyn as a butler and Walter Plinge, Yootha Joyce and John Thomas in the coffee stall scene are worth special attention.": A promising start, then. The Assistant stage manager on that production was listed as Peggy Forbes-Robertson.

On 27th August Yootha had a part in the next Arthur Lane production, Dodie Smith's *Autumn Crocus*. She was 'The Young Lady Living in Sin': a type of character role that would follow her around in the years ahead. It was in this production that she was credited as assistant stage manager. Her memories of this time are especially interesting. Speaking about it in 1976, at a time when she was becoming limited to the role of Mildred Roper, she said that most of the cast at Croydon had fallen down with flu, and she was called on to play multiple roles: so much so that the play became a kind of "monologue" for her. However, the local reviews at the time make no reference to this amazing feat; in fact, on 31st August, one review referred to the performances of all listed cast members. Could she have been exaggerating; promoting her versatility as an actress at a time when she was becoming afraid of being typecast as Mildred?

All the same, Yootha got good credit for her performance in this play: the local press said that "if her current performance is any criterion, Yootha Joyce is a young lady of whom we may expect great things. Let us hope that the producer will show equal discrimination in casting her for future presentations."

The review also picks up on a mistake in the sound effects that might have been Yootha's fault. It remarks on the "blows of a hooter on the O.P side, when the bus is supposed to drive up on the prompt side?"

Yootha remembered her work as an assistant stage manager as tough going: "in those days five sets had to be changed in 30 seconds, and if you missed a single fork in the restaurant scene, you were had up." Once, she recalled she had to "hold up a fireplace for an act while the stagehands cursed and bashed behind her off-stage."

This was her last performance at the Grand; that September, she returned to RADA. The experience had given her greater confidence in her acting abilities, knowing she could "make money at it" too.

CHAPTER 8

Now in her fourth term at RADA, Yootha had progressed from upper middle A2 to upper middle 1B. This was the moment she chose to provide herself with a stage name by dropping the Needham, and using Joyce instead. "It's a family name, and seemed less of a mouthful than Needham. Being stuck with Yootha is enough," she would say. Some of her fellow students had left, after staying for just three terms: Roger Moore says of himself: "I did all that they told me but I was developing the principle of taking none of it too seriously. As far as I was concerned I was leading the life of Reilly and it was great. Later on, of course, I'd get around to being a star."

For Yootha, however, the studies continued. In the autumn and winter of 1945, she was reviewed in two productions:

Heartbreak House. George Bernard Shaw – 13th & 14th November 1945.
Role. Lady Utterwood - Yootha Joyce. "Improvement maintained."

Cymbeline. William Shakespeare – 12th December 1945.
Role 1. Lord - Yootha Joyce. "Spoke well."
Role 2. Imogen – Yootha Joyce. "One of the better ones."

Her attendance was still an issue. She once said she was "usually pathologically late for everything but her work." Perhaps she never saw her time at RADA as real work? It's known that she applied for a scholarship to continue with her studies at RADA, but according to the Academy's librarian Clare Hope "she never got it." Now that she knew she could act and make her living as an actress, there was, as she said, "no way that I wanted to stay" – we don't know if her failure to get support affected her too.

In early 1946, now in her fifth term, Yootha had not progressed beyond upper middle 1B. Her attendance was suffering, and was remarked on in her fifth term report: the reviews she got, though not bad, were not great either.

Her memories of her last term at RADA were not pleasant: she recalled that, "The head said I was no good, but he usually said that about everybody," and that "all the awards went to Juliets and Desdemonas, and I'm a bit strong for them." Here are the (mixed) reviews of her final performances at RADA:

You Cant Take It With You - Moss Hart & George Kaufman. 18 February 1946.
Role. Essie - Yootha Joyce. "Unattractive."

She Stoops To Conquer - Oliver Goldsmith. 25th March 1946.
Role. Kate Hardcastle - Yootha Joyce "Showed vitality and charm."

She didn't take her final exams, and didn't get a diploma, "I guess that's why she decided to leave" Clare Hope said. Yootha claimed she was not discouraged by some of the comments made to her by "the head": Was this Sir Kenneth Barnes? She said he thought she "wasn't a lady and in acting, you needed to be just that." And again: "They all thought I was the worst actress they ever had in the whole of their history, and I'd need a further two years before I could make a living, so I left." "It was not really my cup of tea," she confirmed. She also maintained she didn't finish the course because she was "offered a job," saying that at this point she went to work at the Croydon Grand. However, we've already seen that this isn't true.

It's uncertain what Yootha did do when she left RADA. She did say that touring with ENSA [The Entertainments National Service Association] was "something she had done in her next long RADA break." In those days, plays formed part of the basic service entertainments repertoire. Perhaps this was what she did, but the list of actors that toured with ENSA is immense, and it is impossible to locate individual performances, the more so as we have no knowledge of where she might have gone. For years I have scoured charity shops and internet sites to find any concrete evidence of when and where she might have performed, but with no luck. Most performers in the post-war period had some experience of working with ENSA, jokingly also called "Every Night Something Awful." It was still fully operative in 1946: tours were organised with actors who registered at London's Drury Lane Theatre, where they would send them all over the world as well as in Britain. If Yootha did perform with them, her performances apparently had little impact – perhaps not surprisingly, since she was a beginner. I remain hopeful that some real evidence will turn up. She also mentioned doing some BBC radio for a year after RADA: but Glynn Edwards told me that he was "not sure what radio she did." He couldn't remember her doing any at all when he was with her.

Recently, a rumour was brought to my attention that Yootha had claimed she had performed in sketches at the Butlin's Skegness holiday camp, and had in fact appeared with Laurel and Hardy. The two comics did perform there, in a show organised by Bernard Delfont in summer 1947: it ran from June 23rd for six days, and featured Len Clifford and Freda, Slim Rhyder, and Marioa, the 'Amazing' girl juggler as support acts. But Yootha is not mentioned on the billboard, nor does she appear in the images of cast members, so there is no way of proving the truth of the rumours.

CHAPTER 9

Yootha was now getting a lot more stage experience. In 1948, she joined the Harry Kendall players, a repertory group, where she got her first taste of theatre in the north of England, mostly in Lancashire and Yorkshire. She became adept at observation of the local people, and particularly at mimicking their different accents, for which she had a real talent, as any serious fan knows. This skill is evident in some of her later performances, perhaps best as the Blackpool landlady Mrs Rowbottom in the 1972 film of *Nearest and Dearest*, where she hits the nail on the head, getting every vowel and consonant right. She was always very serious about this kind of character acting: "I consider my work to be the most important thing," as she said. Yootha had the capacity to play a wide variety of parts, and enjoyed contrasts and challenges. She said she found "top people so boring in the classical theatre," and was determined to experiment and be adaptable. She could lift the most passé and "dead" scripts.

One of Yootha's early parts with the Harry Kendall Players was Peony Barker in the Guy Bolton play *Humoresque*, a "comedy of youth" as its author called it, set in various music students' apartments. It was also categorised as a "light and breezy, after dinner play" whatever that means: perhaps it helped the audience digest! Harry Kendall himself was the producer, and, according to one review, "set a pace that did not slacken." The young cast entered into the tempo of the play with "good spirit," though "apart from the two leading male parts, there is little chance of characterisation." However, the actors "all work to make a success." Indeed, Yootha's performance was singled out: "Yootha Joyce is successful as a 'boisterous' young lady student." Favourable comments like this must have bucked her up, and help to get rid of any insecurities her family may have created.

Yootha did talk of her early repertory years later in life, in particular when she was achieving success as Mildred. She enjoyed looking back to her early touring days, when she had played in "Shakespearian scenes." In this same interview with Alix Coleman in the *TV Times*, she said, "apparently, I wasn't a bad Portia," though she also added that she "always thought she [Portia] was a drip." In her repertory days, she said, there was "a Shakespeare voice" and a "Shakespeare attitude," and that "everyone was trying that, or all sorts of Christopher Fry things."

Again in this interview, she talks of her approach to making her stage entrances, and mentions a supposed "fault" in her acting that was used against her at RADA. "I used to think, 'God, I'm an actress. I don't come on as if I were a lady,'" she said. This was criticism that rankled, and she couldn't let go of it. I think it's possible to see this conflict in her acting. At times, she would put on "ladylike" airs in parts that had no call for such mannered falsity. I think it held back her flow as an actress, most notably in her later performance as the hard woman/ex-lover in *Charlie Bubbles*. I am sure that without the airs she puts on in that performance, she'd have given the part more depth and strength, getting her nails deeply embedded in the character's bitchy dialogue.

These years are a bit short on concrete facts, whether about the parts she played – I have no idea where she played Portia –, or where she played them: information on the repertory companies is hard to come by. We have no knowledge, either, about her private life at this time.

In spring 1949, Yootha joined another company, the Reginald Salberg Players. In June of that year she appeared with them, along with Peggy Mount in Noel Coward's *Hay Fever*, where she gave a "droll performance as Judith Bliss." Peggy Mount had come from a repertory theatre in Bradford, the Prince's. [When she left the Prince's in 1947, her job was taken by Coronation Street actress Pat Phoenix, or Pilkington as she was called then, an actress who I believe later impressed Yootha.] The *Hay Fever* production produced "almost continuous hilarity," with "adequate support from Yootha Joyce and fellow actors including Derek Benfield and Jean Burgess."

In the autumn, Yootha got news from home that her uncle Williamson had died on 28th September 1949, at the age of 60, in Pinner: he left a widow, Grace, and £293: no doubt she would return home to provide some comfort to her family. Within a year came worse news – her grandmother Rebecca died on 27th August 1950, a week after Yootha was 23. Rebecca had continued living with Maude and Hurst, in Croydon, at 35 Gladstone Road. All her effects (including the sum of £653 12s 6d) were left to her only remaining son Henry, who was a film-booking manager. I have no idea if this caused any family tension, though it may have done. Understandably, Yootha took on few engagements at this time.

CHAPTER 10

After her grandmother's death, Yootha returned to the northern repertory theatre circuit, this time with the Jack Rose Players. The company had taken the lease of the Theatre Royal in Ashton-under-Lyne, which dated from 1891, and mainly housed variety shows – it had become a cinema for a time in the 1930s, before reverting to its original use. It may even be that Hurst Needham had played there in earlier times, for Bransby Williams went there with *Mi Padre*. It finally closed in 1953, after two years with repertory companies – before this happened, Yootha had moved on. But with the Jack Rose Players, she would have lived in digs, or "combined chats" as they were known – they were very basic, nothing but a bed and an armchair, and a shared outside toilet.

The Jack Rose Players opened at Ashton on Monday February 26th 1951, with *Peace Comes to Peckham*, in which Yootha played Grace, the elder daughter. They usually performed one play in the evening, and rehearsed another during the day: titles included *Nothing But the Truth, The Light of Heart, Mountain Air, Night Must Fall, Grand National Night, A Lady Mislaid* and *The Perfect Woman,* a farce by Wallace Geoffrey. Yootha would have performed in most if not all these productions. Here is one amusing anecdote from this time: "There was one incident when I was meant to descend a huge staircase looking very glamorous. I was the ugly duckling turned into the beautiful swan, and as I was holding on to my leading man, my knicker elastic broke, and they slid down my thigh, I was walking crossed legged trying to keep them up, and as I got down to the bottom of the stairs they fell round my ankles, so I just bent down and picked them up, rolled them up and put them in my leading man's pocket. I don't think anybody noticed. Then we walked around and he said, 'what was that you put in my pocket Yootha?' 'My knickers luv' was my reply." In another play, *The Seventh Veil*, she remembered: "I left the piano to rush into my sweetheart's arms, and the piano went on playing." Yootha's time in the North was a success. She also recalled that when she was in a play called *Mother of Men*, on 14th June 1951, she missed one of her matinee performances: "I went to a matinee to see the film *All About Eve* with Bette Davis" (which is supposed to be based on the life of Tallulah Bankhead, whom Yootha would later work with). She usually had Thursday afternoons off: "we would usually work in the morning and evening, however, sitting there I overheard two ladies behind me saying how lovely it was to have Thursday afternoon off to go to the pictures. It was three in the afternoon and I was supposed to be on at 2.30! I completely missed my performance. That was the only time in my life I'd missed one, and I sweated blood. I should have been fired but they didn't do that, they were very sweet about it." She must have been too valuable a performer for them to sack.

Yootha was still at Ashton in 1952, no doubt developing her style and loving it. On 31st January 1952 she starred in *The Young in Heart*, with several new members of the company – no doubt she would have made them welcome. The play had good notices: "the blend of comedy and sentiment gave full scope to the players," it was said, and "Yootha Joyce played a loveable teenager" [she was 25].

On 18th February 1952 the company celebrated its first anniversary with a two-tier cake, which was "cut by Yootha during the interval and shared amongst cast and audience in front stalls."

After this success, Yootha decided to leave for a job in London. Her last appearance in Ashton was on 5th May 1952, in *Heaven and Charing Cross*. In 1953, as I have already mentioned, the lease expired, the company disbanded, and the theatre closed. Their last performance, when Yootha had already left, was in *See How They Run*. As a matter of fact, Pat Phoenix made her first appearance in Ashton in November 24th 1952, but sadly their paths never crossed.

In May 1952, Yootha joined a couple of London repertory companies. With the Royal Players, she took the part of Audrey Foster in *The Happy Marriage*, by John Clements, an adaptation of Jean Bernard-Luc's *Le Complexe de Philémon*, which had had a fourteen-month run at the Duke of York's in the West End before transferring to the Theatre Royal, Chatham.

More interesting was the role Yootha took in 1953, in *Wide Boy*, by Ian Stuart, who also produced and starred in it, at the Regal Theatre – unfortunately, I have no idea where this theatre was. It was a full on, gritty kitchen-sink drama, a genre that was already beginning to take hold. It is set in a lower class cockney home, and focuses on the influence of home life on two delinquent teenagers. Ethel, their mother, is in a second marriage with a special constable, and finds bringing up her children difficult, as her new partner stands for no nonsense. Yootha played one of these delinquents, Clara, a sophisticated good time girl who gets two visits from a probation officer. It seems to have been a role that suited her, and she got a very favourable notice: "Yootha Joyce as the sullen yet graceful Clara, is always true to life." Still, this wasn't yet the wider success she wanted, beyond the theatre, in film and TV: instead, in April 1953, she was offered seasonal work with the Harry Hanson Court players in Westcliffe, Southend.

CHAPTER 11

The Harry Hanson companies operated in various theatres, including The Prince's, Bradford, the Leeds Theatre Royal and the Grand, Swansea. They were known for being resourceful with props and sets, recycling them and adapting them for each new show. Their productions were affordable and very popular with audiences, especially in the holiday season. Harry Hanson himself was a formidable figure, reputed to have a different coloured hairpiece for each season; it's said that when presenting Dracula he wore a white hairpiece, and once told his actors; "My Dears, you have played your parts so well that my hair has turned white with fright!" Harry Hanson gave employment to many, and enjoyment to tens of thousands. "Long live the name of Harry Hanson's Court Players."

Whatever their background, Harry Hanson was known to pressure his actors to always appear glamorous, on and off stage. This filtered through to the other associated Harry Hanson companies. He always insisted his actresses were well turned out, which may explain why Yootha never looked anything but glamorous in public.

It seems that when she was at the Palace, Westcliffe, the Hanson Company worked Yootha hard, for she appeared in a large number of plays. She began her stint with *Charlie's Uncle* in late May 1953, and immediately was boosted by a favourable review: "Yootha Joyce, a newcomer, made a palpable hit as Sylvia." A large variety of work followed, with very encouraging comments from theatregoers; she never got a bad review. In *The Deep Blue Sea* she "gripped audiences with some tense acting." In *The Happy Prisoner* she was "properly downright as the farm girl." It was the time of the Coronation, and they put on a special show *Our Family*, a farce, which, according to the reviews "depended too much on the striptease element; but Yootha Joyce and Harry Bowers lent distinction to their roles." In June, in *Widows are Dangerous*, however, they gave "a really funny farce," in which "Yootha Joyce scored hearty laughter": "The players got along very well with their one-scene comedies and occasional mystery play." On 22nd June she played once more in *Autumn Crocus*: the review said it was "a scrupulously well staged and acted presentation, with Harry Bowers and Yootha Joyce in tenderly played love scenes." *Music for Murder* "had its thrills, especially in the last act, where Yootha Joyce shone as Priscilla."

The review and support for Yootha seemed never-ending. Again, in *The Outsider*, about an unorthodox healer, she "was delightfully sincere as the crippled girl."

Worms Eye View, put on at the end of July, seems to have been the funniest play: "all the company combined to make merry." The manager-producer and (sometimes) actor Jan Fogarty "had the ability to tackle any play and provide great results."

August was the height of the summer season in Westcliffe, with large audiences. Yootha played one of the main characters in *Maiden Ladies*, the month's opening production. Mostly, they put on comedies and farces: they were in direct competition with Laurel and Hardy, who were also appearing in Southend. Her performances were still appreciated: Yootha Joyce was "commendable for artistic work," "scored once more as Iris," in the farce *Wild Horses*: in *Relative Values*, she was "outstanding." In *Waters of the Moon*, "co-stars Edna Hart and Yootha Joyce gave fine portrayals." *My Wife's Lodger* was "enjoyed by typical holiday audiences," and contained "spectacular sword fights" – perhaps Yootha's training at RADA came in useful! After a break in October, they returned in November with *Having a Wonderful Time*, which sounds typical of the kinds of shows they put on: it had "little plot, but plenty of slapstick nonsense, reminiscent of former times" and as a result "gained much laughter." "The company seemed to revel in its absurdities and duly fell on the floor (once there were six lying prone) and engaged in other antics." Again, "the best of the acting came from Yootha Joyce." *Glad Tidings*, by R.F. Delderfield, was considered "a much better piece": "the humour came naturally from the plot and gave happy opportunities to all concerned" "Yootha Joyce and Paula Flack played a less youthful couple dexterously."

Yootha's time with the company seems to have ended that November, when the company travelled north to the Gaiety Theatre in Ayr with *My Wife's Lodger*, and then back to Westcliffe once their pantomime was over. We have no records of what she did – there is no sign of her in Scotland.

CHAPTER 12

We don't know if Yootha got much work after she left the Harry Hanson Players, but it would not be surprising, for a relative beginner, if this was a relatively dry period. In 1976, when she had become a successful actress, she said "On the whole, my situation has been marvellously trouble-free. One's had one's despairing, despondent moments if work wasn't coming in. I used to think if I was out of work for three weeks I'd commit suicide. Now I can think of other things." We can see that work was her central preoccupation: to lose it meant to lose control of her destiny; she was more fragile than she perhaps appeared, even perhaps to the point of destructiveness.

However that may be, in May 1955, she was touring in *Murder at the Vicarage*, at a few venues, including the Bristol Hippodrome and the Palace Theatre, Chelsea. Yootha remembered an incident from this time: inspired by seeing *A Star is Born*, she fancied herself as Judy Garland, and started singing "I was born in a trunk" in the empty theatre, on the edge of the stage. "I got so carried away one day that I fell off the stage into the pit and sprained my ankle."

She had to leave the production to recover. Soon, she applied to the producer of a company at the King's Theatre, Gainsborough, Lincolnshire [currently up for auction]. It was run by Glynn Edwards, an actor, soon to be Yootha's husband. Glynn's background was a total contrast with Yootha's. He was born in 1931 in Malaya: his father John was employed in the rubber business. His mother died when he was young, and he returned to Southsea, to be looked after by his grandparents. His father later returned to England, and opened a pub (The Rose and Crown) in Salisbury: later, he remarried, to "a marvellous woman," as Glynn remembered. He died in 1946, just as Glynn was leaving school: "I left school at fifteen, I was a total dunce," he confesses. "I was talked into sugar-cane farming in Trinidad but had little enthusiasm for it. I was helping to manage a country club in Port of Spain, with acting as a sort of hobby. I came back to London aged 21 and joined the Central School of Speech and Drama. Nobody wanted to employ me, so I employed myself by putting on a play. That led to me forming my own small touring company."

"I suppose I'm the envy of many an actor," he said, "I hardly knew what it was like to be unemployed. In fact, I only had to sign on once at the Labour Exchange."

He was 23, and "full of arrogance." The company would perform a new play every week, he told me: "We usually did West End hits." He went on tour with Rex Arundel's *Vile Inheritance*, later renamed *The Call of the Flesh*. "It was a terrible show actually" he says, "all about venereal disease. It was popular because at that time the theatre was very puritanical; and of course you had the Lord Chamberlain's rulings, where you were only allowed to say 'bloody' twice, but it was considered by the standards of the time to have been a little bit naughty. We did very well with it, actually, but I had to recast at one point for the part of a hooker from London. Yootha auditioned, and in fact I auditioned two ladies, who both performed very well. Yootha wanted £12 a week as her fee, whereas the other actress said she would do it for £10 a week. So I thought to hell with the expense, and employed Yootha. She was a lovely lady." I asked him what it was that made Yootha stand out? He chuckled: "well, she obviously read the part very well, and she looked very sexy on stage, in everything, and she'd been very successful in the Harry Hanson Players. I took her on, so I must have fancied her. She was quite a girl. We went on tour and we hung out together. There wasn't much to do in the afternoons, so we just sort of slid into bed together, and that was it. We did the show for about six months," he remembers. *The Call of the Flesh* was billed as a "sensational story of crime on our streets – for adults only", and promoted as "daring", "naked", "raw" and "gripping"; it's no wonder it was a success. They appeared with it in Leeds, Wolverhampton, Boscombe, Swansea and other venues, including London. Glynn remembers that "The play turned out to be so popular that I took it on tour: it ran until the panto season. After the run, however, I never produced again and went straight into the acting profession, and did that for the rest of my life. After it finished, I joined the renowned Theatre Workshop, with Joan Littlewood. Yootha joined a few months later."

Joan Littlewood, of course, had a huge effect on British theatre in the mid-century. In 1953, she had taken the Theatre Royal in Stratford East, in the East End of London. Born in Stockwell in 1914, she was the daughter of a servant girl, "a cockney bastard" as she once said. She was raised mainly by her grandparents, who took in lodgers as a way of making ends meet. It was these lodgers, leaving their books behind, who supplied Joan's hunger for reading; she managed to acquire formidable social and historical knowledge.

Her journey into the theatre is well documented. She won scholarships to The Old Vic and RADA, and it was there that she first encountered Rudolf Laban's movement technique, which had a great influence on her. Aside from that, however, she was never impressed with what RADA had to offer her. She also met many left-wing actors, among them her future husband, Jimmy Miller, himself influenced by Brecht, and involved with agitprop theatre. She began touring with the Theatre Union group, from which Theatre Workshop eventually formed. Many others were involved, including one key figure, Joan's future lover Gerry Raffles. They produced their own manifesto.

"Theatre should be free, like air or water or love": that was Joan's enduring philosophy. They encouraged those without theatre experience to join up, with the aim of producing plays featuring the British and Irish working classes, attractive to the local community: where possible, they supported new writing from untouched voices. Their aims, above all, were anti-West End, aiming to break its dreary predictability and middle-class predominance. They also toured, in the North and in Europe.

It took some fifteen years, after attempts in Manchester and Liverpool, to find a permanent base for the company. They eventually settled for the partially derelict Theatre Royal. It was in a cheap, working class area: "the place was falling down" as the actor Murray Melvin told me, when I interviewed him in the famous theatre bar.

The members of the theatre worked day and night, multitasking as painters, stagehands, cleaners, adapting to whatever was needed to get the theatre in working order. Everything was done on a very tight budget: some members even slept in the attic. Before they came to Stratford, in fact, they were offered the Royal Court in Sloane Square, together with the huge grant that the stage company would get if they took it on. "Joan refused it because of its wealthy ambience, so they came here," Murray Melvin said: "Joan turned down that comfort for something real. She would have watered down her principles if she'd have accepted the Royal Court, and she would have never done that till the day she died. Life had been too tough. She had a reason for her day and she wasn't going to compromise. Miss defiant."

With her penchant for new ideas and for plays with a challenging content, Joan got wind of Glynn's production of *The Call of the Flesh*. She came to see the production deliberately because of its content, Glynn recalls: "she actually came to see it when Yootha, myself and our company played a big date at the Empire in East Ham, a venue that's since closed. I hadn't known that Joan had been to see us perform, but of course it was because of that performance that she offered me a job at Stratford. She was preparing a production of Jaroslav Hašek's *The Good Soldier Schweik*. I went on to work with her for nearly ten years, almost exclusively."

It was a good break for Glynn, but we have no idea of what it meant for Yootha. Probably work was becoming a bit scarce: her great fear. As she once said in an interview: "I'm desperately imperious. I hate failure. One survives, but that isn't enough. You can survive in almost any way. I've never come to terms with failure and there's no way I'm going to change now. This is me, and if you don't like it, hard cheese."

Yootha was very competitive, as Glynn recognised. "She was fussy too. I remember when we were together; she went up for a role in Agatha Christie's *The Mousetrap*, the famous long-running play. I know she was offered a role in that. We'd only been together for a very short while and we were also pretty poor. She went to see it, read the script and said no. She wouldn't do anything just to be in work."

CHAPTER 13

In 1956 Glynn and Yootha rented a flat together at 223 West End Lane, Hampstead. At this time, *The Good Soldier Schweik* was being transferred to the Théâtre des Nations festival in Paris. Glynn remembers, "Joan was looking for more women for the production." She asked Glynn if he knew anybody, and he suggested Yootha for the tour. Whether she auditioned for Joan is not clear, though she did once say that aside from one film, she had "never had to do an audition." It does seem somewhat likely that Joan was happy enough with her performance in the earlier *Call of the Flesh*.

Yootha, then, joined the Theatre Workshop cast, which included a young Brian Murphy, who remembers being awestruck by her. The workshop decamped to the Théâtre Sarah-Bernhardt on 7th July 1956, where they lived in nearby digs in a brothel, "We didn't know it was a brothel," said Yootha. "When we came down in the mornings there was a policeman outside who was a bit suspicious and kept asking us for papers - until he realised we weren't the girls who worked there."

By all accounts, the production was a great success, as was Yootha's handling of her small role. Some said that it made a distinct impression on Joan, who believed Yootha was "a great comedienne," With this in mind, she asked Yootha to join the company on its return to Stratford, "the one in the East End darling, not the one on Avon" Yootha once quipped; she thought this request from Joan was "lovely."

How "lovely" the experience of Theatre Workshop really was for Yootha is difficult to know: she always found it difficult to convey her innermost thoughts. The Theatre Workshop was not just avant-garde: it was fundamentally a group effort. The initial audience figures were not great, but gradually word got about. Jean Gaffin, who later worked in the office, remembers that "there was a sort of pioneering spirit" in the place. As Murray Melvin said, when he studied there, he "learnt, we all learnt from the company as a whole; we were all in it for the good of the company. Of course, with Joan, there was the old adage that 'The play's the thing'! What did the play demand and why aren't you giving it to the play? Egos were certainly not allowed under Joan."

What Yootha and the other performers attempted to do was find a way of learning, so as to change and reform the theatre together. Often, they would have to write, rehearse and perform a production in the space of two weeks! In that sense, one could think of all the group experiences as Yootha's; experiences that were vast and are well documented. Joan's approach was basic: she was never a slave to any accepted practice or acting method, but this doesn't mean that she was undisciplined. On the contrary, as Brian Murphy said: "People thought Joan's work was free form, it was in fact very tight." Murray Melvin commented: "The plays were all sharp and political in some way or other. Joan wasn't interested in entertainment, it was education she was interested in." She joked that she was prepared to "boil them [the actors] in oil in if it would help." Actress Julia Jones remembers her saying "I want actors who act with the whole body, not just from the neck up, and can create real working people." Joan said she would "start with the actors' feet, and "go under the stage and make sure they were not shuffling."

Yootha herself said that studying under Joan's directorship was a "rather nice" experience. Other company members were more critical. Richard Harris was impressed by Joan's force as director; but she could also "humiliate and destroy you," and Miriam Karlin too remembered that Joan had "said terrible things about her": "you love her but can't bloody well trust her" she said.

Joan's drive to achieve her goals didn't make for an easy life, and along the way she experienced a great deal of hostility: "It was a struggle – the Arts Council hated me, so that wasn't good, they'd have pissed on my grave." She was known for her socialist ideals: so much so that during the war, her home in Cheshire was under surveillance by MI5: for two years she was banned by the BBC! Politically, in fact, she was "a mass of paradoxes, a lifelong committed socialist with a love of luxury and gourmet tastes." She even described herself as "the synthetic prole." Jean Gaffin remembers her time in the theatre office, when "People were always talking politics, and I remember sending telegrams and things over things like Cuba." Asking Jean whether Yootha had similar political ideals, or whether Joan had any political effect on her, she told me she had "no memory at all of such discussions with Yootha."

Dudley Sutton, who joined the Workshop a few years after Yootha, remembers something of the political ambience in those days. His views are very fresh and worth quoting at some length: "Well, there was only one card-carrying Communist at Theatre Workshop that I knew of, and that was John Bury, the company's set designer. But Joan was a very very confusing sort of a person. I think she was a Communist, or she might have been at one time. And the nice thing about it is that Communism wasn't frowned on. But Joan was very bigoted in a way; for example if you didn't agree with her you were a load of shite, and if you were a middle-class, arty, public school type, you really couldn't open your mouth. It was tough if you didn't come from a working class background. You had to shut up, and there were only about two of them at Theatre Workshop that did come from that kind of working-class background. I mean, Murray Melvin came from a very genteel background. I knew his parents Victor and Maisie quite well, and they were very educated and politically active."

In fact Murray told me that his parents "Were both members of the Labour Party, but when Blair arrived, Maisie, disillusioned by him, left." But Dudley went on to tell me that "Yootha - I had no idea what her political views were, we never talked about it much really, because Joan talked such a lot of shit about it: maybe that put Yootha off it! But it's funny, I was talking to the playwright Mike Bradwell recently about Joan's politics, and the thing about Joan was that her politics were more to do with 'style'; it was more to do with acting. When performing, she would say 'don't talk to those capitalist c***s in the theatre stalls, talk to the workers sitting up in the back of the gods.' What she meant was, lift your chin up, and speak to those that mattered. Once you understood that, performing on stage, you could relax."

But, I came across a quote, I think it was Chatterton, who said any writer worth his salt must be able to argue both sides of a question, like Arthur Miller or

Bernard Shaw, but with Joan, in the plays we did, all the bosses were c***s and the workers were geniuses, and you know, I'd been around, and I knew that this was rubbish, and having spent four years in the company of mostly working blokes, I knew that they were just as venal, devious and wonderful as everybody else."

Dudley remembers his time with Yootha with great affection. But he too had little knowledge of her childhood, or her work before they met: he did say, however, "She was an absolute joy when I first met her."

His own route into Theatre Workshop gives an insight into the scene that Yootha was a part of. Before coming to Theatre Workshop, he had been a mechanic in the Air Force. He'd also been an amateur actor for four years.

"By the time I came to the acting game I had officers up to here. All that bullshit. I loved the English language as it was spoken in this country and loved the fact that I would be billeted with blokes who spoke English in about twenty-odd different ways. But up until Littlewood's appearance, the English theatre was completely middle class. It was run by the officers, and when an ordinary man or woman came onto the stage, they'd always have to be stupid, comic or both. That sort of representation would really piss me off, because the English language was so much richer than what these people were given. Joan was the first person committed to putting the realities of the English language on the stage, as it's spoken. I'd been thrown out of the RADA: that was the only qualification I had when I joined Joan Littlewood and the others at Theatre Workshop. I never had any problem recognising what was so wonderful about her."

"I was in tears in the student kitchen once when a bloke said to me: 'Why don't you go down the East End and have a look at a play they're doing called *The Good Soldier Schweik?*,' and I went down there... God! It was such a revelation. It was amazing. There was Brian Murphy, playing the part of an officer with a dog, which was a bit of rag on a piece of string. By the time he'd finished, the dog had fucked everybody else, running around, tried to piss on his leg, I mean everything! I was just in heaven. Yootha would have been around all this as well as all the other girls in the company, and they were not posh girls! They included people like Fanny Carby and Avis Bunnage. To me, Bunnage was one the best actresses I ever came across. She never became the star that she could have been, because she didn't fit in, none of us did, the worst thing is now people just don't know her! She was the best person I ever stood on a stage with. She'd got more presence and more talent in her fingertips than these so-called geniuses with their knighthoods and damehoods. It's sad that theatre all seems to have reverted a long time ago, to the fifties."

Dudley couldn't say what Yootha gave for her audition for Joan, if indeed she had an audition. His own, he told me, "was so awful." He told me he had later had access to the audition notes: "I wanked my way through lots of misery as Romeo, to show how much I could suffer, then I did an ad lib of a man in a cave finding his way out - then I did an improvisation with mime and that's how I got in! I also improvised with a cockney accent because I'd studied teddy boys so much."

"Joan asked me what work I'd done before, and I told her I'd been thrown out of the RADA: to her, that was like coming in with a medal." When I asked Dudley whether Joan appreciated or valued the experience and teachings from RADA, which she, as well as Yootha, had attended, he gasped, "No, God, are you kidding? That was deeply despised." "As an amateur actor in the Air Force, my nickname was 'Curly'. I'd stand on the stage kissing the commanding officer's daughter, and my mates would be shouting and egging me on, and I'd have my back to the girl, piping her up with my fingers. I've worked in a holiday camp; you know I come from the vulgar end of it all. But with Joan the actors had to have a relationship with the audience. And when I was at the RADA, the lights were shone in the actors' faces so that you couldn't see what they called 'the enemy' – they actually called the audience 'the enemy'. The critics used to assault Joan Littlewood because she used the techniques of amateur theatre, the music hall, street entertainers, busking and juggling, and strangely, they condemned her for all the things that made her special and wonderful; she made the plays breathe, I think we were one of the first theatre companies that would have music in a play that wasn't called a "musical""

Brian Murphy had joined Theatre Workshop earlier than Dudley, in 1955; he remembers his own audition for Joan, which he got through his teacher at evening classes. "It was a wonderful company and quite different to everything else that existed in the West End. I went along to a show and I was wildly excited by what I saw, when I auditioned to join the company. Joan was very kind and sweet."
Like Dudley, Brian had to pretend he had got lost in the dark and fallen down a pothole. Joan said, "you're young and you're not up to it yet - get some more life experience and come back later." "I regarded that as the big elbow," Brian recalls "but that Saturday I received a telegram from her saying 'you can start Monday'. I was so excited. I don't know to this day whether somebody had dropped dead or whatever. I had a wonderful learning experience there, it was marvellous."

I wondered whether Glynn and Yootha would take their work home with them when they were at Theatre Workshop, and perhaps discuss it over breakfast or doing the washing up! Glynn told me while he was there, "Joan ran very chatty rehearsals, so we did a lot of discussing things at the time, and she would always rehearse the first ten days or so sitting on the stage with her actors and actresses. After this, she would move into the audience and into the gods, taking and giving notes as she went. So there was always a lot of chitchat between Yootha and me as well as the other members of the group. However, we would focus more on the piece, as we would be busy doing it!" Clearly they would learn as they rehearsed.
Julia Jones remarked that for her, "A strange thing happened one evening when the curtain came down on *Johnny Noble*. Joan pounced on me. 'Your performance is letting down the whole company!' she said angrily. I was suitably shocked: 'What do you mean?' She didn't reply, regarded me for a

moment and swept away. Fellow actor David Scase was nearby. I asked him what Joan meant. He laughed. 'Don't you know you're getting very good notices?' Thinking it over later, I wondered was Joan in some way jealous? An Achilles heel in this remarkable genius?"

Barbara Windsor, who Joan thought 'edible', joined the group later, starring as Rosie in *Fings Ain't Wot They Used T'be*. Asked if Joan was domineering with her actors, or whether there were any clashes or difficulties with Yootha, she confirmed that Joan did have a jealous streak. "She would insult you if she didn't get her way, she was a toughie, there was no doubt about that, but I never saw Yootha in any conflicts with Joan, creative or otherwise." "Yootha, along with most of the 'Theatre Workshoppers', just loved the experience of working with Joan Littlewood at Stratford East. Joan'd call them all her 'nuts'."

Glynn said that "When you work with a director you have to learn to respect them, and when you look at all these people she trained up, such as Richard Harris and Harry H. Corbett, you can see why she was such a successful director. Of course, being given the chance to work for Joan later on was great; I got on very well with her."

After Yootha's initial experience in Paris with Theatre Workshop, she returned to Stratford. In 1956, her next projects were not on the stage, however, but as box office manager for the company's productions of *Captain Brassbound's Conversion* and *Treasure Island*. She was busy now with office duties with Jean Gaffin, who, at 17, had signed up, after a start helping with a group of friends. "We redecorated the theatre when the Workshop took it over. When I was asked to clean the lavatories, I asked Gerry Raffles what else I could do, and I ended up in the office with Yootha. From what I can remember, Joan didn't rate Yootha too highly and put her in the office, wanting her to do something useful." Jean remembers that she was herself "Quite shy and timid, so I didn't ask Yootha how she felt about this decision. I do remember liking her, and a few years down the road I remember feeling incredibly pleased that such a nice person did so well."

Jean told me she felt a bit guilty about implying that Joan didn't rate Yootha: "but it was true; I remember liking it when she was in the office, she was friendly and fun." "Joan said that she put Yootha in the office because she wasn't good enough to act in the company. And she went on to be one of the most famous ex-Theatre Workshop actresses, and do brilliantly. But that was at that phase, when she was very young - she didn't sort of please Joan greatly." Jean also remembers that she "didn't have a relationship with Joan." Brian Murphy, on the other hand, remembers that Joan "adored" Yootha. Dudley Sutton has a different explanation: "I'm not sure, but I think putting Yootha in the box office probably meant that Gerry Raffles fancied her. I would think that would be definitely it." Murray Melvin's opinion is different again, and kinder to Joan: "There was no principle behind putting Yootha in the box office. Perhaps it was for experience? It was all done because there was no money, the principle was poverty, we did everything, we made the sets, you sewed your own buttons on your own costumes - when you weren't painting the building that is! It was a shrewd way of running the ensemble. You pulled the curtains, you mopped, and I cleaned the drains."

Christine Pilgrim, who joined Theatre Workshop much later than Yootha, told me that she thought working with Joan Littlewood was "a challenge for most women." She said, "Toni Palmer and Barbara Windsor seemed to manage but I know of few others." "Yootha and I didn't talk about our respective Theatre Workshop days. I worked there long after she, Glynn, Murray Melvin, Brian Murphy and Joan's other 'nuts' had moved on. By this time, Joan was more interested in creating her Fun Palace than in theatre. It was Gerry Raffles who thirsted for another West End hit and persuaded her to try out new plays. I was in a play called *Macbird*, based on Lyndon Johnson's rise to the presidency after the assassination of John Kennedy. I played one of Johnson's daughters, while Myfanwy Jenn played the other. I also transcribed for Joan (I do shorthand). I remember working with her through the night, rewriting Vanburgh's *She Would If She Could*. She not only rewrote the entire play; she renamed it, *Intrigues and Amours*. *Macbird* suffered the same fate. I remember hearing the author say on opening night, 'Good play. Who wrote it?'

"I think Joan might have 'redistributed' actresses whom Gerry Raffles fancied. I suffered a similar fate. Gerry tried his hand with almost everyone. He'd say, 'Well, I had to try, didn't I?' He was a rogue, but an honest one!
But Yootha obviously weathered her 'redistribution' and, as Murray says, it may well have been a practical solution to a staffing problem. Yootha was sharp-witted and would have been a dab hand in the box office. That said, it wouldn't surprise me if her posting there had more to do with politics than practicalities."

Watching Yootha perform it would appear somewhat obvious that she had a tough side, as did most of the women at Theatre Workshop, including Joan. Murray remembers: "Yootha was very feminine, but underneath it, very strong, and of course that was Miss Littlewood too." "Joan didn't get on with many female actors, and you'd think that Yootha would be the last thing that Joan would get on with, but Yootha had all that femininity and all that pizzazz, but she was a toughie and that's what Joan liked, that's what Joan saw and that's what Joan used to bring out in the characters. I think Joan knew how tough it was for women in those days. Because Joan had been through it long before Yootha was born. Imagine the patronising Joan went through as a young girl when she told people she was going to be a theatre director. Can you imagine that male chauvinistic behaviour? So all the women who had to get through to a certain stage had to be pretty tough to win through, and Joan saw that."
Julia Jones remembers Joan's toughness too, but was prepared for it "Joan had more ideas in half an hour than most of us have in a lifetime; thus, in rehearsals, she would so overwhelm actors with her suggestions and ideas that they could become confused and lose their own creative impulse. I learned from this that I must go into the first rehearsal sure of the core of the character I was to play before Joan got to work."
Glynn said he had no idea that Joan didn't rate Yootha as an actress. "I tell you

something," he said, "Joan really did prefer male actors. Yootha didn't do all that many shows with Joan, but Joan tended to do a lot of men-only productions such as *The Quare Fellow* and *The Hostage*. She wasn't really that hot on the women, and of course she had some brilliant ladies there such as Barbara Windsor, Miriam Karlin and of course Yootha, but she didn't really hit it off so well with ladies as she did with blokes. She would often talk of her favourite actors, such as Jimmy Booth, and Roy Kinnear, but she never really cracked on for her ladies, I don't know why!" Dudley agrees: "there were usually two or three she would totally favour and the rest would just sit around. Of course it would get on my tits and I'd go outside and sulk, but looking back on it I wanted to be a star, and that was just ridiculous. I found it very difficult being part of a company, I wanted to be the lead all the time, but really, what I was best at was dance and mime as well as supporting roles. That's why I enjoyed working later on in *Fings*, because I could play gamblers and teddy boys, and play to my strengths.

CHAPTER 14

Yootha married Glynn on 8th December 1956; she was still at the Theatre Royal box office during their production of *Captain Brassbound's Conversion*. She took Glynn's surname Edwards, and they had a small ceremony with close family at Hampstead registry office.

Though they were very close, the marriage was not as strong as they both expected. Dudley Sutton recalls it was "a strange relationship really!"

In an interview in 1975, Yootha admitted she didn't know why she married Glynn: "I suppose everyone expected us to marry. It was more important 20 years ago. I must have thought I was in love when I married. I remember standing in the registry office and looking at Glynn and thinking, 'What the hell have I done?' Glynn would say exactly the same."

Glynn remembers their arrival at the Registry Office. They drove to the event in his trusty little bubble car. Yootha couldn't drive herself, but he told me how useful the vehicle was to them both. "We used it as our wedding car and had a few pictures taken getting into it. We would have to be careful if we'd parked it up and not left enough room, because as you know with those cars, the door opened from the front, so sometimes we couldn't get in! So you had to be very careful that people didn't back up to you."

Brian Murphy remembers being impressed that they had a car: "none of us had cars. Yootha and Glynn only had one of those converted aeroplane cockpits, a bubble car, but it seemed grand to us. They used to go abroad in it on their holidays." This was true, Glynn said to me. The size didn't put them off: "We used to take it all around Europe too, it was good value, because when you haven't got too much money, which we hadn't at the time, it gave us a lot of opportunities. We'd take a tent or whatever and off we'd go. No matter what people say about those little three wheelers, they were very economical for us, and I had three wheeler cars quite a bit actually, all a question of economics. I think they did 80-90 miles to the gallon."

Glynn remembers little of Yootha's parents. When they were living in Croydon, he said, "We used to pile in sometimes for weekends." He met Yootha's father a few times but never heard him sing. Knowing Glynn was keen on boating, I asked how keen a sailor Yootha was: "I've had many boats, but one of the boats I remember having when I was with Yootha was a canoe, and she used to call that "Splash," because we always used to get rather wet. There was also my first little sailing cruiser and there was one where we had an accommodation adaptation, and we used to buzz around the Solent. Yootha really didn't like it when the weather was rough, but what she did like was the harbour life. She loved mooring up at the harbour and going to the pub restaurant or a local viewpoint. Sometimes if the weather was bad and we were going back to, say, Portsmouth or whatever she would insist 'Now you take the boat now, Glynn, and I'll take the train luv.'" Glynn chuckled, "sometimes we would do a bit of camping too, but only if the weather was good."

Murray Melvin too had happy memories of Yootha and Glynn, and I felt privileged that he shared them with me, telling me on no account to rush the book: "It was always Yootha and Glynn, they were a team," he remembers, "and I don't know why, but Yootha mentally, not physically always had an arm round me, and that's why I would always get the lift home in the bubble car, 'how are you getting home?' she would ask, because we'd be around until about 1 o'clock in the morning, 'Glynn', she would shout, 'we're taking him home.'" "It was a great time for me" he said, "it was my university. I learned so much." As I switched on my voice recorder he said, "Whenever I talk about Yootha and Joan, I go, I just go, I miss them so much."

He recreated his first meeting with Yootha for me, as if making a theatrical entrance. I widened my eyes in anticipation, "My first meeting with Yootha," he announced, "I came here to the Theatre Royal in 1957 and my very first job was painting the foyer. I was up a ladder one cold morning; I was painting the gold on the filigree and suddenly this figure in a two piece sunflower yellow suit with trousers and high heeled shoes, which was new and rare combination in those days, said, 'morning luv, you're the new dogsbody are you?' I said 'yes, I was just painting the foyer.' 'Yes well the whole place needs a coat of paint, and until they can afford it, they'll have to put up with me - make sure they don't grind you into the ground.'" Murray lifted his finger as if to show me Yootha's firmness at such an instruction, and I really felt her personality come alive. "She was Miss Practical after all," he added, "she just glided into rehearsal of *Celestina*, [the fifteenth-century Spanish play about a madam] I was very impressed," he said.

It was good to hear Murray's description of Yootha's ensemble, and nice to know of her insistence on looking her best, even in her early days. Perhaps she got it from her time with the Harry Hanson Court Players, when the directors demanded that she always looked glamorous, bringing elements of theatre into her everyday existence. Talking about this in a 1976 interview, she said: "I'm desperately conscious of my appearance and I'll go to rehearsals in false eyelashes, the lot. I don't care if false eyelashes are out of fashion. I hardly have eyes, let alone lashes." And again: "I like clothes, but I don't work to a style. I'm inclined to be overdressed rather than underdressed."

Dudley Sutton recalls that Yootha "was always extremely well turned out, she had great style. I didn't know whether this was thanks to Joan, as Yootha was already in the company before I joined, and married to Glynn Edwards." Dudley joined Theatre Workshop in 1958, and his memories of Yootha were as fascinating to hear as Murray's. Asking him what it was like to appear on stage with her he said "To be on stage with Yootha was such a delight, she had such a wonderful way about her. I mean I was very young, hopeless and completely lost by it all and there were people at Stratford, like Brian and Yootha, who seemed to know exactly what was going on. I seemed to have spent my young life, in fact most of my life being confused, until I got much much older and I began to understand a few things."

CHAPTER 15

Not everything at the Workshop was a work of genius or a stunning success. Early in January 1957, Yootha took on the role of Susan Brady in John Millington Synge's *Playboy of the Western* World, which played at Stratford for three weeks. It was an ambitious play to attempt, particularly because of the strange, rather artificial Irish English that it's written in. Reviews were not great. The *Daily Telegraph* review was headlined "The Playboy Lacks Poetry" and called it an "uninspired revival." *The Times* was particularly harsh on some cast members, and noted that "Theatre Workshop's approach to Synge is that of a company who modestly doubt their capacity to deal with his speech rhythms. They hope to make up for the deficiency by sheer acting; but it is, of course, a fatal deficiency."

After the three week run, the company tackled their next project, John Webster's macabre revenge tragedy, *The Duchess of Malfi*, produced and directed by John Bury. Though the play is now frequently performed, Murray Melvin says that Theatre Workshop were the first to produce it. It starred Philip Locke, Howard Goorney, Glynn Edwards, Dudley Foster, Brian Murphy and Avis Bunnage. Yootha played Julia, Castruccio's wife and the Cardinal's mistress; she was the last in the billing. *The Times* welcomed the revival, and noted that it was "played with simple vigour." The actors, however, were "at the mercy of Mr John Bury's quite spiritless direction" and that "only Dudley Foster breaks the spell, occasionally to afford vivid and exciting glimpses of Bosola, that strange tool of villainy with a tormented conscience." *The Observer* commented somewhat sarcastically on Avis Bunnage's performance: "flung on a bed by her incestuous brother, she registers nothing more momentous than: 'oops!'"

During summer 1957, the theatre closed, as the company rehearsed a production of *Macbeth*, which didn't include Yootha – a pity, we might think, for she would have been a brilliant Lady Macbeth, and it would have given her something to get her teeth into. Murray Melvin told me that Glynn took over the title role at very short notice. Ewan MacColl [then known as Jimmy Miller], was the original choice, but "walked out half way through the rehearsals." "The production was all mapped out, with plans to perform in Moscow, when Ewan suddenly left. Glynn was the next one in line and within two weeks he had to perform it. Everything was given to him by the team to get him through, and Joan got him through to the level of everyone else. I was so impressed with him." This was typical of Joan's company: they had the ability to pull together for the common good of the play. First night was 3rd September, and it lasted into October.

The remaining months of 1957 seem a little patchy: I have very little information on what Yootha did. The London Resident Company took the Theatre Royal over at this time for a production of Wycherley's Restoration comedy *The Country Wife*, and I have discovered that Yootha in fact briefly appeared with this company in *By Candlelight*, an Austrian comedy that had been made into a film in 1933. She played Countess Von Baltin. Geoffrey Wright played the Baron; the production also featured the talents of Joseph Walker and Margot Evans, amongst others.

Yootha was not billed in any Theatre Workshop production until the beginning of February 1958. Now, however, Yootha clearly began to make an impact. Joy Jameson, later her agent, tells me: "I'd say Yootha was quite a mover and a shaker in those days." She was clearly developing her craft. However, the roles she played during the rest of her time at the company tended to be mainly prostitutes. Much as she was well received in these roles, they would be her first experience of being typecast.

When she returned, in February 1958, it was in *Celestina*, the Spanish play already mentioned, by Fernando de Rojas, which centres on an old bawd (originally it was a novel in dialogue form, which they must have given in abridged form). It was another daring challenge, and an original choice. Joan Littlewood herself produced it, with sets by John Bury and costumes by Una Collins. The music was selected and arranged by Michael Ivan. Murray Melvin played the part of Calisto, the young man in love with Melibea, and who uses Celestina [played by Eileen Draycott] as a go-between to get his way with her. Joan herself played the part of Alisa, Melibea's mother. Yootha played Lucrecia, Melibea's maid, who also falls for the old bawd's wiles. Murray showed me some of the photos of the production from the Theatre Royal archive: a dramatic-looking Yootha, with him. "There she was in *Celestina*, look at it, just look at it!"

The reviews were mostly positive. "Outstanding performances" from the company, said Peter Roberts in *Plays and Players*. "*Celestina* must be the best thing Theatre Workshop have done to date, and I can only hope that they will take this production with them to the Paris International Festival where theatregoers less parochial in outlook will be more likely to appreciate its great merits. The quartet of low characters (two prostitutes and two servants) were nicely rendered, though James Booth's conception of Sempronio as a twentieth-century barrow boy, whilst most striking, struck an anachronistic note."

Joan may have been impressed. Yootha's performance led to her taking a lead role in the company's next play, Jean-Paul Sartre's *The Respectful Prostitute*.

Set in the American Deep South in the thirties, it explores freedom, moral choices and dilemmas, all in a context of systematic racism and sexism. Yootha played Lizzie, a white prostitute who witnesses a crime committed against a black man. As a result, she comes under enormous pressure. It's a real challenge of a part. Glynn Edwards told me "she was good in that, one of her greatest performances. We were both in that show and I was 27 at the time, I'm now 82! So forgive me if I can't remember too much about it. My character was involved in all this awful business with the Klu Klux Klan, and he was about to be lynched! Her customer, I remember, was played by Jimmy Booth. There was a bit of a conflict within a scene as she had me hidden in the room with the customer!" Murray Melvin remembered being really taken aback with her performance, and told me that she became "something else" – "alive sexually," he added. "It was strange to see such a transcendent performance, it was remarkable." He also admitted that "Apart from playing prostitutes, Yootha didn't play many leading parts at Theatre Workshop." Murray's comments echo Joan's. A "stunning performance." As she put it in her book "I knew she had hidden depths, but that dead pan face, gently sinuous movement and cynical delivery, it was unforgettable."

The critics were favourable too. According to *The Times* "the company did their best with Sartre's play." It singled Yootha out: "The prostitute was very justly drawn by Miss Yootha Joyce." However, it went on, "the characters lost their edge, and the performance, jolted out of the deliberately casual style of the opening, found no level on which to hold a steady course."

Murray remembers that in the production "Joan didn't want Glynn to black up for the part. Looking at his blacked up face, she said 'Glynn, what have you got on?' He replied: 'I can't come on white as me!' 'Well,' she said, 'when you come on, they're all ignoring the play and thinking ooh look, there's Glynn all blacked up!'" "But", he went on, "when you watch Glynn's movement, I don't think he needed the make up, because he WAS a black man, I don't think he needed to do it, and today we aren't supposed to notice colour, are we? Was Miss Littlewood ahead of her time? But he went against Joan's wishes, which was a rare thing." I asked Murray if he ever did such a thing. He replied with raised brows, "no! I was the student, I wouldn't."

Glynn remembers the incident differently, "I didn't honestly know what Joan thought" he told me, "she certainly never told me she didn't approve, but she may have said that it wasn't necessary to black up if I didn't want to, but I did think it was essential for the role. It was a racial subject about skin colour, and I needed to have it for my character, but that was a jolly long time ago."

Around this time Glynn was considering branching out into television work, which he enjoyed; no doubt he communicated his enthusiasm to Yootha, who later came to enjoy working in the genre too. His television career began with an ATV series about and entitled *Sir Francis Drake*, in which he played the ship's drummer. He remembers filming ten episodes, which featured Jean Kent as Queen Elizabeth I. Glynn met Michael Crawford, later his co-star in *Some Mothers Do 'Ave 'Em*, who was also in this series. He recalls that "It was early days for TV: we were never, ever put to sea. The ship was made of cardboard and they wobbled the cameras to make it look like we were sailing." After this dabble in television Glynn returned to join Yootha and the company to Stratford East for a festive production of *A Christmas Carol*. Yootha took on two roles, The Spirit of Christmas Past, and Mrs Trossit [An additional character Littlewood specially brought in for this 'worked on' production]. She was also joined by Brian Murphy, Dudley Sutton, Murray Melvin, Avis Bunnage, Anna Beach and Stella Riley. The *Daily Telegraph* called the production both "salty and snappy."

The memories of Yootha's fellow-actors, however distant, all tell us how much she was loved and respected. Dudley Sutton told me he "really liked the way both Yootha and Avis would walk across the stage, they didn't look like ponces. I loved being on stage with Yootha. She was 'real,' that was the greatest thing about her. I used to love her because she would always slightly take the mickey out of everything. Before we went on to perform once, there was somebody rambling on on stage, and she said 'Oh God, another great speech bites the dust.'" Joy Jameson, her future agent, told me that "when she was at Stratford East – unhappily before my time with her, in spite of the fact that I already represented Murray Melvin – it seems to me, discussing those times with Murray, that they had a heck of a good time down there although they'd have been paid tuppence and a toffee apple."

I asked Dudley how they did support themselves financially. He said, "Theatre Workshop jobs were the best in the world, but we got lousy wages. Our wages on a good week were £12, but we started on £6. 16s. 6d. However, my first wage was £3. 13s. 3, plus £7 if you were performing, and £10 if you were abroad."

Talking to Glynn about those days, I asked him about his and Yootha's drinking habits: "I drank a lot when I was married to Yootha and she kept up with me. Wine was only 5 shillings a bottle then, and I could down a bottle as easy as a pint of beer. Yootha liked a good time. But I never thought she had a problem. She never seemed to drink any more than anyone else and no one ever saw her drunk."

Yootha was always up for a good time, and would always attract attention. Dudley Sutton remembers that "she would always have plenty of admirers." He liked her "because she had good sense, you know? Yootha was kind, generous and warm. She knew about life, and would get me out of trouble with girls. She was like a mum in a way, so if I had gotten into trouble with some girlfriend, Yootha would sort it out. She just looked after us. She was like a den mother. Oh! And she loved a good gossip! Avis Bunnage would look after us too; they were really wonderful women. Interestingly, the only actress I can compare them to now is Maggie Steed, who plays wonderful serious Elizabethan drama, completely without bullshit."

CHAPTER 16

In late 1958 and early 1959, the Theatre Workshop were preparing and rehearsing their best-known projects, which enabled them to give most of the actors in the company a "ticket to ride". Brendan Behan's *The Hostage*, according to James Booth, was "only a 17 page script which Joan brought to life through her direction." The first performance at Stratford was on October 14th 1958. The cast list would change: Yootha took over the part of Colette from Leila Greenwood. Murray Melvin originally took the part of the young Cockney soldier Leslie, who is taken hostage by the I.R.A. After a few months, it would be taken over by Alfred Lynch, of whom more later.

The Hostage was an immediate success. Lisa Gordon, who reviewed it in *Play and Players*, wrote that "It certainly has the seeds of greatness in it, and the first night was an occasion which I shall long remember." Lisa Gordon was aware of Murray Melvin's work in *A Taste of Honey*, and said that it was "entrancing to see how he developed under Joan Littlewood's policy of training," : proof, if any were needed, that all Joan's actors, including Yootha, were indebted to her for their coming successes.

Fings Ain't Wot They Used T'be, one of their most famous and successful productions, also appeared in February 1959. The idea for the show came from Frank Norman, an ex-convict, who submitted a few pages of script based on a Soho gambling den. As he himself acknowledged, the piece owed much to the improvisation during rehearsals at Theatre Workshop. The piece was comic but played straight, with the music composed by Lionel Bart. Glynn Edwards played the part of Fred Cochran, a gangster who lives with his loyal moll Lilly, and provides a gambling den for the underworld's failures, including ponces, prostitutes, Teddy boys and corrupt police officers. Fred has a windfall on the horses and tries to establish himself as top dog; the play ends with him marrying Lilly. The initial run was from 17th February to 2nd April, and Yootha took two roles, 'a tough policewoman' and 'Murtle', playing it up as posh. It was the beginning of fame for Theatre Workshop. The reviews describe Littlewood as "one of the truly heroic spirits in the London theatre;" "she knows how to get the best out of actors and plays alike." Yootha was singled out for praise: she "holds the eye whenever she appears" noted the *Observer*.

After its first run, *The Hostage* was to be taken to Paris for the Théâtre des Nations festival on 3rd to 6th April 1959. In Murray Melvin's excellent book *The Art of Theatre Workshop*, there is a photograph of Yootha pointing to the billboard.

According to the show's choreographer and teacher of the 'Laban' movement technique, Jean Newlove, it seems that the digs in Paris were the same as used on the previous visit to the festival. "Apparently we stayed in a brothel. I was so innocent I didn't know but it seemed strange. I was pregnant at the time with my daughter Kirsty," she said; "and I do remember Yootha had stayed up all night playing cards with actors Howard Goorney, Brian Murphy and Stella Reilly while awaiting news of her birth. But sadly, after that we lost touch."

When they returned to Stratford, the production of *Fings* was undergoing a process of fine-tuning, in which some of the parts were switched. Murray Melvin recalls that, although he was still in Shelagh Delaney's *A Taste of Honey* in the West End, he only saw a run-through of *Fings* before the later first night transfer at the Garrick (*Honey* having finished by then). "It was Joan's method of working. Once a show was opened, Joan would then, what she would call, 'start working on it,' so things would change on a daily basis. It came as no surprise that a scene from a production would change or disappear. In the original production, the original two ladies of the street were played by Ann Beech and Carmel Cryan, later replaced by Barbara Windsor and Toni Palmer. It was all part of the working day at Theatre Workshop." Carmel Cryan recalls working with Yootha in the earlier production of *Fings*. She was later to marry Roy Kinnear, a particular favourite of Joan's, who later featured as the popular character Jerry in *George and Mildred*. She remembered how sophisticated and experienced Yootha seemed.

Working for Joan Littlewood was a very intense experience, and it didn't suit everyone. Yootha herself never gave the impression that Joan was hard on her (and on actresses generally), but there is still some evidence she might have been.

An interesting case is that of Pat Phoenix, the famed Elsie Tanner of *Coronation Street*, who briefly took on the role of Lilly Smith in 'Fings'. Pat's insightful account of her time at Theatre Workshop, from her autobiography *All My Burning Bridges* showed she believed she was: "a conventional actress, trained in conventional ways, and the clever routine of Theatre Workshop was not my cup of tea. It works for many, like Richard Harris and James Booth who were in *Fings* along with me and Yootha Joyce but it does not agree with all artists and it did not agree with me. Miss Littlewood has done great things with many actors but I found it difficult to work in her extremely novel way of production." Pat expanded on this experience in an interview with Morrissey for *Blitz* magazine in 1985 – here, she actually mentions Yootha. "Joan treated her players very harshly, nobody was beautifully paid. You barely had enough to exist on. Joan and I clashed because I thought she was a load of sounding brass, and not enough violins, and violins are very important in the theatre. She nursed the men, like Richard Harris and James Booth. But she was very hard on the women, women like Yootha Joyce and Barbara Windsor."

Even the men could be critical of her: Alfred Lynch was known to have had "some problems with Littlewood's improvisational techniques; while recognising her as a remarkable director, he felt she also had a frightening power to destroy, as well as animate, actors." Dudley Sutton remembers that his struggles were mostly bound up with class.

"Oh, she gave me a real hard time, took the piss like mad. She was a sod, but you didn't mind because I was there to learn something that was so unique that you were prepared to put up with it. I suppose there were some middle-class, contrived, arty things within me that she felt needed knocking out! But there was never any point in trying to defend yourself with her. I was never any good as an actor until I left her, never any good at all, except at dancing. But what she had taught me had never left me and will be there for the rest of my life." There was

a battle all the time to avoid sentimentality: "that was the main battle between us, I was sentimental, all my reactions and responses were sentimental and she knocked it out of me, thank God. Whether she did that with Yootha before I arrived I do not know. Littlewood despised me because I went to a public school so she would deny that I knew anything. Publicly she would despise you, unless she fancied you of course, like she did with Richard Harris and Jimmy Booth: then you could do no wrong. But looking back, my background was as genuine as everybody else's. And I think it's bullshit to think that you've got to be working class to have any veracity." I asked him whether he thought Joan was possessive towards her actors: "Oh yes, of course she was, especially towards her actors, including Yootha. I will use the word 'genius' for Joan. The woman created a university for me, I was never really any good – except that Murray Melvin and I were the two in the workshop that were good with mime and dancing so I studied that a lot, what I couldn't do was open my mouth." Dudley recalls that Harry H. Corbett was one of her great loves as an actor "He was the best of the classical actors , and wasn't at all romantic." But though even he on occasion mentioned Joan's power to "destroy," Yootha never mentioned it as having happened to her.
Dudley remembers that as part of the improvisation "We did wonderful mock cockney for *Fings*. Language is the richest part of our culture and it's ignored, to me everything is about language."

Throughout 1959 *Fings* continued to change and develop under Joan. Yootha's involvement in the production increased. She took on a role as 'The Brass Upstairs' in addition to the two she already played. She needed more exposure to display her improvisation skills, and give the show more punch. Murray says she was great at playing so many varied roles, "Posh one minute and brassy the next, she was brilliant." Dudley remembers Yootha "playing the whore at the top of the stairs in *Fings* where James Booth comes on and says 'You say that again and I'll come up there and 'do' you,' and she said 'You couldn't afford it!' When we performed it, it brought the house down. She was great with one-liners like that; I'd love to see the stumps flying. Instinctive with a good attack: that was Yootha. That was a part that she was brilliant in, these sort of parts are great, playing whores or gay men; better than being the boring romantic lead… really boring!" Dudley told me how much he enjoyed movement, mime and dance when he was at the Workshop, "A few of us used to go down to Cambridge Circus where there was a bloke called 'Yat'. He had come from the Ballet Russe, and he taught dance for actors. It was staggering and I was absolutely in love with French mime, after seeing *Les Enfants du Paradis*. I remember with Yootha, I did a wonderful tango with her in *Fings*; we danced across the stage, and my hand was going down and down, lower and lower and when it got to her crotch there was a big rap of her hand and I pulled my fingers away as if they were burned. She was great."
Theatre Workshop shows were rehearsed to very tight deadlines. Between April 24th and 9th May 1959, the company revived John Marston's *The Dutch Courtesan*, from 1604. Their first production – according to Murray Melvin, the

first for three hundred years – had been put on four years earlier. Joan was the producer, and Glynn and Yootha took leading roles as Master and Mistress Mulligrub. Other members of the cast were Howard Goorney, Richard Harris, Rachel Roberts, Dudley Sutton, Ann Beach, Carmel Cryan and Brian Murphy. The set was designed by John Bury, and fixed on a gradient. It was "exceedingly easy on the eye and remarkably hard on the actors," according to *Plays and Players*. According to *The Times*, "Mr John Bury's set, with its raked floor of diagonally aligned cheques, encourages a mannered elaboration, which Miss Yootha Joyce avoids by comic acting based on direct attack." According to the critics, the actors couldn't be heard - again according to *Plays and Players* "The overwhelming impression was that the speech was that of a 'mumble school.'" Perhaps it was nerves, but *The Stage* Review didn't think so: "Under- rehearsal was evident on the opening night, but players with the experience of Rachel Roberts, Yootha Joyce, Howard Goorney, Glynn Edwards and Brian Murphy should have little difficulty in tightening up their scenes." Praise was evident though "There was an outstanding performance by Howard Goorney as Cockledemoy, a prototype of Til Eulenspiegel, and excellent work from Yootha Joyce, Glynn Edwards and Rachel Roberts as sundry fruity characters of dubious reputations and fortunes. When the cast have looked at the script more carefully, this play richly deserves a transfer."

Dudley Sutton specifically recalled Yootha's performance in this play. Her responses were incredible, he said: "She was playing this rude Elizabethan-type landlady, so her tits were on display. I was playing the gauche young boy, so she was sticking the tits out into me all the time and they just made me cry out whoorrrrr!, which normally I wouldn't have done! I loved that honesty and directness in her performance. Yootha was an inspiration."

For most of 1959, Joan was working on versions of *The Hostage*. She had an amazing ability to remember huge numbers of changes; the actors too must have been working flat out. She used to have them improvise an hour before curtain call, to warm up and create a team spirit. Yootha was still Colette. Other cast members included Glynn Edwards, Stephen Cato [later Lewis], Brian Murphy, Leila Greenwood and Eileen Kennally.

As has been mentioned, Alfred Lynch took over as Leslie, the hostage, from Murray Melvin. He and Yootha would often discuss their performances. Joan had spotted Alfred at the Royal Court's production of Willis Hall's *The Long and the Short and the Tall* and asked him to join the company. Yootha immediately warmed to him, and they would become firm pals. Alfred was a loner and chose to keep out of the mainstream. He was the son of a plumber, brought up in the East End, and left school at fourteen with strong ambitions to become an actor. He was inspired by visits to the cinema, and hated the routine of his work as a messenger in a printer's office. Working as a lorry driver's mate, he would spend evenings at Toynbee Hall at acting classes, where he also appeared as William Mossop in *Hobson's Choice*. It was here he met his lifelong partner, Jimmy Culliford. He failed a scholarship to RADA, but continued his course at Guildford Repertory after a stint as an assistant stage manager at the Midland Theatre. It was with George Devine at the Royal Court that his work progressed. Sadly Alfred died in 2003, aged 72, before I had chance to talk to him about his friendship with Yootha, but in a collection of Yootha's photographs I was given, one of Alfred was there, at the top of the pile. Toni Palmer, who joined Theatre Workshop in *Fings*, told me she knew Yootha liked Alfred very much. "She used to talk about him a lot and of course he used to help her with her life's problems." For Yootha one such problem was nerves, and it didn't disappear with age. "Maybe Alfred helped her deal with them?" Toni said.

When things went wrong on stage at Theatre Workshop, the actors would simply turn to the audience and say "sorry, folks." In rehearsals and performances of *The Hostage*, Yootha remembered, the author would occasionally turn up. "If Brendan Behan turned up drunk during his play, and started singing in the auditorium, we would bring him up on the stage and he would do his little blackbird dance and then we'd get on with the show," she said. Dudley, who played a Russian sailor in the production, compares this to modern instances: "The Irish had immense respect for a song; if Brendan began a song he'd finish it, just like in the TV show *The Royle Family*, when the Thomas P. Westendorf song "I'll Take You Home Again, Kathleen", ' was sung, the respect that was given to that song, with the camera panning round, with the people listening; the Joe character sang the whole song. This wouldn't happen elsewhere, but it certainly would with Joan Littlewood, the thing was given such respect. To me stylistically that's really important."

The list of actors who appeared alongside Yootha at Theatre Workshop is breathtaking, and I am very grateful to those who have given their time to share the past, helping me to piece Yootha's life together. One of the most important was Barbara Windsor, well known for her vast and varied experience in the entertainment industry. When I asked her about her time at Theatre Workshop, she told me that her mother was so happy for her to do the West End: "she was always keen for me to get away from where we started out; she was a cockney snob, and she loved the West End. She sent me to elocution lessons and wasn't happy with me playing the cockney roles." However, for her first project with Joan Littlewood, a cockney was what she had to be, replacing Carmel Cryan in *Fings Ain't What They Used T'be*. Talking about Joan Littlewood, she was very revealing about her attitude to her performers.

Barbara first auditioned for Joan in 1959: "My audition for Joan was at the Wyndham's Theatre; I went down there and I wasn't really in the mood for it; my agent really sent me, as she thought it would be good for me. It all started with a chat, with what I thought was the cleaning lady in the foyer. I wasn't that keen on the job, and as I was more your West End performer, I'd been used to the way things were done there, so I told this cleaning lady I didn't really want it. She was questioning why I didn't want the work, so I just gave her my honest opinion. Then, come the time to do my audition, I was pleased to see my mate Lionel Bart there alongside Frank Norman, who was sitting on a stool. It was so nice to see them. Blinded by the light, I was told by the director, who I couldn't see, that the part was for an Irish prostitute. Being awkward, I told the director that I couldn't do Irish – I could, but I was just not keen. She said 'well where are you from?' 'Shoreditch,' I told her. 'Go on then,' she said, 'Give us your version of a Shoreditch prostitute.' I went all out with it. I knew a few from the theatre area that I'd always say hello to, so I'd recall it all off from my observations, saying '£10 a hand job, wank etc.' After that she said, 'Can you sing then?' 'Yeah' I said. Bart jumped in, 'Oh yes Joan, She's a fantastic singer.' So I walked over to the edge of the stage with the music I'd brought: 'Where's the piano player?' I asked. 'Oh there isn't one,' came the voice from the footlights. 'But if you're such a fantastic singer, just sing.' I gave my rendition of 'Sunny Side of the Street.' After I'd finished, the cleaning lady I spoke to earlier on appeared again from the darkness of the auditorium. 'Where have you been all my life?' she said.

She told me I'd got the part as Rosie! It was such as shock, as this was Joan. She told me she actually auditioned me in the foyer and that I had gotten the part out there too. Talk about crafty!" Rosie in *Fings* is famous for the magical musical number 'G'night Dearie,' Yootha sang alongside her and at the time of a cast recording, Yootha played her three parts, a brass, Murtle, and a policewoman. A review in *The Stage* noted they were "three well constructed studies."

The musical number also included another fine actress, Toni Palmer, who played Betty, another prostitute. The critics insisted that "notice should be taken of" them, both her and Barbara. Toni, like Barbara, told me that before taking on the play she "'did almost everything that you could possibly do in show biz.' 'I was a dancer in all the West End shows like *The Original Coliseum Show*, *Guys and Dolls*, *Kiss Me Kate* and *Can-can*. Then I met with Danny La Rue; I worked 21 years for him, I never left his side for 21 years; I worked at the Winston's Club, Danny's own club in Hanover Square in shows. I only left when they were doing pantomimes, because I couldn't cope being in those as well! But the rest of the time I was always there with him. And throughout that time I was in lots of plays and television and God knows what. I never stopped working, God knows why, dear, because I'm not that good, but I got regular work.'"

"Being with Danny was a very happy job, we changed the shows every three months to keep them fresh, we were always doing something new, and they were great times. I remember writer Barry Cryer was doing the shows and one of my characters was called 'Mandy Rice Puddun'; theatre was so much fun in those days. When you talk about satire today! Well in those days we didn't spare anybody, they were all set up and made fun of, and people we were making fun of would come to the shows and laugh at themselves."

Toni, like Barbara, had to audition for Joan. She said she never knew Theatre Workshop existed until she went to audition for *Fings*. " I was working with Victor Spinetti in The Winston's Club when Victor said to me, 'Joan's looking for a couple of old tarts! You and Barbara better get yourselves down there,' so I went. We were wondering what on earth we were going down to Stratford for, we didn't think it was going to be any good, because we'd never even heard of it. Barbara had been the day before and they thought she was wonderful. I just did my usual audition, and before I left the stage Joan said 'would you like to be in my show?', and that was it. I think it ran for two years and I stayed with it until the end."

As *Fings* developed, so too did the interest it aroused. Spin-offs now included a big hit record from Max Bygraves with the title song, and a cast-recorded LP for Decca. I asked Glynn whether this recording caused any problems for Yootha – was she embarrassed about her singing voice, as she had been years ago in front of her family? He said: "Yootha sings well on the record of *Fings*. I haven't got a good voice, but I think we both had the ability to put them over. Joan would always want the acting to be right and the singing would follow."

In February 1960, Joan decided they had to transfer to the West End, to the Garrick Theatre, seeing it as a necessary evil. They had to sell themselves to the West End market, and some say it "weakened the energy." *The Hostage* had also transferred in June 1959 to the Wyndham's Theatre. Now, it seems (though we can't be sure) Yootha was appearing in both productions. If she was, she had certainly spread herself very thin.

The Hostage was so successful at the Wyndham's Theatre that it was prime for a run on Broadway. Unfortunately, this didn't involve Yootha. Glynn explained to me why: "Yootha, I recall, was very successful playing the three parts in *Fings*. Joan didn't want to send her over to the USA as she didn't want to disturb that success, and of course American equity at the time was pushing for their theatre parts to be taken by their own actors. Engaging American actors was its priority – though I did go. Yootha's part, [Colette] was played by an American actress. That's why she didn't go, but you know, she was very happy in *Fings*, and they were smashing roles. Of course it would have been very nice for 'us' to be working out there together, but unfortunately, it just wasn't meant to be. She was never really offered Broadway roles by Joan."

So now Yootha was only playing in *Fings*, which itself was changing. As has been mentioned, now there were new cast members, like Barbara Windsor and Toni Palmer as Rosie and Betty, who brought in new life. Barbara Windsor, speaking to me about her early experiences of the company, described her first impressions: "The list of actors that had worked at Stratford East was long. As well as Yootha, they included Harry H. Corbett, Brian Murphy, Richard Harris, and Victor Howard. When I appeared at rehearsals, I thought what the bloody hell is this? I was used to a different way if doing things. I was used to having everything prepared; scripts and lines learned, all very formal and professional. Joan would just sling the script on the floor and say 'lets all do it in our own way!' Which I didn't like. I didn't really like her direction at the time."

Barbara remembers observing Yootha working under Joan's direction: "Yootha always seemed to work well. I never saw her confront or question Joan's methods. Joan would say that everything was for the sake of the company. There were difficulties here and there. The actor Victor Maddern walked out; he didn't like working under Joan I remember, and I walked out too on one occasion. But Joan's work was well known, fabulous productions were being shown, such as *A Taste of Honey*; it seemed sensible to be involved in the company. The work we were doing was fresh and new, it was a real talking point, and not just in theatreland." She also remembered that even though Brian and Yootha both were lovely and were great friends, they "had very different personalities."

Toni Palmer told me she had never met anybody who didn't like Yootha, "I liked Yootha very much and we got on really well, she was very very popular, she had her own style and her own way of living, she did what she wanted to do, she seemed to me to be a very nice person, but sadly, I never seemed to get to know her terribly well. It's funny, we didn't have much contact outside of the show, not that I didn't like her, it's just some people you see and some you don't."

I asked Toni if she knew of any places where Yootha would enjoy hanging out: "Yootha used to like 'The Kismet'" [a famous Soho dining club frequented by Marty Feldman, Frank Norman and Francis Bacon, among others.] "She used to like a restaurant in Charlotte Street, but sadly, the name escapes me. She would love going out for meals and things, and she was quite sociable at times, but at the same time she was very private,"

Yootha was indeed a very private person, and for that reason tracking her life can at times be difficult.

CHAPTER 17

Was Yootha ever one to advise her fellow actors? Especially in the rehearsals for *Fings*, the actors must have bounced ideas off each other. I asked Dudley Sutton if Yootha ever received notes from Joan, or if they would advise one another. "No, not really, we would just watch and listen to each other on the stage; we weren't giving each other notes, we just listened to Littlewood all the time. It was wonderful for me."

Barbara Windsor in *Laughter and Tears of a Cockney Sparrow*, says that Joan "always made sure we were kept up to scratch. Instead of typing out discreet notes for each individual actor, she used to scrawl them in longhand and pin them on the notice board inside the stage door for all to see. The only person who never seemed to get a note was little me. 'What is it with you, you jammy cow?' said Yootha Joyce." Toni Palmer, in contrast, told me that they would get endless notes from Joan, "every time she came in we got notes on the board, forever, but I think most people never took much notice of those, we all carried on in our own sweet way": "It's very hard to describe Joan because she was such a mixture herself. There was lots of improvisation, you made it up yourself and then she'd go away in the evening with all the pages she'd scribbled down of what we all said: then it was all typed out next day and put in the script. You could always say that half of the shows were written by us. Now, though, it's so different, it's all very cut and dried and laid out. I'm glad I worked when I did, because now, I couldn't stand it! I'm so lucky now, I know," said Toni.

Toni's memories of the theatre in the late fifties and early sixties convey a great sense of fun, but there were times when voices where stifled through censorship. The Lord Chamberlain had to officially approve shows' content for approval. *Fings* was certainly on his list. Toni recalls a letter sent to Joan during the production. "Oh, it was so funny, and of course I remember the exact wording," she said. "We all got asked to gather and listen to the letter, that Lionel Bart had to read out. It started: 'The actor playing the part of Tosher will not get the actress playing the part of Rosie, up against the table in an attitude indicative of copulation. The actor playing the part of the builder's labourer will not cross the stage carrying the plank at an erotic angle.'" Toni thought the letter "So loony. We were all doubled up laughing as Lionel was reading it out, thinking it was the most stupid thing we'd ever heard. Of course we never took any notice. Joan, though, wanted to work it into the show in some way, but of course it would have caused a lot of aggravation, because they were quite capable of closing a show down in those days, you see, so we just thought we'd ignore it, as chances were he wouldn't come and see the show again, the Lord Chancellor or whoever it was."

When I talked this incident over with Dudley, he asked: "It's interesting, why does censorship go down the social scale? Maybe the working class should decide what's legal and illegal. These other people make expressions used by the ordinary person illegal. Why not punish people who use words like 'quantitative easing?!'" According to Barbara Windsor, it was "all a shake-up of the theatre that we were involved in, and it was part of Joan's breakthrough. In the production of *Fings*, it was all about unmentionable things; the subject and language content were challenging for the audience. Until then, they'd only seen tame, cleaned up versions of the numbers, from Max Bygraves who performed them at The Palladium. But ours were quite risqué and bold, we even had dirty versions of songs that we'd perform. The language didn't bother us. It was the critics that were shocked, but as Joan's work was a breakthrough, we were allowed to be outrageous on stage. We got away with a lot."

Ironically, it was this sexiness that audiences wanted to see. Theatre was changing, as new forms of expression came to the surface. As Dudley said, Yootha and the other women "didn't pretend to be sexy, they *were* sexy. Posh actors tended to express their sexuality in their voices, whereas Theatre Workshop actors did it through their bodies. Yootha could become very sexy in her performance, as could Avis Bunnage, Rachel Roberts and Maggie Steed, too. People like that. They were women and they wore their sexuality with pride; they certainly didn't hide it, but conveyed it in a joyful way - not a salacious way. Toni Palmer was incredibly sexy too!"

Performers like Yootha, Barbara Windsor, Toni Palmer and Avis Bunnage, [an underestimated actress, even today] undoubtedly conveyed strong, tough, female characteristics in their performances and probably in their own lives, too. When I asked some of the people at Theatre Workshop who worked alongside them whether they thought their attitudes intimidated or threatened Joan in any way, Jean Gaffin told me "At 17, I found Joan so intimidating. I can't imagine her being intimidated by strong women. Avis was lovely, a fine actress."

Yootha herself later talked about her toughness, claiming that "Professionally, people have said I've a masculine temperament." Murray Melvin agreed: "Yes, they were toughies. Yootha, Avis, Fanny Carby, Miriam Karlin, even Barbara Windsor, and they don't come tougher! That toughness was what Joan saw, and they all had a rapport. Joan knew what it was like and saw their strengths, and used that well in all their characters. But as well as being a toughie, Joan was also very feminine too, you see. You wouldn't necessarily see this on TV interviews though, because she was always up against those men like Malcolm Muggeridge; did she ever have a woman interviewing her? No, they were all establishment boys who she loathed and put up with, just for the moment; she never stuck much from them. We still haven't broken through yet. For instance, how many statues of women are there in this country? We're getting one of Joan here outside Theatre Royal, but the battle still goes on. Apart from the obligatory royals and Thatcher in the House of Commons, there aren't that many female statues, are there? I think it's about bloody time we got one up for her!" It's true, of course. At Thames TV, where Yootha later filmed her hit comedies, they have plaques on the walls for the men like Tommy Cooper and Benny Hill, but only for one woman, Irene Handl! Yootha obviously didn't make the grade. With all these strong personalities, who was really in charge? Barbara Windsor said that Yootha and the other actors all thought Joan was great, and they learned a lot. "They all seemed used to her, not scared of her so much. Toni Palmer may have been a little scared. She hoped Joan wouldn't discover her wealthy background, as she thought it might have displeased her. I remember she said she was from Brixton, just like her husband, the writer Ken Hill; of course Joan loved this type of working-class background, and it really fitted in with her way of thinking."

It seems Joan rather liked female toughness in her company. Barbara again remembered one time when the costume woman said she should wear tatty clothes for her as role as a cockney: "I told her cockneys wouldn't dream of looking so tatty, 'I'm not 'avin it'; of course Joan liked the fact I could stand up for myself." Murray Melvin commented that "You could never say 'thank-you' to Joan. If you did she'd give you a clip round the ear and kick you out. 'Thank-you' simply wasn't a word that came into her vocabulary. Neither did you touch her," he said.

Dudley remembered "Littlewood really hated the fact that I'd been to a public school, she couldn't stand it. The fact that my father managed to arrange it through the black market cut no ice with her at all. Even my grandfather, who had worked in the mills in Lancashire as a kid wouldn't do it for Joan, because *I* hadn't done it." Commenting on Toni Palmer's fear of her, he said: "I think generally that was the case in the theatre in those days, you had to be known as working class. It was terrible snobbery, but it was the height of fashion. The whole thing became such a nonsense because everybody was calling themselves working class. I mean members of the Workshop included Richard Harris, who came from a wealthy flour milling company in Limerick. Dudley Foster went to a public school, I did, Brian Pringle did, in fact a lot of us did, but I de-public-schooled myself by going into the Royal Air Force, which I was lucky about, because I became equipped for standing on both sides of the fence."

Performances of *Fings* at the Theatre Royal were noted as "remarkably at ease," and more so when it then transferred to the Garrick Theatre in the West End. Yootha's characters were getting lots of attention; Glynn remembers that he, too, "got a year's work out of it." Barbara recalled that "Yootha, Toni Palmer, an assistant stage manager and I shared a dressing room for two and a half years during the run. Even though I was only in one show with Yootha, we had a great time. There was never a cross word between us, we bonded really well. Yootha was a smasher, and she would never take over. We would occasionally go out to the pub and have a few drinks and all talk about our work together. We were the talk of the town. We all made such an impact."

The list of people who came to the show was very impressive – Princess Margaret, Noel Coward, Judy Garland and the Kray brothers, among others. I asked Barbara about the Krays: "I remember when the Krays were around, everybody was nervous and excited, especially Yootha. She couldn't get over their presence, she was so jittery." Toni Palmer added, "I remember the Krays. When we were at the Theatre Royal too, they used to come into the bar there, and they were just treated like friends. Joan quite liked them, and they presented a very nice façade. They were very keen to be with showbiz people, but as everyone knows, they weren't really very nice!"

I asked Toni what it was like, sharing a dressing room with Yootha and Barbara: "I think people would assume that us three sharing a dressing room would be like a load of cats fighting but we never were," she said, "In *Fings* we also had Miriam Karlin in a neighbouring dressing room. Miriam used to do her voice exercises; well she couldn't really sing, but she sang the way she was supposed to in the show, she'd be screeching! I'd open up the adjoining window and shout to her "Shut that fuckin' row up" and she'd return, "Mind your own bleedin' business" of course we'd all be doubled up laughing. We really had a great time in that show."

When I asked about Yootha's performances in *Fings*, Barbara particularly remembered her playing the tough policewoman: "she was brilliant, that performance even scared me," " I respected her abilities and strengths as a professional actress. You know, she would drive us mad a times. I remember us all working hard, slogging our guts out, and trying to make something funny. Then she would appear; come down the stairs, say her line, and wallop! Job done. Everything about her seemed so effortless; this lady knew what she was doing. She could play anything, any role, housewife or prostitute. She could be so sexy."

Toni Palmer echoed this too: "When you saw Yootha on stage, she was always very strong, and when she would be playing the brass upstairs and she'd be walking down a little staircase into this gaff and we were all lounging about doing bugger all and she'd lay into us. She was that strong that you never thought she had a nerve in her body, but obviously looking back, she did. I think basically she was quite an insecure and nervous person."

Barbara Windsor said: "there was a part of Yootha, I felt that I couldn't quite get? Not sure why! But it never stopped me from loving that lady." When I asked whether Yootha ever talked about her past, she replied: "No, she didn't. I never really knew anything of Yootha's childhood, none of us would really talk about the past, everything we discussed was about the here and now, we were so excited to be starring in the West End."

Toni added "Yootha was very funny, she never seemed to realise how good she was. She said to me once, 'I always think the current job will be my last, and I'll never get another' and of course she got the *George and Mildred* role alongside Brian Murphy and I think it was one of the most popular sitcoms ever made in Britain, and it's still being repeated endlessly on television and everywhere else. Of course as an actress she could go much further than that, and I can imagine when she was in rep she probably played every part going. When she was with Joan, long before me, she used to go round with the ice creams in the interval, and took the money into Gerry Raffles and he used to pay some of the artists' salaries out of it because there was no money."

The West End transfer of *Fings* to the Garrick Theatre brought positive reviews: "the company was excellent all round" said *Theatre World* and Yootha in particular was thought "amusing." She was also attracting the attention of Frank Muir and Denis Norden, who worked in television at the BBC, and were well known for discovering great comic talent. In a letter from Denis Norden, he remembered that "it was her performance in *Fings* which so impressed me. It was an amazingly entertaining show with, I think, a first rate cast, from which Yootha Joyce absolutely shone."

Yootha recalled that "when Frank Muir and Denis Norden saw the show, it was then that she got her first television work, in *Brothers in Law* [a sitcom starring Richard Briers]. - From then on, people just phoned up" she said.

This was the start of a new genre of acting for her: she liked it a lot, and thought she could "get things right." She and Glynn were beginning to move away from live theatre, partly no doubt drawn by the money to be earned. Theatre was in decline, with repertory companies beginning to struggle, but there were jobs to be had in television, and, of course, it brought much wider exposure, even if creativity perhaps suffered. Glynn recalls that when the run of *Fings* ended at the Garrick, he was involved in Theatre Workshop's production of *Oh! What a Lovely War*, but at the same time, was offered a part in the film *Zulu*; "it's not often that you get the chance to being asked to work in two lovely roles. And I decided as I hadn't done much filming in those days so I went with *Zulu*." He never regretted his choice, he said: "I was the big hero, not Michael Caine or Stanley Baker. They had me play Corporal Allen, winner of the VC for his heroics at Rorke's Drift." From then on, while he still did theatre occasionally, film and TV work poured in.

At times, Glynn worked alongside Yootha, in shows like *Dixon of Dock Green* and *Man About the House*. He went on to feature in programmes like *The Paper Lads*, *Some Mothers Do 'Ave 'Em*, and most famously as 'Dave' in the hit show *Minder*. In fact, much later, in 1989, when *Minder* was still being filmed, I met Glynn when I was working as an usher at the Liverpool Empire; he came to the door and asked me where he could find the theatre bar. He was starring in the Agatha Christie play *Towards Zero* with Michael Cashman. Even years after *Fings*, then, theatre was something that had stuck with him. I was 17 at the time and a bit shy. I didn't mention my interest in his late wife, but it was nice to see the face that shared a laugh with Yootha.

Fings lasted at the Garrick for about two years. Glynn stayed with the

56

production for its first six months and then headed for Broadway with *The Hostage*; after that, he returned to the show for the last six months. "Yootha and I weren't in a whole lot of plays together, *Fings* was the longest show that we were working together," he said. Like Barbara Windsor, Toni Palmer was only with Yootha during that time: "before that I didn't know her from Adam, and after that I hardly ever saw her," she said.

After the run at the Garrick, Yootha's work with Joan began to fizzle out. Perhaps she got tired of it, like Dudley Sutton, who said that "Littlewood's shows were less fun in the West End. I got fed up with it and wouldn't go in. I didn't want to go and just dress the stage. I thought if I wanted to go in to the West End, I'd go into a proper West End show and get a decent wage. I went into the West End version of *The Hostage* for a few weeks, but didn't do the West End version of *Fings* at all."

Whatever Yootha's reasons, she certainly never mentioned any spats or dissatisfaction with Joan; I'm sure she was extremely grateful for what Joan had given her. Apart from a touring version of *Fings* at the Opera House, Manchester in which Yootha was assistant director to Miriam Karlin, and a tiny role in the film version of *Sparrows Can't Sing* in 1962, Yootha only appeared in one more stage show that Joan Littlewood directed, another adaptation of Stephen Lewis's *Sparrows Can't Sing*, entitled *The Londoners*, in 1972.

All this must have given Yootha and Glynn some financial security. They moved from their flat in West End Lane, Hampstead and bought one near to Hyde Park. It was the basement flat at 198 Sussex Gardens, Paddington, and had previously been used as a storeroom. It would be Yootha's base for the rest of her life. Alfred Lynch, Yootha's pal, lived next door.

Obviously, both of them had immense respect and gratitude for all that Joan had done for them. The work at Theatre Workshop continued, of course. Joan became known for pursuing ambitious projects like the 'fun palaces': she worked with architect Cedric Price to produce an experimental model of a participatory social environment, with places where people could learn, enjoy and express themselves. She had a huge impact on the creative scene, and made an enormous difference to the lives of those who had worked with her. In 1975, following the death of her beloved Gerry Raffles, Joan became the companion of the vintner and poet, Baron Philippe de Rothschild, and gave up directing. Joan died in 2002, aged 87. As Murray Melvin said: "We thought she'd outlive us all, she was such a domineering character in our lives."

~

Toni Palmer said, "I certainly achieved something in working in *Fings*, because everybody then knew who we were, and Barbara and I had two of the biggest pictures you would ever see on the walls of the Garrick theatre. You could see them all down the Charring Cross Road. Of course you did get stuck for years playing the tarts with hearts of gold, but it was a lot better than not working at all."

"After *Fings*, I worked for Joan once more in something else which we won't go into because it was dreadful."

"Joan in the end used to call me the old fraud! But it never stopped her giving

me work though. She liked both Ken and I; she treated us very well and we got on very well with her,"
Toni Palmer

"Joan would call me little bird's egg. And I felt quite protected, but I'm not sure she wanted any of us to leave the nest! She could have a jealous streak at times. Joan had asked me to work with her again in a show she was putting together on Broadway, Philadelphia, this was after the success of West End show, but after the first time on stage, which I did purely for her, I wasn't that keen, and I said no. She then questioned my career direction, moaned about it being too commercial, as I was loving the films. Joan, rightly or wrongly, hated the success and money that television brought.
However, I relented, and went on to work with her in *Oh! What a Lovely War*, but at the interval on our opening night in Philadelphia Joan burst in at the end of the first half: she was furious with Victor Spinetti's performance, she went mental. 'What are you fuckin' doing being the star?' she shouted. She really upset him, it was just awful. It was terrible to see Victor just on the verge of tears, especially as we had to continue into the second half. Of course I turned round and said 'Don't you talk to my leading man like that, do you know what it's like to get out there and do what we're doing? I don't see our names outside on the billboards, I only see yours, so why don't you sit in the front row with a big spotlight on your head?' At this point, I left the stage, quite upset, and Victor handed over his hat and said to Joan 'OK, I'll leave, you can play my part in the second half', According to Victor, Joan said "Don't you dare talk to the director like that!" Which was not like her. However, Joan would have loved that row, and of course she was winding us all up!'
I learned so much, I never thought that at the time but it prepared me a lot for the future. I know she loved me in *Eastenders*. I went for dinner with Joan two weeks before she died."
Barbara Windsor

"I was brought up with a company that was family, you don't often get that anymore. She was our mum and we were her children. Even right up until Joan died, if any of us was in trouble, she'd be on the phone, saying, you know so and so? Well, they're not working just now, so why don't you give 'em a call and make sure they're all right."
"It was a privilege to work with Joan and if she said 'no!', you didn't argue, Joan would never say no for no reason, there was always a reason. Everything is not for the good of everyone, but it was for the good of the play. "Joan has to be marked with a statue. If the kids climb over it and chalk on her, she'd love it."
Murray Melvin

"They have some sort of altar to Joan down there, I don't do that. I don't worship anyone except myself. Littlewood has influenced my life, but it was half a century ago. We've moved on, no actually we've moved back! The West End is full of David Cameron look-alikes! They kicked the working class actors

out pretty thoroughly, mainly by withdrawing funding from drama schools."
Dudley Sutton

Maude, aged 17 (Left) and
Yootha's Grandmother, Rebecca.
(Right)

Hurst (Bottom
Left) in Egypt 1917

Hurst and
Maude,
Ilfracombe 1919

Maude. Brighton,
1926

Yootha's birthplace.
The site of
Bolingbroke Nursing
home as it is today.

57 Bennerley Road,
(Right) and basement flat
(Below) as it is today.

Yootha, (18 months) on
the beach at Brighton.

Yootha's all time
favourite photograph of
herself. Image © Rex
Features.

Yootha as a child. Image ©
Rex Features.

ARTHUR LANE presents

"ESCAPE ME NEVER"

By MARGARET KENNEDY

Characters in order of their appearance :	
Sir Ivor McClean ...	WALTER LEYBOURNE
Lady McClean ...	EDWINA HOWELL
Fenella McClean ...	JOAN LALLY
First Tourist ...	JULIA PLINGE
Second Tourist ...	KAREN BOYSTON
Caryl Sanger ...	MICHAEL GOVER
Butler ...	JACK MARTYN
Herr. Heinrich ...	LEN LAURIE
Gemma ...	PHYLLIS BAKER
Sebastian Sanger ...	ARTHUR LANE
Waiter ...	IVOR HOPE
First Spinster ...	LAURIE ADAIR
Second Spinster ...	DOROTHY JONES
Mrs. Brown ...	MARY BARLING
Petrova ...	MARJORIE DENVILLE
Dresser ...	PEGGY FORBES-ROBERTSON
Wilson ...	PERCY FOX
Understudy ...	ELLEN-MARIE WORGER
Messenger ...	BERTHA BLEACH
Coffee Stall Keeper ...	WALTER PLINGE
Girl ...	YOOTHA JOYCE
Man at the Stall ...	JOHN THOMAS
Tourists, Coffee Stall Customers	

Synopsis of the Scenes :

ACT 1

Scene 1 ... The Salon of the Palazzo Neroni, Venice. An afternoon in May.

Scene 2 ... The same. The following afternoon

ACT 2

Scene 1 ... The terrace of an hotel in the Dolomites. Six weeks later

Scene 2 ... Caryl's room. An afternoon some six month's later

Scene 3 ... A studio in a mews. Evening, some weeks later

ACT 3

Scene 1 ... The Practice Room of the Theatre. The same evening

Scene 2 ... A coffee-stall on the Thames Embankment. Later that night

Scene 3 ... The studio. Late the next night

Play Produced by LEN LAURIE

Ellen-Marie Worger is a pupil of Miss Harrison, Purley School of Dancing. Scenery by Capes of Chiswick. Furniture and Furnishings by Studio Here, Fulham. Wigs by Gustave. Books by Foyles. Crockery and Table Dressings by Allders of Croydon. Cigarettes by Abdulla.

General Manager	...	...	...	R. GEOFFREY WOOD
Manager and Producer	...	...	...	LEN LAURIE
Stage Director	...	...	...	JACK MARTYN
Stage Manager	...	...	...	WALTER PLINGE
Assistant Stage Manager	...	...	...	PEGGY FORBES-ROBERTSON

For the ARTHUR LANE THEATRICAL ENTERPRISES

First professional outing in *Escape Me Never* at The Grand Theatre Croydon July 1945.

GRAND THEATRE & OPERA HOUSE
CROYDON

Box Office open daily 10—7   Tel.: Cro. 0011-12

Early billing in *Autumn Crocus* at The Grand Theatre Croydon August 1945.

ARTHUR LANE
proudly presents

AUTUMN CROCUS

by

DODIE SMITH
(Author of " Dear Octopus," " Call It a Day," etc.)

with

PHYLLIS BAKER   MICHAEL GOVER

WALTER LEYBOURNE   RUTH SHAW

LAURIE ADAIR   R. GEOFFREY WOOD

YOOTHA JOYCE   CATHERINE SUMMERTON

and FULL LONDON CAST

Production under the direction of
R. GEOFFREY WOOD

Week Commencing Monday, August 27th
Evenings at 7.0   Mats. Wed. and Sat. at 2.30

65

As Stella Loman in
The Call of the Flesh
1955.

PROGRAMME

Week commencing MONDAY, OCTOBER 17th, 1955

GLYNN EDWARDS presents

"THE CALL OF THE FLESH"

A Play in Three Acts

By R. HOWARD ARUNDEL

Characters :

Robert Loman	...	...	...	GLYNN EDWARDS
Dora Loman	...	....	...	... MAY DANA
Eileen Loman	...	...	...	... LINDA BELL
Ted Ryder ...	...	...	...	... RICHARD OWENS
" Rip " Dawkins	...	...	...	WILLIAM RIDOUTT
" Jockey " Bates	...	...	...	... ROBERT JONES
Stella Loman	...	...	...	... YOOTHA JOYCE
Michael Vallance	...	...	...	... IVOR SALTER
Mrs. Lovell ...	...	...	..	... LESLEY SCOTT
Det. Inspector Winter	...	...	HOWARD CHARLTON

Produced by R. HOWARD ARUNDEL

Our Bars are at your Service. Tea, Coffee and Snacks also obtainable.
Delicious Ices obtainable from the Usherettes.

**Early (damaged)
publicity shot**

Yootha and Glynn lighting up.

Wedding photos. Hampstead Registry Office. 8th December 1956. Courtesy of Glynn Edwards.

As Collette in Theatre
Workshop's *The Hostage* 1958. ©
The Cowan Archive

As Collette in *The Hostage* with Glynn Edwards, Howard
Goorney, Avis Bunnage and Dudley Sutton 1958. © The
Cowan Archive.

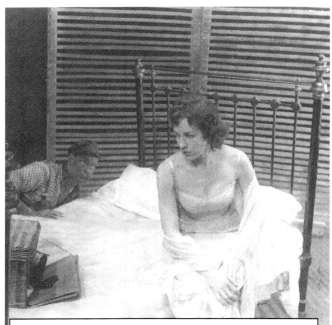

As Lizzie with Glynn Edwards in Theatre Workshop production of Jean-Paul Sartre's *The Respectful Prostitute* 1958. Image Courtesy of Theatre Royal Stratford East Archives Collection.

Joan. Image courtesy of Joan Littlewood.

PART TWO

CHAPTER 18

In the early sixties, after she left Theatre Workshop, Yootha dedicated herself to building an acting career, mostly in film and TV. Both for her and Glynn, it seems, offers of work came in steadily: on the odd occasion they would appear alongside one another. Did their work get in the way of their marriage? We can't really say; though since both of them were ambitious and serious-minded actors, the long and irregular hours must have been hard on the nerves – a bit like starting a new job every other week.

Yootha's route to success was through television. At this stage, she was getting supporting roles, in comedies or dramas: she alternated between the two. She was lucky in her first role, in Dennis Norden and Frank Muir's BBC TV comedy *Brothers in Law*, cleverly adapted from a novel by Henry Cecil Leon about the travails of an idealistic young lawyer. She appeared in the seventh episode, 'The Separation Order' which aired on 29th May 1962, as Mrs Trench. As has been mentioned, Denis Norden had been so impressed with Yootha when he saw her in *Fings*, that he gave her a part. In a letter to me, he remembered that she was "scared stiff before that performance." For all that, Yootha felt that her performance was a success and as Yootha said, people kept ringing her up, offering work.

Brothers in Law was also aired in Australia. In a notice in September 1963, the TV critic of the *Sydney Morning Herald* noted that a lot of talented character actors were breaking through in British television in those days. They "seem to be on permanent tap for British casting directors" and said that the show was "first class in all departments and a winner."

In the intervals between TV work Yootha got a job backstage as an assistant director in a production of *Fings* at the Manchester Opera House. The director was Avis Bunnage, who of course she knew well. The production only ran for six nights, in July 1962: some say that when Theatre Workshop moved to the West End and into the mainstream theatres it had compromised its own principles, and was losing its edge.

At this point, Yootha returned to work for Joan Littlewood, though now in the world of film. Joan was then making her first venture into direction with a version of (curiously) one of her less successful stage productions, *Sparrers Can't Sing*, by Steven Lewis (himself an actor); the film is about a sailor, Charlie Gooding, who comes back from the sea only to find his home has been demolished and his girlfriend Maggie is living with Bert, a bus driver, James Booth and Barbara Windsor played Charlie and Maggie. Yootha only had a brief and bright appearance in the film as a barmaid; it's a pity she wasn't given more space, but we have to remember that in all Joan's productions it was the ensemble that mattered.

For Joan this transition from theatre into film was fraught with issues, which have been well documented. Barbara Windsor told of some of the difficulties she had with the cameramen, who told her off for being too theatrical for film – Joan, so possessive of her 'birds egg,' exploded, as Barbara recounts wonderfully in her memoirs. She told me that on that production, Joan was very resourceful with her casting: "she would get the kids off the streets to appear in it" she said. "Calling them over she would say 'what are you doin' 'ere? You wanna be in a film?'" Barbara's memories really bring her remarkable history in show business to life; she even remembers her friend Lionel Bart taking her out for kippers and champagne after the premier of *Sparrers*.

At this time, too, Yootha made a brief return to the theatre. In February 1964 she played the neurotic Sally Thomas in *Signpost to Murder* by Monte Doyle, at Castle Theatre, Farnham. According to one reviewer, there was "an enthusiastic reception for this lively and colourful production". Yootha's pal Alfred Lynch took over as guest producer.

Following the success of *Brothers in Law*, word got out about Yootha's comic talents, and other projects followed. Throughout the sixties, her career in television grew: she was a capable and versatile support in most of the leading comedy and drama series of the day. She next embarked on a couple of television plays: an adaptation of John Wain's novel *A Travelling Woman* for the BBC, and another for the *Play of The Week* series, when she had a supporting role as Vera Maine in *Gina*. A reviewer remarked that "the supporting cast were admirable." She also had a part in ABC's *Armchair Theatre*'s *The Fishing Match*, a comedy about three people stranded in a riverside pub during a summer storm, with Peter Butterworth. The play "introduced redheads Yootha Joyce and Jo Rowbottom," "characterisations were all excellent, and worthy of special mention (Cissy-Yootha Joyce)."

Yootha also featured twice in Benny Hill's TV show, then on BBC. Christine Pilgrim, who was herself a guest on the show, told me "Yootha really wanted to do 'legit' theartre and I wouldn't say Benny's show quite fell into that category. So I don't think she enjoyed it that much. And Benny could be difficult to work with at times." Her contribution to Benny's show was as Bella and Elvira Crudd: most often she would be the "Funny Tart," a regular character on these shows, played by other actresses too.

The clearest and most famous example of her playing this part, however, was in *Steptoe and Son*. She was Delia in the episode 'The Bath,' broadcast on 10th January 1963. At one point, Yootha appears to adjust her stocking suspender: during the recording, there was an audible snap of elastic. Yootha, it seems, improvised at this point, emphasising the character's sexiness by stretching her leg out to adjust it: no doubt she impressed Harry H. Corbett, also a product of Theatre Workshop. His daughter, Susannah, herself an actress and now a successful children's author, told me that "Obviously dad had met Yootha at Theatre Workshop. He had mentioned actors he knew personally and that were at the top of their game. Yootha obviously made the cut."

Some time ago, the actor Ian Burford, who worked alongside Yootha in a radio recording of 'The Bonds That Bind Us,' an episode of *Steptoe and Son*, remembered that the producer, "who was also the warm-up man, introduced her to the audience in a less than subtle way, 'well Yootha Joyce, what can I say.... Whaaaaarrr!' Yootha was less than pleased and entered through the curtains to face the audience with a face like thunder. I'm sure that in such circumstances Yootha was not a person to hide her feelings."

The BBC was impressed with Yootha and used her for other *Comedy Playhouse* productions: *Impasse* and *A Clerical Error*, and in further episodes of *Steptoe and Son*. A review of the episode 'A Box in Town,' recorded on 10th October 1965, where she played the part of Avis, noted: "I think Yootha Joyce was one of the funniest girlfriends Harry H. Corbett ever had. I wish we could have seen more of this romance."

The writers of *Steptoe and Son*, Ray Galton and Alan Simpson, told me that "we attended all script read-throughs, and because Yootha acted the parts well, she was re-booked on numerous occasions." They remembered that "Both Harry and Wilfrid Brambell warmed to Yootha in *Steptoe and Son* and they all worked very well together." When I asked them about what they remembered of working with her on the *Comedy Playhouse* series, which they also wrote, they told me "she was very good in *Impasse*, as she was in anything on which she worked with us. We certainly had lots of admiration for her."

I also asked them whether they saw beyond the "Funny Tart" image, and whether they had considered her for a series; they said that they hadn't. However, she did appear in a Galton and Simpson episode of the BBC's 1965 *Frankie Howerd Show* (which was unfortunately wiped), as a tipsy vamp, who tries to have her wicked way with a seriously alarmed Frankie. Thankfully, a recently unearthed copy of the episode; the final one of the first series, originally broadcast on Friday 15th January 1965, is currently being restored at the British Film Institute. At this time, broadcasters regularly wiped TV shows so as to re-use expensive videotape and save space in their archives. It's pity that so much historic work, by a lot of talented people, has been lost in this way, including some by Yootha.

The list of comedy shows Yootha appeared in shows a steady build-up of parts: no doubt this led to casting directors thinking of her as most suited to that genre. [See Appendix B] In dramatic roles, however, she had similar energy: sadly, later on, at the height of her career, this type of part never came her way. At this time, in contrast, she had multiple roles in serial dramas (usually crime-related) and TV plays, such as *Z Cars* and *Dixon of Dock Green*. This was what she once classified as her "tortured woman" period. A particular case in point is 'Ask Me If I Killed Her,' an episode from the crime drama series, *No Hiding Place*. Here, she plays a convincing, vindictive wife, who tries to set her husband up as a murderer when he tries to leave her for another woman. Yootha's performance as this obsessively vengeful woman is accurate, strong, and at times even scary! This performance led to further 'sinister' roles, as the hard KGB agent Manlinov in *The Saint* in 1967, alongside Roger Moore, and as the tough German, Sister Dryker, in *Jason King* in 1972. But of course the "funny tart" characters, along with occasional convicts or prostitutes (as in the 1960's series *Cluff* and *Redcap*) never seemed that far away.

CHAPTER 19

Yootha's film roles in the sixties, although varied, were mostly short and snappy. Following *Sparrers Can't Sing*, she appears briefly as a laundry woman alongside Rita Tushingham in *A Place To Go*. It sounds as if her only speaking line is unusually high pitched – maybe it was dubbed over! Her next three films; *Catch Us If You Can*, *The Pumpkin Eater* and *Die, Die, My Darling* give her greater focus and fixed her in the public eye: the last two, in fact, starred Anne Bancroft and Tallulah Bankhead.

Catch Us If You Can was one of a group of films appealing to a new breed of crazed pop music fans: they were promotional vehicles for the likes of Cliff Richard and The Beatles, in famous films like *Summer Holiday* and *A Hard Day's Night*: *Summer Holiday* was one of the first, inspired by others starring Elvis. They relied on British character actors to drive the story forward; a bunch of young singing stars wasn't enough, and they needed a contrast of types and other baggage to make them more appealing. *Catch Us If You Can* was director John Boorman's first film, and featured The Dave Clark Five. The light-hearted story involves a stuntman and a model, Steve and Dinah, disenchanted with their showbiz lives, who escape to an island, with Dinah's manager in hot pursuit. Yootha, given a larger role than in previous films, plays Nan, a bitter, uptight, middle class wife, stuck in a dull marriage with her equally dull, middle class husband, Guy, played by Robin Bailey. The pair have roving eyes, and are dissatisfied with their lives, just as Steve and Dinah are. In the film, Yootha is at her best as a predatory man-eater. In one scene, she walks in on Steve while he's having a bath; her suggestively hungry looks are very reminiscent of Mildred – it almost seems that she was warming up for the role. The film has a lot of tiresome romping scenes, including Yootha running around Bath (the city, that is) in Charlie Chaplin costume. Still, she looks as if she's having fun.

This was the first film in which she appeared in the US: it was meant to appeal to an international audience: there was a huge appetite for the emerging British pop explosion. It was very good news for Britain's film actors. Yootha certainly seems to have chosen her work carefully, and one of her criteria would be this possibility of international exposure.

Her next film, *The Pumpkin Eater*, would certainly travel. It was based on a novel by Penelope Mortimer, adapted by Harold Pinter, directed by Jack Clayton, and filmed at Shepperton studios in 1964. No doubt her friend and neighbour Alfred Lynch gave Yootha some advice on working with Pinter: he had played Aston in *The Caretaker* at the Oxford Playhouse in 1961. The part Yootha played, a woman in a hairdresser's, had to be specially written, she said, because in the novel the woman was only mentioned in a letter. As we know, she said she never had to audition; but for this project, it seems she did: "I did do a reading and a screen test for that tiny bit, which people still talk about." It's only a small scene, but it had a great impact. Jo, played by Anne Bancroft, is in the salon escaping her problems, only to be confronted by a woman under the nearby hair dryer, played by Yootha, who brings her dilemma back to her. It is a brilliant performance, leaving the audience on tenterhooks. Yootha once said in jest, open mouthed and holding her chest, that she "never knew she was like that". In his biography of Jack Clayton, Neil Sinyard says that the film contained "The best screen acting miniature cameos from Maggie Smith and Yootha Joyce. The best that one could hope to see." Also telling me that he thought that Yootha was "a terrific actress: hard for me to think of a more remarkable single-scene cameo in a film than her performance in The Pumpkin Eater". It is true of course; Yootha tackles the schizophrenic character in a very natural, seamless way, as her mind drifts between gentleness and aggression. Her work at Theatre Workshop had made her study art from life – that must have contributed to the portrayal. Yootha in a TV interview once said that it was her first film, which wasn't strictly true. She also remembered that the experience was very exhilarating for her, mainly as she was working with "lots of wonderful people." To interviewer Tony Bilbow who in 1980, remarked on how different the character in the film was from Mildred, she quipped "yes, but the same problem." Harold Pinter never said anything about the performance, as far as I know. I asked his then lover, Joan Bakewell, if she could perhaps expand on their time working on the project, but she replied "I just can't help. I don't know who Yootha Joyce was and never heard Harold speak of her."

It has been difficult to research Yootha's relationship with Tallulah Bankhead. She starred alongside her in the Hammer film *Die, Die, My Darling.* Yootha hinted at a friendship that was worth investigating, but little or nothing is known about it. She claimed, in fact, that Tallulah gave her a West Highland terrier on the film set, and she promptly named it after her – later, this same Westie gave birth to another, Samantha. Tallulah is not on record as saying anything about working with Yootha, and those involved with the film who kindly replied to my enquiries had nothing to report. Christine Pilgrim, for example, told me that she "never remembered any discussion with Yootha about her association with Tallulah Bankhead."

The film is based on *Nightmare,* a novel by "Anne Blaisdell" (a pen name for Elizabeth Linington) adapted by Richard Matheson. Mrs. Trefoile [Bankhead], a religious fanatic, loses her son Stephen in a car accident. She is later visited by his ex-fiancée Patricia, who confesses she would never have married Stephen. Mrs. Trefoile, in a fit of religious mania, imprisons Patricia to cleanse her of her sins, for the sake of her beloved son. It was shot at Elstree, and on location at Letchmore Heath in Hertfordshire. Hammer Films were keen to follow up the success of the then aged Hollywood stars Bette Davis and Joan Crawford in *Whatever Happened to Baby Jane?* Apparently, Tallulah had turned it down. Tallulah herself was not in great shape; she suffered from bouts of pneumonia. However, she prepared herself intensely, drinking less alcohol and embarking on a strict health regime. On set, she would usually be the last to turn up. On some days, her health was good, on others better, depending on how motivated she felt. This frailty is curious, considering she is seen with Anna, the housekeeper played by Yootha, giving Patricia a good and (to me) strangely satisfying beating. This is when we see Yootha's physical strengths as an actress. She clearly has a side to her, matching her so-called masculine temperament. She is certainly not to be messed with! Naturally, the reviews focused on Bankhead: a review in the *New York Times* said "Although she towers above the cast and story, her present effort adds little to her record."

Yootha was also acting in TV at this time, and took three parts in consecutive episodes of ITV's *Play of the Week*, 'A Tricycle Made for Two,' by Arden Winch: 'The Gambler,' ' The Sophisticate,' and 'The Innocent.' She appeared in this series a few times, along with other actors trying to get into the industry, like *Eastenders* actress June Brown and Yootha's future co-star in *George and Mildred*, Sheila Fearn.

Increasingly, in fact, television was becoming her main career, but she perhaps wondered whether she was making any serious inroads in the medium. Did she think she was destined always to play the funny tart? Still, she was being welcomed as support by the great British names in TV comedy, such as Harry Worth, Peggy Mount and Sid James. Her work on two series, *The Wednesday Play* and *The Wednesday Thriller* (was this to be Yootha's night forever?) did offer her a chance to work on scripts from the best writers of the day, including Dennis Potter. She was slowly pushing herself forward, usually playing scary, somewhat sinister roles: sometimes she was the lead character. She had good reviews: in *Theatre 625* for BBC2, she caught people's eye. When she played Miss Binnington in 'Portraits from the North: The Nutter,' *The Stage* wrote that the production was "a masterpiece of observation from performers and writer", "the cast rose to the challenge" and "the actors concentrated on playing it perfectly straight: the operative word is 'perfectly.' Yootha Joyce gave a performance which was all the funnier for the way she steadfastly ignored the absurdity of her own and everyone else's behaviour."

In the same series, she played Jane Matthews in Basil Warner's *Try for White*. *The Stage* again noted that "The play sprang to life after a slow and noisy start"; "All the characters were well drawn and seemed taken from life. No one stood out as a star because, although some had longer parts, all seemed too real to be regarded as leads and supports. Joss Ackland's uncouth lout, so demonstrably unworthy of Yootha Joyce's intelligent and desperate Jane, had perhaps the most difficult role, calling as it did for enough good nature to make her fond of him yet enough underlying viciousness to make his cruel spurning of her part of a believable whole." "Yootha Joyce gave a striking and moving performance."

How seriously was Yootha taken back then in the sixties? These television performances are never, or very seldom, given repeats – some of them may have been deleted or wiped. Unfortunately, we seem likely only to see her in reruns of *George and Mildred*, and nothing much else.

CHAPTER 20

In 1966, Yootha had a part in the film version of Robert Bolt's *A Man For All Seasons*, about the execution of Sir Thomas More, Henry VIII's Chancellor, which ultimately won many Academy Awards – it was filmed at Shepperton studios. She played Averil Machin, a smallish part, and though she got no award herself, the association with an Oscar-winning film must have furthered her career. It was nearer to what she would have done at Theatre Workshop years before, but this was the only historical costume drama that she played in. It's a pity, for she was capable of playing strong female characters from the past. She appeared in only two scenes. In the second, in which she is intensely questioned by Leo McKern, playing Thomas Cromwell, she looks a little nervous, and the hands don't seem to work in unison with the face. This might be intentional: whatever the truth of the matter, you are certainly left wanting a little more from her.

Yootha returned to the theatre in 1967, alongside some big names, in Robert Shaw's *The Man in the Glass Booth*. The play, directed by Harold Pinter, was later made into a film. It concerns a Nazi war criminal who is arrested and sent for trial to Israel. Yootha plays Mrs Rosen, an Israeli agent who interrogates the central character, Arthur Goldman/Colonel Adolf Karl Dorff, played by Donald Pleasence. The play also featured Lawrence Pressman and Sonia Dresdel. Yootha's agent, Joy Jameson, said that "Pinter must have been impressed with her in *The Pumpkin Eater* as it was he who asked her to join." The play was premiered on 11th–15th July 1967 at the Nottingham Playhouse, then went to Brighton before settling in the West End, at the St. Martin's Theatre. The play got a mixed reception in London, though *Plays and Players* described the whole presentation as "impeccable." Lary Spurling, in *Theatre Magazine*, commenting on Donald Pleasance as the lead, reported "Our hero is arrested as a Nazi war criminal and sent for trial to Israel. When he offers a million bucks to save his life, 'Not Christ's blood could buy it!' answers Miss Joyce crisply through clenched teeth."

The play's success led to a transfer to the U.S. Joy Jameson told me "Yootha was VERY good in the play. Alas, because of American Equity, she wasn't allowed to play the role in the transfer to New York, because they decided to have a big fat typical New York Jewish woman in the play there." "The woman who did play it [Ronnie L Gilbert] was more physically right for the role but Yootha had much more power and menace," Joy commented. She remembers that Yootha was disappointed about not going to New York: "But there was the work visa to be got, and at that time Yootha was not a big enough name to automatically get a work permit, plus they would have had problems with the U.S. trade union at that time." The play went on to succeed in America, which led to the later film. Pinter never used Yootha again, for reasons we can only guess at. Donald Pleasence, however, was plainly a friend: for she called on him, together with her neighbour, the theatre dresser John McNicoll, to witness the signing of her will.

Shortly after the West End run of *Man In The Glass Booth*, Yootha decided to take on a new agent, Joy Jameson, who represented Yootha until she died: she also acted for Donald Pleasence: we don't know who her agent was before that. Joy told me "Yootha had asked Donald Pleasence for a formal introduction. So he put in a word for her and subsequently she phoned me, suggesting we met with a view to me taking her on. Of course I was happy to do so..."

Enquiring about her early days with her, Joy said, "You'll find I'm very bad on dates. Mostly because when I moved my office three years ago I lost all the stuff

I had in books and then at a very grand age had to start using computers...what a horror!"

From this point, no doubt in part because of Joy's support, Yootha's career seems to have developed at a steady pace. She was photographed glamorously by Gerry Cranham for a page in the actors' directory *Spotlight* in the 'younger and leading women's page': It gave all the relevant particulars, including her height: 5 foot 5 inches. She worked alongside Albert Finney, Billie Whitelaw and Liza Minnelli in *Charlie Bubbles*, which was filmed in Manchester. The plot concerned a troubled married writer who has an affair with his secretary. Joy recalls, "she appeared as a film star acquaintance; a rich bitch, former lover of Albert Finney's character Charlie Bubbles. Yootha was all glammed up. It was the kind of part she would never get the opportunity to play after she became so popular in comedy roles on television. As Joy said "Yootha was typecast in comedy, which was a tragedy, because in a film like *Charlie Bubbles* she was cast so 'out of the box' as they'd say today. When I watched her performance myself (she was credited as "Woman in Café"), I must say I found her a little lacking in conviction, almost as if caught between being a lady or an outright bitch. The film has a coldness about it, and nobody but Billie Whitelaw seems to have much to offer: in fact it was she who won the "Best Supporting Actress" award from the New York Film Critics Circle.

Joy Jameson's talent for spotting fresh and new work for Yootha was important for building a distinctive future for her as an actress. The role of Kay Fowler in the episode "The Birds and the Business" from the series *Market in Honey Lane* could be considered to be ahead of its time. The programme has many similarities to *Eastenders*, and could be seen as a precursor. In this episode she worked with an old colleague from repertory days, Ivor Salter.

Some of her other work at this time was key to her future exposure and popularity: many projects also had international appeal, which would help her become better known. She featured in *The Avengers*, in the episode "Something Nasty in the Nursery," as Miss Lister, a thoroughly nasty, two-faced woman, who probably inspired the title of the episode. Yootha is at her best, and gives us a special treat by pouting her luscious lips throughout the episode; until that is Emma Peel gives her a good kick up the backside, shoving her headfirst into a wall. There is the compulsory "Avenger" weirdness: Yootha is involved in a nasty scheme in which she and her accomplice, fellow Theatre Workshop actor Dudley Foster, turn fully grown men into daft kids, who give away important defence secrets.

A little later the same year, Yootha caught up with another actor from her past, Roger Moore. She appeared in the 'The Russian Prisoner,' an episode of the highly popular drama *The Saint*. Roger remembers enjoying catching up with Yootha on the set, but finds it difficult to remember details: "it was so long ago." As has been mentioned, she plays a KGB agent, Manilov, very butch and manly with a shock of flaming red hair. She gets another physical kicking, but this time gets her own back, hitting her fellow spies: good practice for the hard characters she was to play in the future.

Also in 1967, work began filming Jeremy Brooks' adaptation of the Julian

Gloag novel *Our Mother's House*, again directed by Jack Clayton. Yootha plays Mrs Quayle, the housekeeper, a very convincing portrayal of a hard woman. Neil Sinyard told me he thought her performance in this was "pretty good; her black gloved hand reaching for the door-chain is pretty scary!" Quayle occasionally visits the house of the group of brothers and sisters who, when they have buried their beloved dead mother in the garden, fear being split up and sent to orphanages. They set up home alone, until their long lost father, Charlie Hook, played by Dirk Bogarde, suddenly returns. He wins them over, but at the same time pulls the wool over their eyes, stealing their mother's savings, which results in an ending that undoubtedly leaves the audience cold. Of course I don't think it would be fair to give away the ending; needless to say it is well worth a watch. The cast, mostly of children, including Pamela Franklin, Mark Lester, and Margaret Leclere, do a superb job. Mrs Quayle is also taken in by Charlie, and is seen messing about with him on the sofa. The *Motion Picture Herald* took note: "Yootha Joyce is amusing as a floozy," it said. I asked Joy if Yootha ever mentioned working with Bogarde, but she replied: "she never talked about Bogarde. He didn't ever get close to anyone he worked with – always cagey because he never ever came out."

In 1967, too, in *Stranger In The House*, Yootha played a shooting range girl, in a slightly incoherent story which follows a reclusive, alcoholic, and once gifted barrister's return to the Bar to defend his daughter's boyfriend, accused of a murder he didn't commit. This time, she worked with James Mason, but again not much was forthcoming: Joy told me, "James Mason I don't think could have been remotely close to Yootha or she would have told me - she knew I fancied him! But she never mentioned him either."

From all the evidence, at this time her marriage to Glynn was losing its sparkle. Later, she recalled, "The marriage slowed off gradually. We drifted apart and in the end we were just good friends living in the same house. It was a marriage without sex. I didn't do anything hideous and nor did he. I never had any of that." She and Glynn "lived very separate lives towards the end."

"We slept in the same room but we had separate beds,. It was just one of those things, we loved one another very dearly, but we couldn't get on." In an interview in 1976 she added, "We were much happier when we were living together. As soon as we married, it was different." However, the picture she painted on another occasion is more colourful. As she said: "There were fights between us as the hole in the ceiling testifies." She went on: "get me riled, get me angry, and they get it darling, wallop! It stops me getting high blood pressure or heart attacks – and let's face it they can always duck," And again: "I can't remember what Glynn had said to me, but he went too far. I was cooking egg, bacon, sausages and chips at the time. I was so angry, I threw the lot at him, wham! Thank God the frying pan hit the ceiling darling. There was sizzling oil in it and I could have killed him." "I have redecorated several times" she chuckles "but I shall never have the hole fixed. It reminds me not to throw things, I'm a chucker you see, I throw the first thing that comes to hand and I've always been a good shot." The reporter noticed that Yootha, when she said this, picked up a heavy ashtray and weighed it in her hand.

She certainly did have a masculine side, and no doubt could be quite scary. She was aware of her temper though, and once said: "I'm awfully quick tempered, after a tiff I expect everyone to be lovely and sunny at once and can't understand why they aren't." And again "If it got really bad, Glynn would go out rather than wallop me. If he'd have hit me he'd have killed me. Nobody has ever walloped me, ever. I'd probably kill them. Men shouldn't hit women. They can drag them into the kitchen and throw a bucket of water over them."

It seems that Yootha had no desire for children: "I think people should only marry if they want children," she said, "I never wanted any, I'm just not the mother sort." Again: "I've never wanted babies, never. It's not that I don't like children. I love children, providing they're other people's," she confessed. Joy Jameson confirmed that she "never thought Yootha was aching to have kids of her own." Yootha said, "My career had always come first. Besides, I know my limitations and I don't have the patience to cope with a baby and a career. Anyway I don't think I'd be a good mum. I'd be far too strict." It certainly wasn't that she was unable to have them: "I'm sure I could have had them like shelling peas." she once said, also saying she thought the whole thing was "slightly undignified." "Towards the end of our marriage we might have adopted one," she said, "but, as we were breaking up, it would have been very silly. I often wondered what would have happened if I'd had a child that was dull. I don't mind if they're not pretty, and if something was wrong, I'd love them to death, even more than if they were normal. But if they were dull, what would I do with them?"

CHAPTER 21

In the late sixties and early seventies, from about 1968 to 1974 (when she was well established as Mildred), Yootha's roles in film and television were at their most varied. She played opposite Robert Shaw's Martin Luther as his wife Katharina in a 90-minute TV version of the John Osborne play about the Protestant reformer. The production was aimed at a U.S. audience, and had great success there, winning both the New York Drama Critics Award and the Tony Award for the best play.

In contrast, she had dual roles as Mrs. Bewley and Phoebe in Jack Rosenthal's *Your Name's Not God, It's Edgar* for Granada's ITV Playhouse series. The production featured Jimmy Jewel and Yootha's pal Alfred Lynch: it showed her at her best. The reviews were good: she was "perfect as Phoebe"; and "a great sense of the comic persisted to the end." She was able to dominate without undermining Alfred's lead as Edgar. Her friendship with him no doubt had some bearing on the quality of her performance; once she said that professionally, at that time, she relied on his opinion on her work "almost entirely." Christine Pilgrim, too, told me "Alfie was very supportive of Yootha." As Yootha said "Sometimes he tells me I was awful when I think I have been rather good, which is a bit annoying, but mostly I think he is right." Lynch , for his part, was aware that in most of his acting he "always seemed to play losers." But he was also known to choose his parts very carefully, and everything he was in had quality: *The Seagull, Look Back in Anger* and *The Krays*, for instance. Perhaps this trust in him gave her something of the same ambition.

At the end of the sixties, Yootha's career and personal life seemed to be both changing: you could say that she was taking the bull by the horns. She took on larger, more central roles in her television work – Miss Argyll, for instance, in the BBC *Comedy Playhouse* sitcom *Me Mammy*, written by Hugh Leonard. She worked alongside Milo O'Shea, who played Irish mummy's boy Bunjy, with Anna Manahan as his widowed 'mammy.' The plot revolved around Bunjy's innocence, which contrasts with an unfortunate taste for sin. Miss Argyll, the rival attraction, the mammy sees as the incarnation of the devil. Early reaction was a bit cautious, though Yootha was singled out for praise. According to *The Stage*, "Yootha Joyce and Diana Coupland made the most if their parts and brought a touch of reality in what had been up to then in danger of falling into the category of a period piece." Ultimately, however, the programme was very successful; it ran for three series, twenty-one episodes in all, from 1968 to 1971. According to Glynn Edwards, it was at this point that things started to move for Yootha.

Sadly, the pilot, broadcast on 14th June 1968, seems to have been deleted. Worse still, the first two series have also disappeared. Only the third series, of seven episodes, survives, on a mixture of Pal and TR 16mm film format; but even so, it has never been shown since broadcast! The British insistence on showing constant repeats of programmes we are forced to accept as "classic comedy" always seems to take precedence over providing audiences with a more varied output, showing something of the history of comedy; and male actors still seem to be favoured over women.

In *Me Mammy*, Yootha is again the funny tart: but, as in the past with *The Respectful Prostitute*, she could give these roles a more serious edge. At this time she took a part as a prostitute in *Twenty Nine*, an interesting short film, by Brian Cummins, written for TV, about a twenty-nine year old businessman with a love of heavy drinking, gambling and womanising. The film is gripping, with a sinister atmosphere that reflects the seedy side of late-sixties London.

How did Yootha react to her growing success? Was she resigned to becoming typecast as a funny tart, or as a hard predatory woman, the two roles people seemed to want to see her in? Did she and her agent decide to concentrate on the mainstream stereotypical sitcom roles in which she excelled, rather than serious dramatic ones? Perhaps Yootha's fear that "the current job would be her last, never to get another" (as she once confessed to Toni Palmer) was beginning to worry her. A *Telegraph* journalist remarked, in a 1970 interview, that she was "slightly vague" and that "she lumps all her work together in a casual way, possibly as a defence against the fright of appearing at all." In the same interview, she said: "most people see me as the funny tart, but I'm fairly good at being all wrought up and edgy, and the best thing I have done in ages was a middle-aged waitress with all kinds of problems. I've given more bad performances as an ordinary housewife than you've had hot dinners. I cannot see why I am offered those parts at all." What is clear is that reviews of her in

ITV's *Sunday Night Theatre* [TV series] as Erica Seydoux in 'A Measure of Malice' showed there were those who were well onto her abilities as an actress, stating "the cast gave the characters the depth they needed" "Yootha Joyce (what a pleasure to see this actress in a role worthy of her talent)."

At was at this time that Yootha's 13-year marriage to Glynn ended in divorce. Murray Melvin was "terribly surprised when Glynn and Yootha broke up, when we were at Theatre Workshop it was always Glynn and Yootha, Glynn was a very gentle man," he said. But they were still friends: when Glynn moved out of the flat in Sussex Gardens, Yootha helped him settle into his new one in Hampstead and even advised him on the furnishings. However on the day of Glynn's move, Yootha said, the tap washers failed in her bathroom, "I thought I'd have a nice warm bath and an early night, I turned on the tap and whoosh, the water went everywhere, the plumbing had gone. Being the last person on earth who is handy with a spanner, I was reduced to instant helplessness. There was only one answer - ring Glynn. He'd only just walked through the door of his new flat with his suitcases, 'don't panic baby' he cried, and he leaped into his car and came straight back. That's my husband all over, bless him.
We spent he rest of the evening watching television and eating tinned soup, then I said 'off you go darling'... and off he went.'" "I loved Glynn dearly," she said: "However I wasn't in love, there is a tiny, tiny bit of difference. I still love him and if I lost his friendship I would be really hurt."
She also remembered that she was "never jealous of Glynn, although I'm on the possessive side of jealous. I don't mean I didn't ever sit down and think, 'This is dreadful.' But I never felt, "What am I going to do now?" My mother says I've never been in love and God help me when I am. I've never sat and pined and phoned. If I've had a good night's sleep, everything's all right. It makes me sound awfully inhuman." And again: "we just came to the end of a lovely relationship, but that's not to say that like most marriages, there wasn't the occasional fight."
The press gathered at the divorce courts on 3rd February 1969, when Yootha, glamorously dressed in black, was photographed outside. Unsurprisingly, the press took a simplistic line, saying that Glynn had "cheated" on Yootha, with Christine Pilgrim as correspondent. Recalling the proceedings at the courts, Yootha maintained that she "had to appear terribly upset and say awful things about the other woman who stole my husband. Getting divorced in those days was a farce. You just couldn't say the marriage had simply broken down, that we didn't hate each other but that we couldn't live together." Christine recalled "Yootha and Glynn's marriage had broken down long before I came on the scene. But as Yootha said, breakdown of marriage was not sufficient grounds for divorce in those days. I was young and naïve and didn't realize that the case would be reported in the national press. It broke my grandmother's heart to see me cited in print as 'the other woman' and that broke my heart."
Christine told me, "it was Glynn's idea to get a divorce so that he and I could wed; we all agreed that I should be correspondent. Yootha was very much in the public eye whereas my career wasn't established at the time, so we thought that

this way would be less likely to attract attention. I remember how Glynn and I offered to pose for the photographer who had to record us 'living in sin' as it was called back then. As Yootha said, it was all a farce, and totally unnecessary. I think she'd have been devastated had she known how painful it became for me and my family, especially when she was quoted as saying it was all 'a hoot.' Of course, I never told her."

Yootha, for her part, said that her lawyer "went potty when he found out the three of us were friends and always going out together. I remember his clerk asked me if I physically tried to stop Glynn leaving the home. Can you picture me trying to stop him?"

CHAPTER 22

On the day of Yootha's divorce, ITV broadcast "Go On It'll Do You Good," an episode of *Armchair Theatre*, which had been recorded some time earlier. It was a comic musical drama about euthanasia by Michael Chapman: unfortunately, it is again listed as missing. Reaction was less than favourable. Barry Norman said there were "plenty of black edges there, but little sign of comedy". Some people thought it was in bad taste, and wrote in to complain it was "offensive," and should never have been shown.

She next appeared in a TV adaptation of Somerset Maugham's *Lord Mountdrago*, and an episode of the *Manhunt* series, again with Alfred Lynch, before she went back to *Dixon of Dock Green*. Her career seemed to be drifting, as if she was waiting round for the right role.

Audiences certainly knew she was a capable actress: by now she was instantly identifiable on the streets of London. A reader of the *Evening Standard*, a Mr. G. Douglas from Glasgow wrote: "Some years ago I found myself living in London, and there was a lady who came along the road in the morning and smiled at me once or twice; there was something familiar about her face but it was the second or third day before I noticed it was Yootha Joyce. The local people had become very fond of her. The most important thing was to see her inside the supermarkets. When old ladies spoke to her, she always took time, no matter how busy she was, to have a quiet word with them. She seemed to be kindness itself." Already in 1970, she shared her feelings about this kind of recognition with an interviewer from the *Daily Telegraph*: "All kinds of people come up to you in shops or in the street and say, 'ooh you were lovely,' but quite often they don't know what you were lovely in, and they hardly ever know your name. It was a bit better in that way working in the theatre where they could have a look at the programme and sort you out a bit. There I used to get letters which started off 'Dear Miss Joyce...' but people are a lot more casual once they've seen you go out with a shopping basket like anybody else."

In March 1970 Yootha's father died in Croydon, aged 75: Maude moved out, retiring to a house in Bournemouth. Hurst must have had some notion of his daughter's growing success. She was filming the second series of *Me Mammy* at the time. We have no idea of how the death affected her. It was at this time that we first hear of her having some problems controlling her nerves, whatever the cause might have been. In the same interview with the *Telegraph*, she said: "I love to work and I am happy to play almost anything in television but my nerves about it are getting worse. What I really dread is having to pick up a cup and saucer in the first five minutes because it rattles so much." She certainly appears nervy in *Conceptions of Murder*, by Clive Exton, which explores the motivations of Peter Kürten, the infamous "Vampire of Dusseldorf." Here, she is the vulnerable victim, visibly shaking at times, so perhaps she turned her real nerves to good account. Still, one wonders if the divorce and her father's death had any impact on her health.

Joy Jameson wondered if her nerves and her drinking were perhaps connected. In a letter, she said: "Many, many times I've seen Yootha shaking with what I thought was nerves but may have been with drinking - but that's the chicken and the egg syndrome, isn't it? Did she drink because she needed it to settle her nerves? Maybe it usually does the trick. I can with my hand on my heart say I never knew Yootha had a drink problem. There was only ONE occasion...dinner at *Mr. Chow's*, Knightsbridge with Yootha, Basil my husband and me. In my mind I thought, God she can't half knock it back! That was because I'd never known anyone drink brandy all through the meal. Maybe three then wine. But Yootha was a smashing lady."

When I suggested to Glynn that Yootha might have begun to drink to help calm her nerves: "Drinking? Well, Yootha was a very professional person, and I had these problems myself, especially when acting and a difficult bit comes up and you think you're going to dry up, but I wouldn't say she was a nervous performer."

Perhaps she found film and television work wearing on the nerves? In an interview, she says that filming work was difficult: "After some ten years of constant appearances, Yootha Joyce still talks about television as if it were a mysterious monster which has risen from the deeps to play merry hell with her nerves. 'The trouble is,' she says shuddering slightly and widening her already large blue eyes, 'that I still don't see how it works. You get onto that set wondering if the microphone boom can possibly be in the right place, watching all those little red lights winking on the cameras. Trying to remember all these things and still give a performance.'"

Yootha always maintained that after the divorce to Glynn, she remained great friends with him and his then wife actress Christine Pilgrim, "in fact I'm godmother to their son." Christine told me Yootha never wanted children, "She was very much a 'no nonsense' person and would have probably been pretty strict. She didn't suffer foolishness easily. But she was delighted to be asked to be godmother to our son Ben. Sadly, Ben, who was born on Christmas Day 1969, died on February 4th the following year. It was a 'crib death' which was another thing that couldn't be acknowledged in those days.

We didn't ask Yootha to become our second son Tom's godmother. I think we all tried not to repeat anything we did with Ben. It was more superstition than anything. Of course, no one ever voiced that superstition. Yootha was always patient, kind and loving to Tom and left him a generous inheritance that helped put him through university."

Yootha was very extravagant and generous with her gifts, Christine remembers. "They were always numerous, expensive and exquisitely wrapped." "One Christmas when Tom was a toddler, his gifts from Yootha included a toy garage and a *Space 1999* Eagle Transporter spaceship. Tom remembers getting his head caught in the cat flap that Christmas. He had been out in Yootha's yard and tried to crawl back in through the catflap." Both Christine and Tom agree that he doesn't seem to have been traumatised by the experience or to have a fetish about cat flaps! And he's a big noise in Corporate America these days so I'd say he came through it relatively unscathed," laughs Christine.

Glynn and Christine remained close to Yootha; Yootha even spoke to the press of her and Christine and getting involved in a music hall double act together! Christine remembered, "We'd talked of doing a double act, but we never actually got round to working on it. We *were* a double act in effect. Yootha was Glynn's senior wife and I, the junior. It really did feel like that. She took priority over me in matters of friendship, work and a history that she and Glynn shared. They were, after all, of similar age and had been at Theatre Workshop together. My work with Joan Littlewood was in a different, later era (in fact, that was how Glynn and I met.) Perhaps if Yootha and I had pursued the double act, we'd have gone somewhere with it. Meanwhile Glynn and I did a little song and dance routine, using songs from *Fings Ain't Wot They Used T'Be*, in Malta. If Yootha had been with us, we could have done a trio, with her playing the copper"

As well as doing the *Fings* double act in Malta, Glynn and Christine went holidaying with fellow Theatre-Workshoppers Roy and Carmel Kinnear and their family: one year they went to Corfu. Carmel remembered "Yootha did not loom large in our lives at the time, as we were all into babies and sleepless nights." Ten years later, however, Glynn and Christine divorced in their turn. Yootha, meanwhile, had her relationship with the pop promoter Cyril Smith - he had moved in with her. Joy Jameson told me that "she seemed to have a good relationship with both Cyril and Glynn - and I have met both with her at her parties." Yootha loved to entertain and was known for being rather lavish. When I asked Dudley Sutton if he knew anything about Yootha's relationships, he laughed and said: "I don't want to go into it." Christine remembered Cyril Smith as "a warm friendly man, as sharp as a tack... a bit like a teddy bear, with a keen eye on the main chance."

In the latter half of 1970, while she was recording for the final series of *Me Mammy*, Yootha also figured in a few films, such as *Fragment of Fear, The Night Digger* and *All the Right Noises*, but her roles don't appear to have developed her talents in any way – they were just means of getting exposure. When *Me Mammy* finished, Yootha spent some weeks in southern Spain, taking a long-earned break and even buying herself a holiday flat in Nerja, then an unspoilt town on the coast south of Granada.

On her return, she received a letter from a Reverend Frank Lishman. I mention this especially, as there seem to be so few letters from Yootha surviving. I obtained this one a while ago from someone who had got it from an album, which also contained a couple of postcards from other people, addressed to the same person. From the contents of the letter, it seems that the Reverend was a fan of *Me Mammy*, but it has been impossible to track him down. Here is the letter, dated July 4th, 1970:

"Dear Rev Lishman, how lovely to hear from you! Sorry I haven't replied sooner; but of course, your letter has travelled quite a lot. Finishing up in Spain! I went there for a few weeks, after the series finished, and only returned last week.

As you will now know, I hope, I relented towards dear Bunjy at the last possible moment - and a lot of good it did me! [*Me Mammy*]

What a marvellous mix-up over Eileen Atkins! I shall tell her the story when next we meet. It will amuse her tremendously.

Heaven knows, if you pardon me! - How it all happened.

Hope you don't mind - but I'm sending a little keepsake snap from us all. Father Patrick took it and cousin Edna and The Mammy are helping to hold the 'likes straight'!

Sincere thanks

Yootha Joyce"

On the "keepsake snap" are the words: "to the Rev. Frank Lishman. With best wishes from "*Me Mammy*" Co. and especially me, Yootha Joyce."

Naturally, the mention of the actress (now Dame) Eileen Atkins aroused my curiosity, and I contacted her to see of she could make some sense of the supposed "mix up". She kindly replied: however, to my surprise she said "I have no idea what the allusion to me in the letter from Yootha is about! As far as I know, I never met Yootha Joyce, though of course I knew who she was. I have certainly never known a Reverend Lishman. I can only think that Yootha and I were mistaken for each other in some way, and in answering the Reverend's letter, Yootha pretended we were friends for some unknown reason." As Peter Errington (who would later work as floor manager on *George and Mildred* and who become a friend of Yootha's) told me: "A lot of people in show biz would make up stories, telling them so many times that even they start to believe them." There seems to be no other explanation.

When she had time off work, which wasn't that often, Yootha would occasionally go to her new flat in Spain. In addition, she could still indulge her hobby of cinema going; later it became more difficult. She once confessed that her favourite film, the one she would take onto a desert island, was *The Lion In Winter*, starring her favourite actress Katherine Hepburn. She thought the timing between Hepburn and Peter O'Toole was marvellous, as was the wonderful score by John Barry. At this time, too, she was beginning to become involved with animal charities, especially The National Canine Defence League. [What we now know as the Dogs Trust]. The Trust's current chief executive, Clarissa Baldwin, remembers Yootha was such a kind person, who always put herself out to help when she could. "Yootha was a great champion for the cause," she said, "and our non-destruction policy was something that was very dear to her heart." Also, Yootha "very kindly lent my husband and I her flat in Nerja; it was on the beach with fabulous views. She went to stay with friends elsewhere but invited us to join them for the day in the Spanish hills."

Yootha herself said: "I've always had pets, but it was quite accidental that I became involved with the NCDL. I always carry a spare lead with me so that I can take a stray dog in tow. Then they go to the League's kennels." "We [the League, that is] never put a healthy dog down - always find a home for it or else find someone to sponsor it, to pay for the League to keep it." She made it her business to promote the League's work; she appeared on radio to promote their good work as well as getting involved at the rescue centres herself.

CHAPTER 23

In 1971 Yootha was off to Twickenham studios with Glynn Edwards and Christine Pilgrim, to play Mrs Hare in the horror film of *Burke and Hare*, about the two Edinburgh grave-robbers and murderers. Christine told me that she played a "Lady of the Night" so they were never on set at the same time. Discussing Barbara Windsor's earlier comments on Yoothas's comic abilities, Christine remarked that "she had extraordinary timing and could drop in a line, and land it faultlessly. Others would chase the laughs. Not Yootha! She had them up her sleeve and slipped them in whenever there was a gap. And if there wasn't a gap, she waited until there was."

"Yootha also knew how to hold a moment on camera; I learned that from watching her during the filming of *Burke and Hare*." I asked Christine whether Yootha gave her any acting tips: "Yootha wouldn't presume to give tips. She didn't give any to me anyway. If she had, she'd probably have said "Demand that you play the other wife Darling!" Yootha as usual gave her best in the film: peeling the potatoes, her face is seriously contorted as she gets to grips with extracting the eyes from them! Later that same year, she played Sister Dryker in 'If it's Got to Go, it's Got to Go' an episode of the popular TV series *Jason King*. She played alongside Peter Wyngarde in the title role, and Ivor Salter, her colleague from repertory days, who played Lorik.

Rumours started to circulate later in the year that Yootha would join Joan Littlewood again at Stratford East in a yet to be disclosed play. This new production, however, was reported by the media as being dependant on funding from the Arts Council, and Joan and Gerry Raffles wanted to be offered more than they usually got. As time went on, it emerged that Yootha was on board, playing Bridgie, a member of the Jugg family in *The Londoners*, a reworking of *Sparrers Can't Sing*. She was joined by Rita Webb, Bran Murphy, Valerie Walsh, Bob Grant, and Ray Hoskins. The play had a new storyline, drawing on the far-reaching redevelopment of the Stratford East area, which was then a hot topic. The characters were shown coping with the demolition of their homes, and in their battles with the council planners. The play also featured new musical numbers from Lionel Bart (who was bankrupt at this point); he also appeared in the production, taking over from Stephen Lewis midway through.

What prompted Yootha's return to the Theatre Royal is a mystery; perhaps she fancied a momentary respite from the film and TV work. Rehearsals started in late 1971, with the production eventually running for 63 performances, from 27th March through to 20th May 1972, at the Theatre Royal. The reception was mixed, but by all accounts it was very lively and inclusive community piece. *The Times* noted, "Miss Littlewood has done a superb job," and said that the characters were "as real as your own neighbours." *The Evening News* first night review in particular "liked the faithful-to-type performances of Yootha Joyce and Valerie Walsh" and *The Stage* found Yootha's performance stimulating. In the view of the *Daily Telegraph*, however, the revisions in the production made "the perfunctory story harder to follow."

As the production of *The Londoners* came to an end in May, Yootha heard that Alfred Lynch's partner, the actor Jimmy Culliford, had suffered a stroke. For Alfred this meant that his career took second place to caring for Jimmy, and they both moved from London to Brighton, where they lived until their deaths, within a year of one another, some thirty years later. Unfortunately, I never managed to interview Alfred, and so have no idea whether the move made a difference to his friendship with Yootha, though it must have been a bit of a blow to her, given that they were so friendly, and lived next door to one another.

Yootha was still working regularly, but at this point in her life she seems rather aimless, merely accepting what came along. More and more, she was used in sitcoms, a world of strong stereotypes. Maybe it was their very safeness that attracted her. For example, she took a part in Hugh Leonard's *Tales from the Lazy Acre* for the BBC, starring again with Milo O'Shea in one episode, 'The Last Great Pint Drinking Tournament.' It was reported missing, but recently, engrossed in writing this book, I missed out on an opportunity to buy a reel of film of the episode on eBay. I even asked the seller later if he still had it, only to be told it had been sold at a car boot sale! I hope whoever bought it informs the British Film Institute, so it can be preserved for posterity. Yootha also took on roles in the film of *Nearest and Dearest,* and in *Never Mind the Quality Feel the Width, The Fenn Street Gang, Steptoe and Son Ride Again, Comedy Playhouse* ('Home from Home'), *Seven Of One* ('Open All Hours'), and *On the Buses*. The reviews were always favourable, but serious dramatic roles seem to have eluded her.

At this time, Yootha become more involved with her charity work. On 25th June 1972 she appeared at the Mermaid Theatre in a show for Vietnam; proceeds went to the Liberation Red Cross of South Vietnam and the Vietnam Red Cross. Here, she rubbed shoulders with Anthony Hopkins, Alfie Bass, Janet Suzman and Brian Murphy, in a series of readings.

During the filming of *Never Mind the Quality Feel the Width* she used her celebrity status to promote the work of the National Canine Defence League. Perhaps she was becoming somewhat disenchanted with the profession, and thought her efforts could be better used by fundraising for the charities she loved. She contributed to the League's newsletters. Here is the "Message from Miss Yootha Joyce," in the Autumn 1972 number of the *NCDL Newsletter*:
"Of course there are a variety of ways in which a dog can suffer ill treatment;

abandonment, brutality and starvation are well known. But I feel most strongly
that many dogs suffer at the hands of the ignorant, particularly in large towns
such as London, in a manner that is less than obvious, and gets little publicity
and is most unlikely to come before the courts."

"Too many people acquire dogs too lightly and then keep them for what they
can get out of them rather than the reverse. People try to keep giant breeds in
towns and flats, as status symbols. The current boom in popularity in Irish
setters has resulted in many being cooped up all the week in tiny gardens where
they never have the chance to get into the free-flowing gallop that they need."

"My Westies are real little terriers and although I live in London I make it a rule
to give them two hours in the park every day. When we are out I encourage
them to sniff around and play with other dogs, to behave as nearly as possible as
they would on their native Scottish moors. So many dogs are over-protected,
snatched away from meeting other animals, kept as little diamond-collared
extensions of their owner's personality. I would always keep two dogs together;
they enjoy each others' company so much, and I enjoy seeing them being
DOGS."

"I know that when a protective owner visits one of the League kennels, steps are
taken to discover whether a suitable home is being offered or not. My main
concern lies with people who, having little knowledge themselves, buy dogs
from sellers who do not care what sort of home life the dog is going to. If only
this type of would-be dog owner could be persuaded to stop and ask him or
herself, 'can I give this type of dog the life that it needs?' then in some quarters
at least, this would be a happier world for dogs."

CHAPTER 24

In autumn 1972, the writers Brian Cooke and Johnnie Mortimer were working
on a project that would change not only their lives, but Yootha's too. Their
writing partnership and their history is impressive. They had devised and written
classic sitcoms like *Father Dear Father* and *Alcock and Gander*. They were
seen as a reliable comedy writing team, providing high quality material for
Tommy Cooper, Marty Feldman, Ronnie Barker, Bernard Cribbins and the like.
Brian Cooke told me that they found their way into TV via radio: "Johnnie and I
did about a hundred radio shows, including the final fourth series of *Round the
Horne*, before we even tried a television show." Brian and Johnnie's climb to
success was clearly a question of talent, hard work and perseverance.

Brian Cooke recalls that their idea for a new sitcom, *Man About the House*,
came through reading the papers. In the small ads, he noticed that "there were an
increasing number of people advertising for 'mixed flat sharing' and as the
subject hadn't been 'done,'" he says, "we twisted it round a little, and made it
two girls and one boy." He added that since the three kids sharing the flat had
"almost total freedom, with no parents to worry about, the downstairs landlord
and landlady George and Mildred Roper became surrogate parents, authority
figures." In his 1983 book *Writing Comedy For Television* (a must for aspiring

sitcom writers), Brian reveals that the writers also gave George "a very low sex drive." It was "astonishing how many bells that rang," he says, "it seems that there are an awful lot of frustrated Mildreds in the world."

The sexual tension between the young people upstairs needed to be counterbalanced by the bored middle-aged couple downstairs. According to Tex Fisher, in his *George and Mildred: the Definitive Companion*, the Ropers were added to stop the youngsters from "turning promiscuous": "they were brought in to break things up, as the subject was rather daring at the time."

When I spoke to Brian Cooke about Yootha's initial casting as Mildred Roper, I was shocked to learn that she was not the original choice for the part. He told me that he and Johnnie had "just finished a series for Bernard Cribbins, and it featured a youngish Sheila Steafel as Bernard's wife. We thought she'd make a great Mildred and approached her for the part. She was happy to do the pilot but admitted she couldn't do a series because she was heading for South Africa, where her mother was unwell. Which was no good to us... And the producer, Peter Frazer Jones, suggested Yootha, which we happily agreed with."

Sheila Steafel herself told me that "Yootha was so loved and remembered"; that she herself had never actually seen a *Man About the House* script, but did remember the time pretty well. She told me "I was with the Royal Shakespeare Company and had to have a week out (which pleased my understudy!). My mother was in fact dying of cancer, so it's not so surprising all else went out of my head! - Yup, I think the Cribbins thing was called *The Man With The Iron Chest*. (Don't ask!) I also thought I'd be typecast if I did any series, so I didn't. STUPID WOMAN! Ah well."

Watching Sheila over the years myself, I must admit she is a brilliant performer, and thought her performances were usually a little kooky! She was perfect for Spike Milligan projects, and later, in an episode of *Rab C Nesbitt* she developed into a fine actress. Remembering her playing a tough wife in the *Tommy Cooper Show*, I think she would have given us a very different Mildred. Peter Errington, the floor manager on *Man About the House*, when he heard about this initial casting, thought that Sheila would have made sense: "I know Sheila and have worked with her, I'm sure if she would have taken the role, she would have made it her own. I can't say she would have been as good as, but she certainly would have developed the character differently."

The casting for George Roper was already quite fixed for Brian Murphy. The writers already knew him from a previous guest appearance in one of their other shows, *Alcock and Gander*, with Beryl Reid and Richard O'Sullivan, in which he played "a very seedy character" – which according to Brian was a "bit near the knuckle," adding that Cooke and Mortimer were "very pleased and relieved that I didn't become offensive." At this time, his situation was a little difficult. In an interview, he says that he was getting a bit desperate as he approached forty." I had a young family and I'd put some money into a revival of *Oh What a Lovely War* that I was part-producing, so things were a bit tight. I was finding I couldn't accept a certain amount of work because it wasn't paying well enough. I got on to my agent and said maybe I should consider selling insurance or something. He said 'don't be silly. You are a character actor, by the time you're forty you'll come into your own.' He said it with such confidence I believed him and he was right almost to the minute. I was just coming up to 40 when *Man About the House* fell into my lap and turned everything around." Brian remembered that Cooke and Mortimer "didn't know Yootha, or that Yootha and I knew each other, but the moment they saw us working together they were quick to recognise the possibilities."

I asked Joan Littlewood in a letter in 1994 for her thoughts about Yootha's performance in *George and Mildred*. In her reply, she told me that "*George & Mildred* was born from an improvisation session at Theatre Workshop." In further letters she told me "The George and Mildred relationship was ad-libbed one morning at Theatre Royal in a frequent practice when 2 characters in a play were too sketchily drawn." Looking around for some confirmation on this, I asked Dudley Sutton about Joan's comments. He said: "It was in a show called *The Londoners*. There was a garden scene in the play and the moment I saw Brian Murphy and Yootha working together on that show *George & Mildred*, I realised that was where it had started. It was probably a little scene; you see, Brian was a genius at improvisation and Yootha was a genius at responding to it. I'm using that silly word genius, but you know what I mean!"
Brian Cooke, on the other hand, said: "I doubt very much that the George and Mildred characters were born out of an improvisation session at Theatre Royal Stratford East. Yootha and Brian Murphy never ever mentioned it to me." It does seem difficult to confirm Joan Littlewood's recollection. In an interview with Tony Bilbow in 1980, Yootha remembered that Brian "phoned me up in great excitement one evening and said, 'I have been offered the most wonderful series about a man and a wife, it's a comedy.' I said 'how funny darling! I've been offered a series about an man and a wife' and he said, 'Let me know how you get on' and I said, 'fine.'" She also said: "the director knew him and the writers knew me! And of course it was the same series! When Brian phoned up he said, 'it's called *The Ropers*.' I said, 'no it's not, it's called *George and Mildred,*' so I said 'oh, it's a different series,' then of course we got together eventually and found of course it was the same series, and we literally did not know that the other one had been cast opposite, they had just picked us out of a hat! It was like a raffle."
Tex Fisher's book quotes Brian as saying "the decision to cast me and Yootha together was serendipity more than anything." "Peter Frazer Jones didn't know me" he said, [Yootha remembered it the other way round!] He knew Yootha Joyce and had suggested her for the wife, a glam and snobbish wife with her overt working class husband." "Brian Cooke, Johnnie Mortimer and Peter Frazer Jones had no idea that we had all worked together at Theatre Workshop and in a few TV shows. It was a great joy to learn Yootha was playing my wife. Yootha too said it was a great joy to her, knowing I was to play the husband."
Yootha and Brian's working relationship in this new project was a match made in heaven. Brian Murphy remembers that they knew each other's timing, "so we had an immediate rapport." By April 1973 the project started with script read-throughs and rehearsals with the rest of the cast, which at that point included

Richard O'Sullivan, Paula Wilcox and Sally Thomsett as the young flat sharers upstairs.

In Brian Murphy's memories of the initial script read-throughs with Yootha he says: "We did some very funny scenes together, which was a great surprise to everyone, as the chemistry was already there. The others had to work harder to find and develop their characters but we seemed to just drop in like old sinners." Later, he adds: "even though we had our backs to one another, we sensed what we were going to do."

Peter Errington remembers that on set, Yootha was always friendly, and glamorous. "She would certainly scrub up well" he said, "We'd have rehearsals in our rehearsal room, for probably two and a half hours, then we'd all go to the pub over the road, or whatever pub was nearest, and stay there till god knows when, not late, but well into the afternoon and it was the same pattern for both *Man About The House* as the later *George and Mildred* series as well; it was very relaxed."

Other members of the crew recall the whole thing as very enjoyable, thanks mainly to the producer and director Peter Frazer Jones, who had worked in the industry with greats like Frankie Howerd and Benny Hill. Peter died in November 2005, aged 75. Peter Phillips, vision mixer on the production at Thames Television remembered him as "a lovely man, totally unflappable and well organised." "Working with him meant a stress-free day" he said, and spoke of the times at the end of series recordings they would all head off to his house "for a cast post-show party." Brian Murphy, in his recollections of working in sitcoms, said that the director "sorts out the timing, the camera shots, and bits of business. It's down to the actors to produce the goods."

Brian Murphy's observations of the production on set and during recordings are of great value, in telling us how the project was put together; his approach to the script was to regard it with the "same seriousness you would the text of a classic play." "At the beginning, the writers didn't know what Yootha and I could do as actors, so we were very small characters to start off with. The writers and director saw what we did with those roles and how well we worked together." "Yootha and I had this close-knit relationship with the two original writers. When we'd guest on other people's productions, they wrote little sketches for us to do. There was a limit to what the actor could do without good material from the writer."

The after-show visits to the pub were obviously a great way for the cast and crew to relax after the rehearsals and recordings at the Thames Television Studios in Broom Road, Teddington. They certainly didn't draw any attention to the fact that Yootha was drinking too much alcohol. When I talked to Barbara Windsor, she told me that she "had heard of the rumours" of Yootha's drinking while working at Thames TV, when she was filming for the *Carry On Christmas* TV specials. "Yootha was always professional, and I would only see her sipping the occasional glass of wine at intervals. But she clearly was a private drinker." The phrase is echoed by Yootha's solicitor Mario Uziell Hamilton, who, at Yootha's inquest, said that she "must have done her drinking secretly in her own home." Barbara told me that she herself gave up the drink, and is glad she did:

now it feels like "acid on her lips," she said.

Clearly, Yootha hid her drinking even from those close to her. Dr Paul Knapman, the coroner at the inquest, said that for at least ten years Yootha "drank upwards of half a bottle of brandy a day." Brian Cooke remembers that "Yootha's favourite tipple was a brandy." Her ex-husband Glynn, however, thought of her as "nothing more than a social drinker." In an interview in 1976, Yootha said that one of her hobbies was giving lavish dinner parties. Sally Thomsett, Yootha's co-star in *Man About the House*, said that her all-night parties were "a blast." Asking others that might have attended these parties, like the writers Galton and Simpson, I was told that "they didn't know her socially and knew nothing about them." "Still starving!" they confirmed. That's really all we know.

CHAPTER 25

The first episode of *Man About the House* 'Three's a Crowd' was broadcast on 15th August 1973, after seven had been filmed: the other six ran consecutively until the end of September. Alan Coren, the TV critic of *The Times*, highlighted the writing the following day, saying that "Mortimer and Cooke ran off a good script." *The Stage*, on 30th August, singled out Yootha's performance: "Yootha Joyce is a superb character" it said. "Miss Joyce is obviously going to have a big contribution to make to this show and I foresee some very funny situations, and this in itself is a mark of success, because I am eagerly awaiting next week's episode to see what this team will get up to. Yootha is a delight and brings a character into the proceedings to contrast the youth element."

Asking Glynn Edwards whether Yootha's performance met with her mother's approval, he told me it did, "and with the sitcom's success after success, Maude was very proud of that." International appreciation of Yootha's work was also noted as far way as Australia. *The Canberra Times* thought she had great abilities as an actress in the show as Mildred, "She brought the character to life with her ability to draw the maximum amount of vinegar from an acid line."

Just before this review, Yootha had taken a part in a TV horror movie, *Frankenstein: The True Story*, with a screenplay by Christopher Isherwood, starring James Mason and Leonard Whiting, filmed at Pinewood Studios. It was aired just after the first series of *Man About the House* had been broadcast. It would be the last of Yootha's dramatic roles: a great shame. Even in this film, she only appears for thirty seconds, as Hospital Matron Mrs McGregor. For this role she is seen wearing a large Victorian bonnet, with little make up on the eyes! I'm sure this would never met with her approval, as she was known to love the false eye lashes, but then she was serious about her career as an actress. The character, unlike the Mildred role, which was now in audience's minds, was, in contrast, rather timid and friendly with no hint of the usual harshness.

It was now that Yootha was asked to appear with Liz Smith, who was also building up a name for herself at this time, in 'A Bird Alone,' a 30-minute TV pilot for a BBC *Comedy Playhouse* production. In *Our Betty - Scenes From My*

Life, her autobiography, Liz says that the show was "never completed because it was considered 'too naughty.'" Liz played mother to Yootha Joyce's character. "It was beautifully written by Hugh Leonard, so you had wonderful real dialogue. Yootha's character was being divorced, with John Le Mesurier as the judge." In Liz's book she recalls, "The description I had to give to the judge of talking to Yootha behind the dress shop she owned while she was 'carrying on!,' was considered too shocking to go out." Very kindly, Liz Smith herself wrote to me recently about this show, which the BBC cancelled. She told me "It was a splendid show, a wonderful cast, wonderful writing and acting, just thrown away, and just look at the things they show today!" I enquired after the show at the BBC, and got a standard reply: not another missing episode, I thought?

Yootha remembered that, away from the cameras and the pop promotion, her relationship with Cyril Smith was quite action-packed. Cyril had a temper all of his own – but he got the same treatment from Yootha. Yootha once spoke of what she called their "wonderful fights," with lots of "shouting and screaming." Speaking to Alix Coleman for the *TV Times* in 1976 she remembered: "He was tremendously strong and once got hold of my wrists, which I really hated. He dragged me into the kitchen and threw a cup of water over me and I began to laugh." She once referred to an incident in a restaurant where she tipped a plate of grilled Dover sole over his head. "We were having dinner with friends one night and Cyril was annoying me. He went too far so I just upturned my plate of sole right over his head. I rushed for the door – because he was a big fella, darling – got a taxi, came home and locked the door. Then the dog wanted to go out, and by the time I got back with her, Cyril had arrived. I looked at him. He looked at me. I thought 'he won't wallop me, will he?' Well, we began to giggle and soon we were laughing our heads off."

Towards the end of November plans were afoot for another series of *Man About the House*: reactions to the first batch of episodes were good. The team were promptly put together to begin rehearsing and recording six new episodes. Richard O'Sullivan once revealed in an interview, alongside Sally Thomsett, that the writers used to come in on the rehearsals, "they got to know us very well, they tended to grab bits of our own personalities and put them in the script." Sally added that she thought the words in the script "came naturally" as a result. Yootha once admitted, "I'm very bitchy as Mildred"! Sally also remembered that, for the rehearsals, the cast would meet up at a church hall in Fulwell. "We worked for two or three hours on a Tuesday and Saturday, a few days before recording, everybody having learned their lines from a delivered script." "Then we recorded all day Sunday". The actor Mike Savage [The Dustman in episode 'How Does Your Garden Grow'] recalled: "the cast would do a rehearsal in the morning for the studio crew and a final dress rehearsal before the audience were brought in. At 7 in the evening the audience would be allowed in and entertained by the warm-up man, usually a retired comedian. The recording started at 7.30 p.m. and would finish by 9 if all went well." "An episode of *Man About the House* was once recorded with the cast standing in inches of water on the floor after a plumbing error with simulated rain." Brian

Murphy said that on occasions things used to go wrong with the sets: "you couldn't go through the door because someone had nailed it shut, so we had to come through the fireplace. The audience would love it when something went wrong."

True enough, in the programme, you can see both Yootha and Brian corpsing in the 'No Children No Dogs,' episode, where Richard O'Sullivan's bandage comes loose, and the audience howl with laughter, while Yootha gives the quivering-voiced Brian a knowing smile at the end of it. Peter Errington told me that Phillip Jones, head of light entertainment at Thames TV, had a job with the cast and crew of *Man About the House*: "God knows what he went through trying to control us all, but working on the shows was lovely and it was so relaxed. And it turned out a good product and we had fun doing it."

As well as the six episodes filmed at studio 1 at Teddington, the team were asked to film a short sketch for the Christmas *All Star Comedy Carnival* show, which ITV used to highlight their best television offerings; it was broadcast prime time on Christmas day. *The Man About the House* sketch, compared to the full shows, was rather weak and lacklustre, almost rushed; certainly not up to the usual standard.

What was clear, however, was that they knew that the programme had a winning formula, and the audiences lapped it up; just to catch sight of the team was a real thrill. Yootha spoke of the new role as Mildred in an interview, comparing it to her previous sitcom hit, *Me Mammy*, in which, she said, "I never got my man, Bunjy. In this show I can't seem to get George interested in me either. I'm glad I haven't got any of Mrs Roper's sex problems. I could never stick a situation like that. They don't really like each other. She's using him as a punch bag for laughs. I'd have gone off and left him. I love saying their lines. I don't have to do any work."

On set, Yootha charmed the crew. Peter Errington always thought her "very considerate to other actors. She was very generous to them; she would never crave for the funniest lines or anything like that. People would leave her stuff at the studios, gifts and things; she was well loved, and she was only ever in the studios for a day."

Andrew Armstrong, the props manager, was at Thames TV from 1971 till 1993, and worked on a few programmes with Yootha. His wife, Zelie (née Smith), worked in the costume department on a lot of shows too. They shared their happy memories of Yootha with me for this book, and told me: "Yootha was a very caring and considerate person and would not say or do anything deliberately to hurt or offend."

Christmas 1973 was a busy time for Yootha, and for the rest of the *Man About the House* cast. They were beginning to get requests for personal appearances and charity events: one such was The Dunhill International Show Jumping Championships Gala Charity Premiere for The National Society for Mentally Handicapped Children at Olympia; Paula Wilcox and Richard O'Sullivan went, with Yootha. Clearly they were very supportive of one another. It also was on the same day that Yootha appeared as a guest alongside Glynn Edwards and Gabrielle Drake on *This is Your Life*, celebrating the life and work of Yootha's fellow Theatre Workshop actor, George Sewell. She was now becoming a celebrity.

The second series of *Man About the House* was broadcast promptly, early in 1974: the six episodes had been shown by the end of February: There was also a new tie-in film with the famous Hammer film company, which was ready for shooting in March. Before the film started, Yootha's beloved dog Tallulah died: but she carried on, also taking a cameo appearance in *The Dick Emery Show*, as the drunk wife of Dick's famous vicar character. Unlike the Mildred character, which was well established in early 1974, Yootha played this one posh: having seen how Harry H. Corbett had been labelled as Steptoe Jnr., perhaps she wanted to show herself as a versatile actress, and not just Mildred. The trouble was the audiences had simply fallen in love with Mildred, and she had made such an impact that there was a great demand for more. The ratings for *Man About the House* were good, and the appetite for the forthcoming film was ravenous.

In his book, *A History of Horrors: The Rise and Fall of the House of Hammer* Denis Meikle says that in those days, "Hammer found itself unable to fund anything more promising than another TV spin-off.," with the cast "descending on Elstree for the familiar routines of *Man About the House*." Maybe so, but as the film was a hit, taking £90,000 in London alone, they had little to complain about!

Sally Thomsett told me that one of her ambitions had always been to star in a Hammer horror, so her dream was half realised, though it's a pity it was a comedy. Sally's memories of the film were that she was never that fond of the movie, as "we didn't have our usual director," as she once tweeted. However there was some fun from the props boys on the set whilst filming, as Yootha once recalled in a television interview. They played a trick on her and Brian, replacing a picture prop of George and Mildred's wedding photograph with "this lovely picture of *King Kong* and a gorgon with lovely snakes coming out of its head." Yootha recalled that it really broke the ice and helped with the nerves. As it was a first scene "it took about thirty takes; we all fell about laughing so much, it was great fun."

After the Hammer film had been wrapped up in April, Yootha went straight into production of a third *Man About the House* series, followed swiftly with the fourth after the third was broadcast in October. She was known to dislike sweet things: in one episode, 'Somebody Out There Likes Me,' as certain scenes had her eating a box of chocolates, they had to be replaced with chunks of cheese covered in marmite! Yootha also appeared in another *This Is Your Life*, this time featuring her co-star Richard O'Sullivan, in November. The two characters George and Mildred were becoming increasingly popular: Yootha recalled that the technicians on the studio floor would say: "'we hear you're going to have your own series', I'd say 'no darlings, not us', and they were right, everybody knew it before Brian and me, we were the last to be told."

CHAPTER 26

By 1975, Yootha's new celebrity status meant that her dramatic roles were replaced with requests for personal appearances in public, often on game shows. People now wanted a piece of her, and as she was a generous person, what else could she do? In January she was asked to appear on the 'other side' - the BBC - as a guest on the TV quiz show *Password*, temporarily hosted by Esther Rantzen. Kenneth Williams, also featuring on the show, describes the journey to the studios in Manchester and Yootha's fear of flying in a letter to Maggie Smith on 27th January 1975: "I sat with Yootha. She was clenched in the seat like a terrified mute and admitted to being scared of aeroplanes. I said, 'They have the lowest accident rate of any transport.' She said that was no consolation to her. She told me her series *Man About the House* was doing very well in the ratings and of course they had to up the money to get us all back for the next series: 'it's ITV not BBC, so I'm surprised the BBC have asked me to appear in this *Password* show, after all, I work for the opposition.' When the stewardess came along she ordered a large brandy: she was obviously enjoying it when they suddenly announced the descent for landing and she had to leave half of it, put the fag out and fasten the safety belt."

Alongside the television shows came the appearances for the charities she cared for. Brian Murphy said "Yootha would never bring her dogs to work: 'animals are not for the workplace.' Yootha was very wise with her animals." Unfortunately, I've no idea where they were while she was filming. The National Canine Defence League made good use of her popularity for their very worthy cause. Clarissa Baldwin told me that she had only had the privilege of knowing Yootha for the last few years of her life, but whenever asked to help with publicity, she was always ready to come forward. She would pack envelopes with other NCDL volunteers.
Yootha was not the type of person to have a dog just to appeal to her vanity. She walked Sammy every morning, afternoon and evening. Sammy, she said, would "bark and growl, but when a burglar came into the house she'd be all over him." She saw them as a "massive responsibility." She used the well-known NCDL slogan invented by Clarissa: "A dog is for life, not just for Christmas." As she said once in an interview: "the fluffy presents become a nuisance. People don't realise what they are taking on when they buy a puppy. And when the find out they often just dump it. Suddenly the animal is filling up the house, eating them out of house and home, perhaps still not trained and it's becoming a nuisance. It gets kicked around or just abandoned. The most common reason for this is because pets are bought for children who think they are going to look after them, until they realise this means going out in the rain, feeding and training. I think there are actually very few rogue dogs – but there are an awful lot of rogue people. There's the odd dog that will turn peculiar, but most problems arise from neglect or ignorance. Dogs do take up an awful lot of one's life. But it's also possible to 'over-love' a dog – that's almost as bad. Pekinese, for example, which are really active little dogs: too many just sit around on laps all day being

fed chocolate, which they cannot digest. They get fat and wheezy and they die early because of it. A good part of our work at NCDL is in education and training people. Just to make them realise what they are taking on. Don't buy a puppy unless you want a dog. Don't buy a bitch unless you are happy for her to have puppies. Or else have her spayed immediately. People never notice what sex they are buying anyway."

Reaction to Yootha's performance as Mildred Roper in the fourth series of *Man About the House*, broadcast in March and April 1975, remained positive, and the scripts were as fresh as ever. Barbara Windsor told me that "when Yootha continued her brilliance in television, I was very impressed, I certainly followed her success as Mildred'; she was just terrific at playing the brassy roles." Brian Cooke said "The Ropers' marriage is like a lot of people's, but in spite of the niggles and arguments, they still stay together. What else can they do?" Sally Thomsett said that "Mildred was strong, yet insecure I think, because she wasn't getting any attention or affection from George, and that's what the problem was there, you know, she desperately wanted someone to love her and cuddle her, and he'd always have a headache wouldn't he?"
But how much of this part was Yootha? Peter Errington told me: "Yootha basically played Yootha, I suppose. I mean she did act but she smoked, she drank, she did all that as the character, as she did in life and it sort of transferred on screen. Brian on the other hand certainly did act, he was nothing like George: he was very 'theatre', not to say that he was a luvvie, but he did love the theatre. Even now he sort of plays parts of those who are a bit down, not flawed but very simple types." Sally said that Yootha, arguably, was like Mildred, "a very flirty lady. She came across as this big fierce domineering masculine person, but she wasn't, she was very feminine and very flirtatious."
As I said at the beginning of the book, viewers would write to Yootha. Sally Thomsett recalled that she had "more fan mail than the rest of us put together." Fans would also contact various media outlets to express their enthusiasm for the show. One viewer from Torquay wrote "Yootha Joyce as Mrs Roper is a knockout. She had the ability to bury her personality in the character. Brilliant, all the way. I am sad that the series is ending!" I don't know where the rumours that the show was ending came from; but the increased fee that Yootha spoke to Kenneth Williams about on the plane trip to Manchester seems to imply that this was not the case.
As soon as series four had been broadcast, series five went into production, though there were occasional strikes during recordings. Yootha had her own dressing room at the Teddington studios, or what the director, Peter Frazer Jones, called the "Inner Sanctum" to which you had to be "invited in." Andy and Zelie Armstrong recalled that at Thames TV: "All dressing rooms were the same, with a single divan and wash basins. There were curtains at the windows. Most of the dressing rooms were quite small. Lyn Harvey, who worked on the costumes, would always provide fresh flowers for the female cast when I was working with her, a touch which was greatly appreciated by cast members. There was no special decor for any artiste in those days. Yootha was one of the

most grounded and professional actresses at the time, and the thought of any special treatment would have made her very uncomfortable."

Sally Thomsett remembered in an interview that when Yootha arrived at her dressing room: "all the cards would go up and the flowers would be there, and the bar would be set up! And the cigarette and the ashtrays, so it was a very homely thing. She usually had some flamboyant dressing gown, none of the ropey old towelling dressing gowns, all with make up round the collar – oh no, none of that."

Yootha's own sense of style was very evident in any images showing her at public gatherings or events, at the supermarket, or maybe putting out the milk bottles! Her clothes were usually bold and vibrant in colour, classy, with a good cut, complementing her amazingly sexy figure. She loved to "drape herself in necklaces, bracelets and decorate the fingers with rings"; so much so that in an interview with *Daily Express* legend Jean Rook at her flat, Rook reported that "Miss Joyce was wearing seven gold rings, I had on five. When we shook hands, we snapped together and locked." Yootha once confessed that she did have a tendency to "overdo the gold jewellery." She was often pictured wearing a Star of David bracelet and necklace; unfortunately I don't know what significance it had for her, if any; sadly nobody could tell me. As well as the jewellery, Yootha had "a love of expensive and beautifully cut clothes." One description of her appearance reported that "she flounced into her little London flat in a stunning, flowing pink number, 'like it darling? I think it's the sort of saucy thing George would like.'" According to Sally Thomsett, "her clothes that she wore as Mildred, well, the taste was not that different to her own: they were a cheap tacky version of the fairly outlandish clothes that she wore in real life."

Christine Pilgrim said "Yootha could make a dress from C&A look like a Dior or Chanel. She did shop at C&A sometimes actually. She never gave me fashion tips, just as she didn't give me acting ones. Although I remember discussing with her what we should wear to the wrap party for *Burke and Hare* ... or the premiere, I don't remember which. Anyway, I turned up in something lower cut and more diaphanous than we'd agreed, and she spat (though with a twinkle) 'Bitch!'"

Putting C&A aside, I asked Joy Jameson if Yootha favoured any particular fashion house or designer. "The only named designer I remember Yootha telling me about was how she loved her Issy Myaki stuff. I think as much as anything for the practicality of being able to throw them in a suitcase and you could just put them on." she said, adding: "I don't think Yootha had any dress-down clothes, but I wonder now what she wore when she walked her dogs?" I was able to send Joy a picture Yootha had kept, along with some others, which clearly answered that question.

Man About the House featured in the popular *Look In* magazine in 1975 [regularly up until mid 1976]. The characters were honoured with their own comic strip of their adventures. The magazine also featured drawings of the cast by Arnaldo Putzu, an Italian who also drew for Hammer Film's movie posters: publicity was very different in those days. Sally Thomsett thought they were "very funny drawings – the likeness of the cartoons to the cast was a popular laughing point," she said. The cast themselves had become very close over the years, including the later addition of Doug Fisher, who played Larry, the fourth lodger. On one occasion Doug was called in as a kind of understudy for Sally Thomsett, who had a suspected appendicitis during one weeks recording, with the writers adjusting the scripts to suit Doug until she recovered. Doug was an Oxford graduate in French & Russian. He had imagined he might be involved in espionage, but he never got the call and turned to acting. He took roles in Shakespeare and Beckett, before landing his role in *Man About the House*. At times, he has the most promising scenes with Mildred, who had the innate ability to sniff out any dodgy characters, including Roy Kinnear's 'Jerry' character, who appeared as an irregular regular member on the team. He was "a great character and sparring partner" said Brian Murphy. Brain remembers that Roy would occasionally "get bored with his performance and would usually do something slightly different each time he performed: he was very spontaneous and we both loved him." Brian's own behaviour on the set was always full of fun, so people said. Yootha remembered herself that "he knows I'm dreadful at remembering lines and when I get to a dodgy bit, his eyes start twinkling and that breaks me up, and then everyone else starts."

After the recording of these shows, the cast would usually have little parties at The Three Pigeons pub in Richmond, or failing that, the Thames bar at the Teddington studios. Sometimes Yootha would give one of her own parties: she loved to cook things up. Sally remembers that "Paula didn't party with us so much because she was married and we were all single I reckon" but when they were all together "the landlords would close early to accommodate them."

CHAPTER 27

In early 1975, Yootha's relationship with Cyril Smith ended for reasons best known to them both. Yootha once said, "I do try and give whatever I have to building a relationship, but I won't give more. In private life, I'm inclined to be extremely selfish. Anyone who's ever lived with me will tell you that." She assumed that there was no point in talking about the break-up. As she said: "When you're working, you go into a rehearsal room and say, 'My fellow's just left me' and they say, 'Darling, what a shame; now, about scene two.' No one tells you to have a good cry. Anyway, I'd hate to go in with red eyes, because I look awful with red eyes." She added "I never cried about Glynn or Cyril and I wouldn't cry about the next one. I've never cried in bed and I never will." Cyril eventually found somebody else, another actress. Joy recalled that she never knew whether he married or whether he just had a romance, but "his new girlfriend came with him to parties." Barbara Windsor remembered that "Yootha had a lot of male admirers, which is not surprising as she had such a charm about her. I would never pry about her relationships, and she would not volunteer a great deal of information about her personal life," she told me.

Many people I have spoken to about Yootha said she was never one to talk openly about her true feelings. Her solicitor Mario Uziell Hamilton said, "she rarely confided in any of her friends, and she kept many problems she had to herself." Perhaps she suppressed her emotions, and that contributed to her loneliness and so to her drinking: it's difficult to say. Dudley Sutton said "I don't know whether Yootha was an alcoholic or not, it's not up to me to say. – Look, alcoholics drink. Don't look for a reason! I would think there isn't any point wringing your hands looking for a reason, because there isn't one."

As Barbara and others have said, Yootha was very sexy and clearly had the ability to attract. Norman Eshley saw this for himself: "she certainly seem to like the men around her and certainly, men were very drawn to her. She had a fabulous figure and she'd walk into the bar and phumph! Every guy would surround her, you'd look over and think, oh yeah, she's doing it again, she was a total magnet as far as men were concerned."

Whatever her emotional troubles, she put her feelings on hold, throwing herself into her work with gusto, "I have great bursts of energy, emotional and otherwise. I don't care whether it's unwomanly or not. I don't sit down and think about it," she once said.

In early 1975, Yootha returned to the theatre to play Bertha, a maid, in *Boeing, Boeing*, Marc Camoletti's French farce, adapted by Beverly Cross, which revolved around a Parisian bachelor and his numerous amours with airline stewardesses. She was joined by some of her *Man About the House* co-stars, Doug Fisher took the lead part of Bernard in the play, Richard O'Sullivan played Robert and Sally Thomsett, Judith. The play began a national tour in March and broke all box office records at the Wyvern theatre in Swindon. It went right round the country, and lasted for a number of months. *The Stage* said: "Yootha Joyce is superb as the maid. The timing and relative economy of her gestures contrast with the aimless arm waving of some of the other members of the cast. And these gestures and her expressions speak volumes of disapproval, resignation."

Some way into the tour Terry Lee Dickson, Yootha's future boyfriend, joined the production as company manager. At that stage, Yootha confessed, she didn't really like him, and was keen to avoid a relationship. She told a reporter, "I didn't feel I wanted to get tied up again." She was quite happy without a "man about the house," so to speak.

While touring, Yootha continued her work with the NCDL: she gave the charity her work schedules, so that when she wasn't working, or if she was near one of their rescue centres, she could gain a little publicity for them. On one occasion, Sally Thomsett joined her in a public appearance when they visited the League's newest kennels at Newbury, singling out the League's mascot greyhound, Czar. It was reported by the organisation: "Miss Joyce had a particular interest in visiting Newbury's Plumbs farm, as she had recently donated a kennel there in memory of her pet terrier Tallulah, who died last year." On another occasion, in the spring of 1975, she attended a benefit show, at the Pindar of Wakefield in Gray's Inn Road. It was chaired by Barry Cryer: Brian Murphy, Roy Kinnear, Christine Pilgrim, and Sheila Steafel were also there, and there was a collection in aid of children with spina bifida.

The popularity of *Boeing, Boeing* grew as the fifth series of *Man About the House* was broadcast during the tour; at times there were outbursts of something like mass hysteria when the cast appeared in public. Sally remembers that the appearances were, "manic; there were many events, and we usually all went to them together." For Yootha, the experience of meeting those who loved her as Mildred was a bit much to take at times. Some of the events were a little disorganised, and the attention and interest was turning rather sour. Talking once about a day out in Edinburgh, she said: "Four of us from the series went to the zoo on our afternoon off, we didn't see one animal, we spent all of our time surrounded by people. You want to cry out 'this is our afternoon off, please leave us alone,' but people wouldn't understand."

Yootha was not to be messed with, and the famous temper would bubble up at times. Sally Thomsett once witnessed it: "we were having lunch or dinner, I can't remember, in a restaurant and somebody came over and said 'I'm terribly sorry to bother you.' She was fantastic, and said 'well don't then!' But then he said 'but could I have your autographs,' and she said, 'well if you know you're bothering us, why are you asking?' Richard and I were sitting there wanting the floor to open up and swallow us. But on reflection it was quite right, if someone's knows that they're bothering you then why are they doing it?"

Yootha was now having some trouble with Mildred. In a later interview she admitted to having "a scorching temper and a lava tongue, which would get her into boiling water with her fans," "I loathe being touched, I can't stand grabbers who come up to you in the street and literally shake your shoulders. The way they grab and shake and shout at you tells you 'I OWN you, you belong to me.'"

To stop future personal appearances from getting out of hand, Yootha employed the help of a specialist organiser, Carl Gresham, better known as 'The Gresh'. He was a big name in the world of personal appearances, who can still be heard on his radio show *Carl Gresham & Friends,* broadcast on www.bbcradio.co.uk (from Bradford) every Sunday morning.

The Gresh told me that the first time he had seen Yootha was as a clippie in *On The Buses*. He has worked as P.A. with many showbiz people: Peter Wyngarde, Pat Phoenix, Morecambe and Wise and Bruce Forsyth among others, as his book on his life's work testifies.

A 'Greshstyle' personal appearance was run with military precision: "For instance when we did an event opening a new Woolworth store in Coventry with Yootha and Brian Murphy I'd arrive with my compère and sound engineer at 4 p.m. the previous day. We'd select which aisle we wanted to block off – so when the celebrity arrived he or she could walk freely down what we called 'The Gresh Way'. I'd already make sure there was a table and chairs with a getaway door (usually into the stores) if we needed a quick and safe exit. We never did. Around 5.20ish, the team would get to the hotel and book in. Myself or one of the team would collect the star from the station and book them into the hotel and arrange to meet them in the restaurant at 8pm for dinner."

Brian and Yootha also spoke about the Woolworth's opening, "The morning arrived and the organisers told us their programme: 'We will collect you and drive around town until a minute to 10 a.m., so that we can be on time for the opening ceremony,' and everything was under control, and we did a dress rehearsal the day before and the police cordoned off the area. We both exchanged smiles. To have the police seemed rather ridiculous. We had done enough personal appearances to know that all it meant was saying hello to a couple of dozen members of staff.

The car whisked us off and several streets away from the store we could see the crowds. There must have been 6,000 there, cheering, even screaming. We certainly needed the police. A podium had been erected in the middle of the floor where we stood handing out autographed pictures as the crowd filed past us in a jostling queue. They had been queuing since 7.30 a.m. that morning. We couldn't believe that scene; we felt like royalty." The Gresh told me "It was almost like a 'Cinderella' moment when the star would arrive at the front of the store, but we left by the loading bay, never to be seen again – till the next appearance."

Away from the tours and personal appearances, Yootha would indulge herself with a few of her hobbies, but her happiest form of relaxation was "doing nothing." She loved to visit antique shops and would decorate her flat often too. She liked filling it with bits and pieces. According to Christine Pilgrim "the flat was always immaculate when I was there" she said; "Everything about Yootha was immaculate" she added. Joy Jameson particularly remembers the interior of Yootha's bathroom: "I remember my joy in noting she'd had her bath personalised with the same material (Dimity by Sanderson) that I'd had my entire bedroom including the ceiling decorated with. I promise you it was not the epitome of good taste. We had a laugh a couple of years later when Dimity was like a snowstorm in West London houses." Yootha also liked to develop her cooking skills for her lavish dinner parties. Glynn Edwards remembers that she did like to socialise a lot: "she was a real social lady, and loved to eat out at restaurants." One of her favourites, as has been mentioned, was The Kismet Club in the West End. She once told a story that on her way to the club she heard a frantic scream from the dustbins. "Rummaging through them all, I found a cat [promptly called Kismet] in a filthy brown bag. She was very ill and practically hairless, we had a hell of a time dripping stuff into her every two hours, trying to keep her alive." Another of her favourites, according to Christine Pilgrim was The White Elephant on the River, in Chelsea, "we went there once when Ray Ellington was playing the piano. I think Yootha footed the bill for that, you know. Money was no object with her." Asking Christine if Yootha was a food connoisseur she said, "I don't think food itself was that important to her. She was certainly no 'foodie'; egg and chips would do her fine, as long as there was a glass of something nice to go with it."

Yootha had other hobbies too. She also loved "roulette, poker and plebby games like whist and solo." She enjoyed visiting the dog tracks, as well as the horse races, often indulging in a mild flutter. Christine Pilgrim told me "Yootha loved the horses. And she'd dress to the nines for a day at the races, that was right up

her alley. I never went with her. Our interaction was always on a family basis."
Yootha's love of horses was so intense that she also approached a horse breeder.
She put her name down for a foal, one from the ten offspring, of the mare Royal
Pat, and the stallion, Imperial Crown, born some months later. Yootha even
claimed she owned the mare Royal Pat, but I was unable to verify this; she
agreed on £2000 for the foal, agreeing to use it as a racehorse.

During breaks from the *Boeing, Boeing* tour in 1975 Yootha enjoyed the
occasional trip abroad, despite her flying fears. Once, she went to Nerja with her
mother and Sally Thomsett. Sally told me on one trip "We had a blast, baby doll.
Her mum was there too and she was fabulous. It was a pretty unknown area at
the time so we had some respite from the fans and spent a lot of time on her
favourite beach." "She was mortal, honey. We had loads of 'Gentleman Callers',
you'd have had a fabulous time lovely," she told me as I sipped my Horlicks.
Yootha's attitude to sex was once picked up in *Titbits*. In an article entitled
'Men and the fallout from female power' she revealed what she and other
woman were thinking about when they took on relationships at a time when
ideas about women and sex were going through fundamental changes (Germaine
Greer's *The Female Eunuch* had been published in 1970). "I'm sure men are
facing difficulties and I'm glad. Women have had it bad for 5000 years and at
last things are changing. Men have just got to rethink their role, and I think
intelligent men are already doing this. It's the unthinking ones that are in
trouble. The average British husband seems to regard sex as a chore – something
he does once a month. But he will have to change his ideas about women now.
Certainly if a man said 'no' to me when I wanted it, I'd try my best to get it –
that's no longer considered wrong or naughty."
When Yootha and Sally returned to the UK, the tour went back on the road;
Sally remembers the time when Yootha began an affair with the touring
manager, Terry Lee Dickson. "We used to go out for drinks and dinner most
evenings. After the show, I remember noticing that Terry and Yootha were
holding hands under the table, and there was age difference; this was way before
lots of people were doing that – women going out with younger men. Richard
O'Sullivan who was with us turned to me and said 'did you see that?' Next thing
I know he was staying in the hotel rooms and they were both having a wonderful
time, fantastic, good on her!"

CHAPTER 28

In autumn 1975, there was the consensus that the team on *Man About the House*
wanted to finish the series and do other things. Yootha said she loved doing it,
seeing it as a "naturally funny situation." When filming began in November, she
confided to a reporter "we would be going to see a lot more of Mildred siding
with the kids in the new and final sixth series." But she felt that "we should go
out when we're on top. Even though we have two great writers, the funny
situations must run out. But I'll be very sad when we have to break the old gang

up. They're a lovely lot to work with, we spend all our time together laughing." she said.
Cooke and Mortimer confessed that "we became aware of the danger that we might start to repeat ourselves or strain believability to get further plots from the flat-sharing set-up in *Man About the House*. Some of the characters seemed to offer more scope for development in a different setting."

Speaking later in her career about the programme, Paula Wilcox, who played Chrissie Plummer, said "we all felt it was time to move on, it was bittersweet really, very sad to leave, but really important to move on." "Nothing else I have done has had such an impact" she said: "*Man About the House* is always hanging over me." When she spoke to Alan Kennaugh about the show's repeat on Channel Four in the mid eighties, she said "I think it was successful because we all had a lot of fun making the series, and the enthusiasm showed." However, once an interviewer when he mentioned the show, noted, "a determined cast to her eye telling you she doesn't suffer fools gladly. And in particular those that want to talk about *Man About the House*." She said, "I'm not paranoid about those shows, it's just they were made a long time ago and I've moved on, I look at that girl on the TV and I don't recognise her, it was another life. She was another person, as an actress I want to move on, but it's hard to shake them off when they're always repeated."

Paula was touching on the typecasting that the show brought and its effect on the work she and the cast were offered in 1975. Her own career continued with a spin-off series about a single mum, *Miss Jones and Son*, written by Richard Waring, but, as she said, it was some time before she could really break free from Chrissie Plummer to work on projects like *Fiddlers Three, Brookside,* or *The Queen's Nose*. She also had a career in theatre to think about; most recently as Miss Havisham in *Great Expectations* in which she got favourable reviews. Richard O'Sullivan also had success with spin-off sitcoms *Robin's Nest* and *Me and My Girl*. Sally Thomsett would star in *The P.G Woodhouse Playhouse* for the BBC, as well as popping up on the occasional game show. She would continue making personal appearances at the most glamorous venues.
Doug Fisher went on tour to Australia with Richard O'Sullivan in *Boeing, Boeing* 1977, and appeared in *The Stud* with Joan Collins and in *Yes Minister*. Sadly, he died of a heart attack in July 2000.
Yootha and Brian Murphy however, of course went on to play the same characters in *George and Mildred*. Thames TV were keen to repeat the success. This was the real beginning of the process that fixed their images once and for all. In Tex Fisher's book, Brian recalled that "Yootha and myself always PERFORMED well, and the writers and directors raised their eyebrows and thought of all the mileage they could get from us. It became obvious as it went along in *Man About the House* that the Ropers were just as popular as the youngsters. We were told that there was a lot of interest in our characters; the feedback was excellent for the whole programme, but especially for us two."
"Phillip Jones, the head of light entertainment, said 'when we finish with *Man*

About the House, we are going to run with *George and Mildred*, the writers would love to do that.' As old pros, me and Yootha thought to ourselves that it would be nice to do our own series, but we didn't believe it would happen, but then it did."

The writers were indeed on a roll and having a great time; their success with selling the idea and the show abroad was incredibly good for them. Speaking about their time writing the new show for Yootha and Brian, they confessed to acting out the characters themselves: "we gave every scene a trial run" they said. They talked about this in a piece in the *TV Times* in 1975: "suddenly Mortimer is the morbid Roper, astounded that his wife should threaten to leave him after 20 years. 'It's physical, isn't it Mildred.' he wails. Brian Cooke skis into falsetto for Mildred Roper. 'Of course it's physical – and mental; it's wearing your socks in bed, and laughing in your sleep and eating pickled onions last night, it's everything.'" Cooke said that George and Mildred "were so well loved by the public, we couldn't waste characters like that. If we hadn't used them again in something else, then somebody else would have."

Brian Murphy confessed that "both Yootha and I had put our other acting ambitions on the back burner while we were doing *George and Mildred*." He also said that they were "inundated" with many offers of stage work, though unfortunately I don't know what they were. When I asked Joy Jameson if Yootha was offered much variety of work in those days she said she didn't have records any more. "I moved from London seven years ago and an awful lot of stuff had to go." She did recall that both Brian and Yootha "mostly guested on other stars' programmes." That's exactly what Yootha did at the close of the year, appearing (as herself) in a special *Christmas Celebrity Squares* on Christmas evening. The programme was only broadcast in London, and seems to have been deleted.

If Yootha was ever unhappy at only being cast as Mildred, or ambivalent about her newfound success as a celebrity, she never showed it in her performance. In 1976, she was in her prime. But there was very little variety in future work offers. Was she afraid of losing her successful status? Would it be possible to just stop playing Mildred? Would that let the team down? Was a return to the constant battle of becoming known as a more intense and dramatic performer just too much of a risk or turnaround? Perhaps it was safer to just let the issue ride and concentrate more on other things, like the charity work? It's impossible to say what her thoughts were.

In early 1976, before the rehearsals for the new series began, Yootha took a brief holiday in Corfu with friends. As soon as she returned to the UK she put her efforts into work at the NCDL. Joy Jameson said to me: "Yootha loved animals (except mice). I think she was on one or two charity panels/boards." And so she was: "Now I'm on the council," she said, "I help out with strays and finding homes for them. I don't get involved with case histories though – just as well I think because I have a terrible temper." She added: "I can be more use in getting publicity and raising money, because it does cost a lot to keep the animals. Ideally, we find good homes for them. We are very strict about vetting homes and keeping a check afterwards. You wouldn't believe the cases we take on.

People can be terribly cruel to dogs. I was at a centre recently when we had a
bitch in whelp brought in. She was literally about to drop her puppies- she'd
been thrown out of a car on the motorway." "I give the Canine Defence League
as much time as I can. I get angry with children, too, when they're badly treated.
I'm not stupid about putting animals before children; I divide my time and
money as well as possible. I work for children, spastics, dogs, old people, War
on Want, and I haven't time or cash for more. It sounds awfully noble, but it
ain't."

Yootha had a deep concern for social injustice, but politically there was nothing
radical about her: "I'm a realist" she once said, "I don't believe in naive
optimism." Joy Jameson said, "I truly cannot remember one single occasion that
Yootha discussed politics (hers or mine) there was usually something else we'd
got to talk about – maybe work, clothes or trivial girlie stuff."

Yootha's work in *Man About the House* brought with it some security, and after
a long career getting there, she knew it. But the security did bring some rather
nastier consequences. Once, in the street, a lorry driver shouted out "if you can't
get enough from George, come round to me!" "Being recognised on the street is
a slight problem, but no one's knocking this," she once told Russell Harty in an
interview, "I still do my own shopping" she insisted. Harty, asking if Yootha
still went to the launderette as well, got a firm "no" from her. When he asked
her if she could afford to buy new clothes instead, she returned "well, I throw
them away when they're dirty, dear" replying with her tongue firmly implanted
in her cheek.

Was she underplaying the "slight problem" of being recognised? Was it more
difficult than she was letting on? One does wonder if the pressures might have
contributed to her drink problem. According to Yootha, Terry, who was living
with her at the time, was often away for six weeks at a time, stage-managing
opera and ballet shows. She would "get brassed off thinking of him with all
those beautiful ballerinas. I'm inclined to tap my feet and bristle a bit," she once
said. Solitude, it seems, wasn't good for her.

When she was with Terry, life seemed to be treating her well. He once spoke
briefly of their time together: "I seem to remember we built a BBQ in the patio.
We did ordinary stuff that ordinary people do. I wasn't having a relationship
with this famous woman on the television programme, I was having a
relationship with a lady who lived in W2 and walked her dog in the park!" Not
everyone noticed her drinking or thought it excessive: Sally Thomsett once said,
"I don't think she had a drink problem, but I know she did like to have a drink,
she quite liked cognac". "She had a fair amount when we were on holiday
together in Spain, she said she had to have a drink because of blood pressure
problems – she said brandy made her feel better,"

Her times in Spain didn't entirely free her from recognition problems. Spain,
waking up to matters sexual after Franco's death in 1975, had taken *Man About
the House* to their hearts, and lapped it up. She remembered sitting outside a
cafe in Granada once, "when a busload of English ladies swamped me and I ran
for my life – but that's the price you pay for being well known and being
allowed into people's living rooms. It's very nice but it can be a bit too much at

times, you feel trapped by the character people feel you are."

Even in Spain, her concern for animals never left her: "when we go out there we feed the dogs and cats. About six in the evening a pack of dogs – virtually wild dogs – come round for all the scraps. Then about an hour later the cats come round. And I rescue donkeys too. The Spaniards think we're quite mad, but it's a question of conscience. I think anyone who throws a dog out of a car in this country is far more cruel than anything in Spain, because we are a society that supposedly respects animals."

Back home at the flat in Sussex Gardens, she was plagued by dirty phone calls: "I had to change my phone number three times. I got really frightened when I went ex-directory and they still came through. When I phoned the police they said they couldn't act unless my life had been endangered. I changed the number again. I'm used to them now. It's a joke to me. If they breathe heavily, I just do the same. One bloke I upset rang again; to get my own back I blew a ship's foghorn down the line. He must have had earache for a week. Men like that don't worry me. Even if one had guts enough to stop me in the street, I could take care of myself."

In an interview with Russell Harty, she expanded on this: "They were quite funny, like 'could I have a part of your old tights' and that sort of thing." All the same, she insisted that part of her enjoyed the fame, "because otherwise you wouldn't be in the business".

You would think Yootha's success in *Man About the House* would have made her a rich woman, but in 1976, she admitted that her bank manager "gently" said to her "I don't want to bother you, love, but you're £500 overdrawn." She admitted to being dizzy about money; but she knew the forthcoming series of *George and Mildred* would take care of that, "It's better to be lucky than rich," she once said. "I'm like my father. I never brood." Her grandmother's advice during wartime still applied, she said: if there were a fire and she had to grab what she could "I think of my dog and my cat and my jewel case, which I'm rather fond of, and I'd walk out and never regret a thing."

The 'dizzy' Yootha did get herself involved with a few business ventures, however, in 1976, she became involved in a company specialising entertainments ventures. Joy Jameson told me "She commissioned a TV series (or a pilot) and as I recall, the character was a kind of Rosalind Russell... yes, more Rosalind Russell than Lucille Ball.... but there were no takers. She wasn't by any means devastated by that." She also told a reporter that she was a "sleeping partner in an après-ski shop just above Granada, in the Sierra Nevada. I've been up there a couple of times, but the shop is really Christine Taylor's. She used to be an actress." "Those people seemed to be good to her and good for her," Joy remembered. Glynn Edwards also told me also he knew that she was "very big in Spain, and the Spanish loved her." It's difficult to know whether she invested in any theatrical ventures, but it seems unlikely, as her opinions about theatre in 1976 seem to have been rather negative, compared to her love of television and film: "I think the theatre these days is too self-indulgent. I don't believe all this money has to be spent, especially when things don't work, and I don't give a hoot if everybody in the audience smokes; it wouldn't hurt my eyes," she once said.

In the time before rehearsing and filming *George and Mildred*, Yootha's social life was vibrant, and there were no signs of unhappiness. Yootha attended a charity fancy dress ball for the NCDL, where she dressed up as Lillie Langtry. She won hands down and donated the first prize (£700) to the organisation.

Brian Cooke remembers that both Yootha and Brian were also very keen on The Stars Organisation For Spastics (S.O.S) and frequently attended film premieres and dinners for the charity. He recalled, "One time I was escorting Yootha and we gathered at the Odeon, Leicester Square for a performance of the film, *Shout At The Devil*. Spotting an usherette guarding the door in the foyer, I suggested to Yootha that we found out what was behind it. The usherette immediately recognised her and ushered us through without question. We found ourselves in a corridor with stairs going up and down. We went down. And found Lee Marvin coming up. 'Where's the goddamn bar?' he said. Now aware that it wasn't down, we indicated up. And so we found ourselves in the VIP room. Along with royalty and the stars of the film, Roger Moore, Ian Holm and Lee Marvin. Yootha was chatted up by all. I lurked in a corner, waiting to be found out, and drinking the free champagne. The screening was delayed by ten minutes. The speeches before the film aired were interminable, praising the director, agents, producers, backers, Uncle Tom Cobley and all... Except for Lee Marvin's speech. He strolled on, and said five words, 'the proof of the pudding....' then strolled off."

In April 1976, Yootha won "funniest woman" award on *The TV Times Top Ten Awards* show, presented by Richard O'Sullivan. She said later in an interview that "awards are wonderful to receive, it gives you such a lift, they're saying you're the best this year, not forever! Just this year. It's lovely, I've got three ITV awards for funniest woman and I never got the fourth so I don't have bookends, so they stay in the loo, I mean you can't put them on the television set because people would have to notice them, but if they want to look at them they know where to go."

Yootha was also gaining maximum exposure, taking part in a number of celebrity-based variety, game and panel shows including *Those Wonderful TV Times*, *Nobody Does It Like Marti*, *The David Nixon Show* and *Whodunnit?* In the last two, she appeared with Brian. In *Whodunnit?*, Yootha was magnificent, in a loud turquoise pink and white print silky dress, with lots of rings. She was smoking throughout the show and was seen catching sight of her own glamour by looking at the studio monitors a lot. At one point, she forms the most exquisite pout with her luscious pink lips. Yootha was also seen subtly perpetuating the Mildred character, giving the viewers what they wanted to see, crying that Brian is letting her down all the time. Brian, in contrast, seemed rather self-contained and cautious. Yootha, who was acting more vivacious and flirty, also coughed throughout the recording and sweated profusely, dabbing herself at times. She made a mistake, giving the wrong verdict. She admitted "I'm sorry my answer isn't good and clear, but then, I haven't got that sort of mind."

CHAPTER 29

The final series of *Man About The House* finished in spring 1976. It was fifth highest in the charts, with 9.2 million viewers. The decision to go ahead with *George and Mildred* came from Phillip Jones at Thames TV, who thought there was a lot of mileage in the characters. Brian Murphy remembered that, privately, he and Yootha thought "we'd believe it when it happened; the crew kept talking about it and Phillip Jones in particular, as we were getting an awful lot of fan mail and letters. The reviews too were picking up on these characters." Yootha said: "We were quite nervous about going solo with *George and Mildred*; we thought the others were the stars." "We knew that *Man About The House* was doing well; we weren't too certain that *George and Mildred* would take off though. We said to the writers, 'funny as George and Mildred are, they won't be that great just on their own; they need something else, otherwise audiences may tire of them.' They told us not to worry, as they had neighbours in the shape of actors, Sheila Fearn, Norman Eshley and Nicholas Bond Owen; this was a relief to us."

Sheila Fearn had a lot of credits to her name. She had been in *The Avengers, Z-Cars, Adam Adamant Lives* and *The Beverly Hillbillies*, and in films like *Catch us if you Can* and *Billy Liar*. Her most memorable role was as Terry Collier's sister Audrey, in BBC TV's *The Likely Lads*. She shone in that role, so having her on board for *George and Mildred* was great for the programme. Fearn, playing Ann Fourmile, was an important character: she held all the others together and almost became the straight woman, but with some very kooky lines coming her way, which she delivered with great aplomb. Brian Murphy remembered that "Sheila was good, as she would underplay; she undercut, which was a good contrast."

Norman Eshley also came to the programme with an impressive career behind him. In fact, he appeared in two roles in *Man About The House*, as Ian Cross, and as Norman Tripp, who marries Chrissie Plummer at the end of the series. He also appeared in TV (*I Claudius, Warship* and *The Duchess of Duke Street*), and in films like *The Immortal Story* and *See No Evil*. Brian Murphy again recalled that during the rehearsals of *George and Mildred*, Norman would observe Yootha and Brian: "he would sit on the sidelines and say, 'I can't take my eyes off you both, I'm learning so much from you,' as he hadn't done much TV. It obviously worked, because his Jeffrey, the put-upon neighbour, is perfectly done."

Nicholas Bond Owen played the part of Tristram, Jeffrey and Ann's son. Brian said he "adored the scenes we would have together." In an interview, he recounts how Nicholas auditioned for the role. He remembers that though there many applicants, "they had got them down to about four. While we were still doing *Man About the House*, I was asked to do a scene with them as part of the audition. Nick was the smallest of them all, and he had a little twinkle; we did a scene in which he fluffed, and had thought at that point he'd lost the role: 'no, I said, we all fluff sometime, let's do it again.' The other three seemed to be rather more savvy and polished and from drama school, whereas Nick didn't. Peter

Fraser Jones came up to me and said, which was your favourite?' 'Well' I said, 'Nick.' He said, 'Thank God for that.' Nick was a natural; he was very adept with his timing too, and would shoot his part separately, as he wasn't allowed to spend the whole day in the studio, so we shot all his stuff earlier on in the day. After three or four episodes he was spot on, he knew what he was doing, a total natural and a great joy to work with."

Nicholas told me he was aware that *George and Mildred* was a spin-off from *Man About The House*, and had seen a few episodes: "but having met Yootha before we even started filming I quickly realised that she was nothing like Mildred in real life and was a very warm and caring lady who was very affectionate and loving towards me. She would often make a real fuss of my entire family and we were all treated like members of her own family. It wasn't until I was a little older that I became aware of just how famous she was and how many roles she had had in the past."

I asked him if his ability and his timing impressed Yootha. Had she given him any tips? "I can remember our first read-through, but the scenes weren't with Yootha, so I didn't read any scenes with her until we started rehearsals. She was always very encouraging, and they would all often tell my mum how well I was doing. Peter Frazer Jones would always tell my mum and dad after a few drinks, that he couldn't believe that he had found me! But apart from my mum (who was the driving force behind my acting career and the reason that I got the part of Tristram in the first place), the person who gave me most tips was Norman Eshley. He was like a second dad to me and helped me all the time."

Other cast members in *George and Mildred* included the "irregular regular" Roy Kinnear. His wife Carmel told me that Roy would appear "several times in their TV series playing Jerry, who always tried to help out with DIY, with disastrous results; he enjoyed working with them." Carmel said: "I know Yootha was an excellent actress, very professional and very funny." Peter Errington told me "Roy was a good mate of Yootha's, and of course between them there were screen sparks. Roy's Jerry character would always enjoy sending Mildred up, calling her 'Mildew.' When he came onto the screen, there would be a definite atmosphere between them both. He played the chancer, and Mildred certainly had the measure of him." Finally, Avril Elgar played Mildred's sister Ethel, "a bigger snob than Mildred" said Brian Murphy. She brought an extra bitchiness to the programme: nobody could beat her in that line. Brian Murphy also said that: "Yootha had suggested Reginald Marsh to play Ethel's husband."

Rehearsals got under way in the back room of the Cardinal Wolsey pub at Hampton Court, and "no props meant a lot of improvising." Brian Murphy said "the Cardinal was good because we would go downstairs for a little drink. If we had a rehearsal room, we would keep it for that series, and it would be taped up just like the set you saw on screen."

Although Yootha made light of the difficult situations she ran into in public and private life, with people shouting at her in the street and unwelcome phone calls, it's impossible to know if it had any real effect on her nerves and performances in the new show. However, in conversation with Russell Harty, she did say, "I didn't feel I had to prove myself in the new series, it was no great sweat filming it, we weren't forced, but the pressure of success is on us."

The intensity of the pressure that was beginning to surround Yootha and Brian must have increased a lot at this time. Christine Pilgrim recalled that when in the company of Yootha, "she loved her brandy. And no one would dare suggest she cut back on it – not her mother, Glynn and certainly not me. I remember her once getting short with her mother – a delightful, mild, caring lady, when she ordered steak tartare, on my recommendation (gulp!), at the White Elephant on the River, "Mother," she said, "It's raw steak and raw egg! Do you think you're going to be able to eat that? Don't be ridiculous!"

"Can you imagine her mother daring to tell her to stop drinking?!"

Peter Errington told me "We were all really really close, Yootha was an amazing lady, great fun, a very loyal and wonderful woman. Yootha did have a time with nerves, and drink was probably one of the things that helped it; I mean actors all want to get it right, but, yeah, she liked a drink. I used to work on another television sitcom, *Birds of a Feather*, and the stars, Pauline Quirk and Linda Robson, would be throwing up before a show, so it was a response to the pressure they were under. It was my job as floor manager to put these people at ease. It was a nerve-wracking experience."

Phillip Jones' wife Florence remembers Yootha as a very private person; "very nervous and also very nice. When she was happy, she was lovely to be with. She was very quiet and retiring. Not at all what you see." Andy and Zelie Armstrong told me that they never saw Yootha drunk: "We all socialised after the show and I never saw her other than being in control and gracious." Brian Murphy recalled, "We all liked to have a tipple, a few of us used to like a bit of wine. 'I think it's time for cold tea' we would say in earshot of Nick Owen. It was a long time before he actually got the courage to ask us, 'what is cold tea?' I still keep in touch with him, he was a very good poker player."

Brian Murphy thought the scripts from the writers were "great." The characters were a direct "follow-on from the music hall traditions, and indeed they explored the characters very well. Brian and Johnnie had got them very tight. We'd have a read-through, and we might just make a suggestion, but very seldom did we feel they would need any changes or additions from us. They would come down to a read-through, and time it, as Yootha and I were quite quick with our dialogue."

Brian Cooke remembers, "Yootha was not a great ad libber. She stuck to the script, as did Brian Murphy. They trusted us to write to their strengths." Brian Murphy recalled once that "at one point we got Brian and Johnnie to act the parts for us which was fun." Recalling the whole set up at Thames TV, he said "The whole thing at Thames was so nice with Phillip Jones; there would be the occasional strike and things there, but they always looked out for us and made sure we were all right, there was always someone around to fall back on, there was never a 'them and us' situation."

With the outside filming set at Manor Road, Teddington in April 1976, Brian Murphy also recalled that, as the initial series of ten episodes were being recorded with an audience at Thames TV's studio 1, also at Teddington, there were the compulsory nerves: "Neither I nor anybody from our little company would drink before a show, we were all too nervous. I'd have the odd fag, but we made up for it after the show, and we sank a few." During the recordings there were also plans being made for Brian and Yootha to appear in the Pantomime *Cinderella* at the London Palladium, and they had secured "over half a million in ticket sales in advance." The work was coming in thick and fast.

Yootha was known to have a temper: "everyone was a little bit, er, careful when they were discussing something with Yootha" said director Peter Frazer Jones: "she had big blue eyes, and if you got a gaze out of them, they could turn black, if she was not well pleased!" "At your own peril did you get the wrong side of Yootha!" he said. Dresser Zelie Armstrong remembered, "Yootha was always consulted on her costumes and what earrings she would wear. She was the most agreeable person and as far as staff in costume was concerned, she was always willing to try anything out. If she felt strongly that she could or would not wear something, she would say so and her wishes were respected. I never recall her being 'made' to wear anything against her will. If anything was said on the studio floor to the contrary, this was in good fun and the costume department were in on the joke as well. Yootha would never single anyone out or behave in an unprofessional manner, and relations with her were always good." Props man Andy Armstrong told me, "She indeed did not suffer fools gladly, but never did any of the props crew suffer from her 'fiery behaviour.' She was a perfectionist and if all around her were doing their job properly, she didn't need to get annoyed." Peter Errington said, "I can't remember any falling out, with any of the cast, especially Yootha, when I worked on all the shows. Of course she would have her bad days, but you'd never tell, she would certainly never make a meal of it: no, she was definitely a pro. She would come to my house and she was a real mate, I never really saw her as an actress, I never saw the temper. Everybody has a temper, but she certainly kept it in check as far as I was concerned at work and in rehearsals."
Brian Murphy said at the time, "we have wildly different opinions on just about everything, but Yootha never bullies me, she just uses her feminine wiles to get her own way!" Nicholas Bond Owen told me he never saw Yootha lose her cool, "but had seen her in the studio and she was always a perfectionist, she would often moan about some of her outfits, and gave the wardrobe ladies some stick about the horrendous earrings they made her wear, but I can't ever remember her really losing her temper in front of me." Christine Pilgrim said the same, "Yootha never lost her temper with me, nor I with her. We had a healthy respect for each other."
Jeanette Farrier, who played the part of the estate agent's secretary in two of the episodes, and who is now a specialist costume and textile designer, told me of her time on the series working with Yootha and Brian. "It was a very long time ago and my part was very small! I don't remember Yootha even speaking to me, let alone talking about her. Unlike Brian Murphy who was warm and welcoming, Yootha was frosty and distant. All I remember was that she was not happy if I got a laugh during rehearsals, or more importantly during recording.

Being a bit of a wimp, I was completely put off by her intimidation! It was only later, as I got older, that I understood her vulnerability."

Christine Pilgrim told me "There were times when Yootha felt awkward standing by while Brian Murphy exhibited his natural clowning ability in *George and Mildred*. He'd have the studio audience in stitches with his slapstick antics while she just stood there with what she called 'a stupid grin' on her face."

Yootha would often wear wigs as Mildred: "she had a selection." She would always keep her hair cut short, saying that "it's so easy to wear under the Mildred wigs." I tried contacting Brian Peters at "Wig Creations," who were credited as her official wig fitters, but in vain: they told me that they had "no record of fitting wigs for her at that firm." According to Tex Fisher "Yootha had significant influence on what she wore, and worked closely with costume designers." It was difficult tracking some of those who were credited on both the *Man About The House* and *George and Mildred* TV series and films, such as Laura Nightingale, the famous 'Avengers' wardrobe mistress. It was impossible to know who did what and on what programme; until the 'Mildred' costume designer Lyn Harvey put me in the picture:

"Paul, just to clarify, I was the Costume Designer on most of *Man About the House*, which is where I met and formed a close relationship with both Yootha and Brian. Yootha loved how I imagined Mildred and asked me to work with them as Costume Designer on the upcoming *George & Mildred* series. I then became the creator of the Mildred look, continued to design all the Thames Series, the Stage Tours, the Summer Seasons, the Australian Tour & even the Movie!

I think Laura Nightingale was a freelance wardrobe lady at that time, I think she might have been wardrobe on the film, but I never worked with her at all and she certainly never worked with me on *George and Mildred*!"

Zelie Armstrong remembers: "I worked as a dresser on the show and so would not have been involved in the purchase of the costumes for the artistes concerned. I supplied the clothes and Lyn was the costume designer. She would read us the riot act and decide what was needed, and then it was passed on to me and a few other girls to get the stuff together. When we were in the studios and were starting the rehearsals for the evening recording of the show, we did indeed have quite a few laughs at some of the costumes and colours chosen for the particular episodes.

I only knew Laura Nightingale through Thames TV. Most costume designers tend to design for each show specifically and, although some have very defined styles, they usually consider the character for which they are creating the design and what the artists themselves feel about the character." Asking Zelie whether she thought Mildred's costumes contained an element of male drag, she told me, "Obviously we all saw how the character developed over the series and what was decided on the costumes. As the script became more established, with Mildred's character taking on a life of her own, it was amusing to see the bright and garish colours being used and the outrageous earrings being chosen. I was not particularly aware that male drag influenced the choices, although that may have been the opinion of some people."

Lyn Harvey, interviewed in the short documentary on Yootha, talked of how she would work together with her on the costumes for the show: "Mildred was great fun, and it was like, let's put the uniform on, with lots of negligees from Brentford Nylons because she used to like her nylon negligees, with lots of frills and things, and also bright colours, pink, and lime green. The earrings for the character were something we really went to town on; we would go out of our way to find the most outrageous and large baubles that you could find, which did catch the public's eye: very garish, but it was Mildred."

"She put this wonderful frock on; she used to smoke like a trooper, and it had got cigarette burns in it – she said 'Oh Lyn darling, don't worry about it' and that we'd 'stick some daisies on it!!' And she made me sew a couple of daisies over the burn holes! The designer would have gone mad if he'd have seen his creation with a couple of fake daisies stitched over the holes, but she was quite practical really."

Zelie remembers that "It was a source of great amusement for all of us and I think that may have helped Yootha to feel more comfortable when wearing some of the more extravagant costumes." According to Kathleen Russell, interviewed by Tex Fisher for his book, and who also worked in the costume department: "most items stayed in the wardrobe until the series ended, when they would be used in a general wardrobe for other productions. Many items of clothing used to sprout legs and walk; it is possible that the cast took old costumes home with them. Who knows where this stuff could be now!" We may never ever see Mildred's famous banana print trousers again!

With the entire first set of *George and Mildred* episodes 'in the can', the cast had to make some appearances for the press. Brian Murphy recalls "whenever we had to be photographed for continuity and just have press stills produced, there would be an appearance of a sudden flash of what I can only describe as lightning, above our heads. When being interviewed and having the discussions recorded on magnetic tape, they would play the tape back and it would be blank. Then they would play it back later on and the conversation would be there: it was weird. No one could understand where this light was coming from, but it happened quite often. We used to have to warn the studios in advance but they always dismissed it, until it actually happened."

There were also personal appearances to be made around the UK. Yootha again relied on 'The Gresh' to make all the arrangements. To promote the new show, Brian and Yootha appeared, for instance, at the opening of 'The Bedarama' in Yorkshire as well at a new Wickes DIY store in Slough. "There was never a slip up and it was an absolute pleasure working with them," said The Gresh, "I never did P.A's with Brian on his own. But we did dozens with Yootha, she was a natural with her fans and they adored her. I remember one elderly lady saying 'It's wonderful to see you in person, Yootha. I haven't admired an actress more than when I was a fan of Pat Phoenix...' Yootha looked at me and said, 'I think we've made it Gresh!'"

When we were discussing Yootha's personal appearances, Joy Jameson said to me: "I'm afraid this is not very interesting; but there are moments when I wondered why? Why didn't Yootha acknowledge Hughie Green at a personal appearance at a Christmas Fayre at Kensington Town Hall? Might that have been two people having the same problem? Hughie Green looked like he might have been drinking – and, if anything, she wanted to get out of there. Maybe he'd met her when he was more popular and ignored her? Maybe. All I know is within five minutes of her clocking him - and opening the fayre, we were out of there. Don't know, but I'm more often right than wrong about those kind of things." she told me.

When I mentioned this incident to Peter Errington, he said: "The only time Yootha and Hughie would see each other is if they passed each other in the corridors at Thames TV when *Opportunity Knocks* was on. I know Hughie was a very larger than life character, so I could imagine that he would probably fawn all over her, as he was known to do, and of course, she would probably have just given him a look."

However, The Gresh told me: "All the people I worked with, Morecambe and Wise, Frazer Hines, Hughie Green, Larry Grayson and many more just loved her and loved being in her company."

On August 20th 1976 Yootha celebrated her 49th birthday. She once said, "I won't tell my age. I think people ought to make up their own minds, I think age is desperately unimportant and, of course, I'm always right; I'm on to that. Well, let's say I'm not always right, but I'm never wrong."

Shortly after this, on 6th September, the first series of *George and Mildred* began broadcasting. Brian Murphy, in an interview with Tex Fisher, said: "Audiences reacted really well," it got huge acclaim and good reviews, audiences loved it. Ten episodes were made for the first series as opposed to the usual six; all went to number 1 in the viewing figures. We were wanted everywhere, to open shops and appear at charity events. It was bigger than us!" It was true. The actual figures on 25th October 1976 showed that *George and Mildred* was number 1, with 10 weeks in the charts. At 9.4 million viewers, for the episode 'Best Foot Forward', it was the 4th highest rating for 1976, the highest being the BBC's *Generation Game* with 9.7 million. Yootha and Brian were congratulated wherever they went on the good figures. Brian recalled, "I think it was so popular because it was a universal theme, the sparring husband and wife. It translates into any language. The countries where the television show was most popular were Spain and Italy." Reviews were good too, with *The Stage* TV critic Ted Willis, then president of the Writers Guild, saying, "it would take a riot squad to keep me way from Yootha Joyce and Brian Murphy's new comedy series." Alan Coren, reviewer at *The Times* said that his "Misgivings on a spin-off were unjustified" and that he had "good cause to chuck a hat in the air this morning. Mortimer and Cooke are strong writers, they work from start to finish, they do not coast, they do not pad out with limp rhubarbing, each line is either a strong joke, or a character delineator, and frequently both. Brian and Yootha come on as strong as the script, her hunger for glamour, her deft scorn, her heart-rending coquettishness, all to watch and savour. Like all fine teams, together they become more than the sum of their considerable parts." Ray Galton and Alan Simpson told me that even they thought "it was competently done." Mrs L.M. Tillyard from Leicester spoke for the viewers: "although just out of hospital after an operation on my writing hand, I just had to write in and say that *George and Mildred* took the pain away. It's the best half hour on television." Even toward the end of the run, the reviews kept coming through. Hazel Holt of *The Stage* commented: "Yootha Joyce's Mildred, lavishly adorned with synthetic leopard, was delicious, alternating between astringent contempt and wistful social aspiration."

Peter Errington told me that, "nobody disliked George and Mildred, but they were flawed. God knows how they managed to afford that house in Hampton Wick." Of course everybody knows that they got compensation from the council! Brian said that both he and Yootha found they got letters from people with "similar" experiences to the characters; "we would also get people coming up to us with similar stories of 'friends' with the same problems. I think the programmes we made would defuse a lot of their own tensions." Brian also found it "astonishing" that children related to the characters too! "We would get a lot of fan mail from children, they loved it, they love to watch this silly battle." And indeed he was right, I loved it.

After the initial series was completed, Yootha again threw herself into guesting on various television shows. When I asked Joy Jameson why she did this, she said it usually was a "contractual" thing, to help promote the series. She was interviewed by Russell Harty for the *Harty* programme, sandwiched briefly in the first half alongside Bonnie Langford, until David Hockney dominated the heavy and long-winded second half. She was very bright and sunny as usual, and trotted into the hot seat wearing a simple figure-hugging dress, nervously clinging to a packet of fags. Kissing a surprised Russell on the cheek, he enquired if she kissed everyone she met, Yootha told him "No dear only the people I like." Russell, seemingly edgy and stuttering a bit, admitted he was very frightened of Yootha." To which she replied "Oh, rubbish, what are you frightened of?" Admitting his fear of being flattened by one of Yootha's looks, she casually returned "If you like," whilst waiting for a taxing question.

CHAPTER 30

Yootha began to reap the rewards from a fantastic start to the *George and Mildred* series: in 1976, jointly with Brian Murphy, she won the Variety Club of Great Britain's award for TV Personality of the Year. Brian Cooke and Johnnie Mortimer also won the Scriptwriters of the Year award. Brian Cooke recalled that when he and Johnnie sat down at the table, "we discovered we were the funniest lady on television! Later on we swapped it with Yootha who had ours." Another glamorous, tough, man-eating female character from the BBC's direct opposition sitcom, *The Good Life*, Penelope Keith, who played Margot Leadbetter, won an award too, as top showbiz Personality of the Year. The day of middle-aged housewife power had started, no matter what the Spice Girls were to say later on. Later that same year, Yootha landed another one, *The Sun*'s Best Actress Award. On 10th November, she was also called to judge and present an award for Pub Entertainer of the Year at the Grosvenor Hotel's Great Room. The winners were 'The Playboys,' a comedy duo from Buckinghamshire. The programme was televised by Thames TV as a *Wednesday Special.*

The increasing public interest in her culminated in an interview she gave to Alix Coleman of the *TV Times*, where she spoke candidly about her personal life. Amongst other things, she talked about her relationship with Terry Lee Dickson, and 'her' new mare Royal Pat, who was "going to drop a little foal next spring," she said. Saying that she had not liked Terry at the start, in the early stages of the tour of *Boeing Boeing*, she admitted that she gradually came to admire him professionally, and before long Terry was "organising her personal life – with the title of personal manager, for his efforts." She said that "Good organisation" was something the "chaotic" Yootha has always been grateful for. Terry reinforced her "jaundiced view of self-imposed discipline."

Yootha told Alix Coleman for *TV Times* that "the three major gentlemen in my life have been good friends as well. Terry organises me. He spends a lot of time directing trips and tours, so he has the habit. He organises me heavily at home, which I need when I'm not working. I lived alone for two years before Terry arrived. I liked it, but it's much nicer now. All my gentlemen come here to live. Oh yes, to my place. I'd never marry again."

Terry was 19 years younger than Yootha, something which the tabloids of course loved, with their contradictory moral codes, but she in fact said that the "age difference doesn't worry us." Terry once said there was a fairly significant amount of press comment at various times, "significant to me as I was not used to being commented on in the press."

Unfortunately, I was unable to track Terry down to interview him. I turned to Yootha's agent Joy to ask how much in love she thought Yootha was with Terry. She told me "We were all a bit dubious about Terry. Younger? Was he pinning a career on Yootha's? Maybe six months ago I saw a documentary on Yootha I'd never seen before. I've no idea how I'd missed it and Terry was on it and I thought no. Terry actually was a good 'un and I know he was a tremendous help to Yootha." Asking Joy if she, as Yootha's agent, felt there were any issues with Terry's involvement as Yootha's personal manager and her working relationship with her, she said: "I thought Terry's involvement was going to be a problem but it never was. He did help to get her places, settle her in. He was a great help to her, and then in time I realised he was more than that and I truly was happy for her. Very hard being an 'icon' and not having a partner to go with. No – that was good."

While the final rehearsal schedules were being put into place for the upcoming *Cinderella* pantomime, Yootha and Brian made a few more personal appearances. On 27th November they were invited to open the new Scansales Bedroom Centre, in Wetherby, Yorkshire. Of course The Gresh was called in for his usual expertise in handling the event and says that although he had "heard the rumours" of Yootha's drinking, he "never saw her drinking silly, she was there to do a job and that's exactly what she did". In December, she recorded an appearance for the Christmas Day programme of *The Generation Game*.

Cinderella was devised and directed by Albert J. Knight, and staged at the London Palladium. She and Brian appeared as the ugly sisters, Georgina and Mildred.
Both had done panto before: Yootha in *A Christmas Carol* in 1958, and Brian as an ugly sister, with fellow Theatre Workshopper, Victor Spinetti. Yootha was very strict about not doing anything too strenuous in the production – "that was left to Brian," as she told the press. The production ran throughout the Christmas and New Year, starting on 21st December. There was a record-breaking demand for tickets, and it was extended for an extra three weeks (thirteen in all), finally closing on 25th March 1977. The show had an evening and matinee performance each day, and lasted a good three hours.
Yootha spoke about her costumes, telling the punters that she was to wear the "highest heels possible" and as Brian "was in pumps," she could tower over him, bullying him as Georgina, much to the audience's delight. Joy Jameson remembers that Yootha was in her element there and "had a great time." The costumes themselves cost around £1000 each, and were designed by Cynthia Tingey. Tingey's original pen, ink and gouache sketches were given to the Theatre Museum by her, and can be viewed online at the Victoria and Albert Museum's website, with a justly elaborate accompanying description. (see link end of book). It is a shame there is no footage of the production. The reviews were good: Sidney Vauncez in *The Stage* noted; "they all do extremely well, and the audience appear to enjoy every moment of it."
While still performing at the Palladium, Yootha and Brian Murphy managed to attend an event specially arranged for Thames TV's controller of light entertainment, Phillip Jones. It was "An Evening of New Dimensions and A Night of Stars Award Ceremony," and took place at The Lakeside Country Club, most famous for hosting the British Darts Organisation finals. Phillip Jones himself was awarded The Club Mirror Special Entertainment Award. The star-studded audience included Tommy Cooper, Danny La Rue, and Denis Norden.
In April, Yootha was also voted Funniest Woman in a *TV Times* readers poll. Then they embarked on a second series of *George and Mildred*. Peter Errington remembered that she was provided with a car to take her to work, and "she was never late." As *Cinderella* drew to a close in early 1977, both Brian and Yootha must have been running out of energy!
Nicholas Bond Owen told me that in *George and Mildred*, Yootha was "definitely the star of the show." When I asked him what this "star" quality was, he told me: "Yootha always had a way of making everyone feel special, she had time for everyone and wasn't stuck up in any way whatsoever, she also had more lines and more costume changes than anyone else in the show and had to look the part in every scene, so she often had make up and wardrobe all over her on set, whereas the rest of us just turned up and said our lines! I also remember that we were often kept waiting for Yootha and she always made a grand entrance."

Towards the end of the first episode of *George and Mildred*, 'Moving On,' Sheila Fearn turned to Nicholas and said "you liked them, didn't you Tristram?" The naturalness of his reply seemed to suggest that he found both Yootha and Brian fun and funny to be around. I asked if he had any special memories of working with them that he could share. He said, "I have lots and lots of special memories of Yootha and Brian as they were both so lovely, in fact everyone involved in working on *George and Mildred* was really nice; the crew and cast members alike would often be cracking up with laughter after watching scenes with Yootha and Brian in the studio, because they were just magical together and sometimes Brian would just carry on being silly after the cameras had stopped filming, just to make the rest of us laugh, he is just a naturally funny person."

"I remember one evening after filming we were all having a meal in the restaurant at the Thames Studios in Teddington with all the cast and crew, and I didn't like most of what was on the menu, so Yootha (who I was sitting next to) asked me what I wanted if I could have anything, so I said I would really like a banana and honey sandwich! So she asked the waiter for some bread, butter and honey and then got a banana from the fruit bowl and proceeded to slice the banana up and make me a sandwich in front of everyone, just to make me happy; that's the kind of person she was and I still miss her to this day! It was a long time ago but I can still remember a lot of it as it was such a special time in my life!"

"Yootha was always very affectionate towards me and she would often cuddle me and ask if I was OK, or if I wanted anything. I always remember her smelling gorgeous, and to this day I have never smelt the perfume she wore on anyone else, so it must have been very obscure and probably very expensive." Sally Thomsett, an expert in such matters, told me that Yootha favoured 'Chloe' by Karl Lagerfeld.

Yootha and Brian continued their outside work too, even offering their names to a Help The Aged advertising campaign in the press, which featured a picture from them as *George and Mildred*, with this mission statement: "life is nothing to feel happy about... Not if you're old and lonely; spending every day cooped up in a dreary old room with only the radio for company." Yootha was also called on to hand over a cheque to a lucky Littlewoods pools winner that year, an event covered by the national news; she also appeared on *Star Turn*, the BBC TV children's show hosted by Bernard Cribbins, in which two teams of celebrities had fun taking part in various acting games. It also featured her old friend Barbara Windsor.

In spite of all this attention, Yootha was having a few concerns again about the direction her career was going. The truth was that apart from Mildred and the TV and events, work was starting to dry up. Joy Jameson told me that although she didn't think actors looked down at her for being in *George and Mildred*, "the real luvvies of our world never considered situation comedy on a level with The Royal Shakespeare Company and The National Theatre. That is changing now, where we are seeing soap stars going to both places, but when you dig right down you'll find those soap stars started in those arty places." She also remembered that "It was impossible to get Yootha the commercials that most people get when in a popular series, because *George and Mildred* were too down market. Brian Murphy got one as a henpecked husband with a Hoover I think. That was a downer, as there could have been tons of money involved and she wouldn't have to have worried too much."

Yootha herself spoke about playing the Mildred character "I hope to God I don't look anything like her off screen /stage – it's the wig that makes all the difference; anyone who looked like Mildred would be a disaster. She is a disaster, a very very sad little lady. She'd love to be like Ann, the posh lady next door. Sometimes she even buys the right dress, but she never can resist adding the plastic earrings and the whole bit. I glitter from ear to shoulder blades. All the jewellery gives her some kind of confidence, it's her front to the world. Mildred's a pathetic figure, most of all in the way she goes berserk over a little dog because she can't have a baby."

Yootha seems at times to be irritated with Mildred Roper. Others said that Cooke and Mortimer captured the actors' individual traits when moulding their scripts; maybe Yootha felt she wanted to break free from Mildred, so she gave her a few knocks. There were those that saw some similarities between the actress and the character, as I've already said, but how similar where they? Robert Gillespie, who appeared in a couple of the *George and Mildred* episodes, told me he thought, "all good writers tailor their texts to suit a performer, provided they have any idea who's going to play a given character." The Gresh realised that Yootha didn't like becoming typecast as Mildred Roper. He said: "it was something we did talk about, but I tried to assure her that her performance as Mildred opened so many new doors. I remember her saying 'God Gresh, you know all the answers!'" He also said, "It's the old story really, but there were certain actions I saw Yootha do that reminded me of Mildred. But she liked to be known as a good theatrical/TV actress."

Robert Gillespie, as well as acting in *George and Mildred*, would work in the future with Cooke and Mortimer in the sitcom *Keep it in the Family* as Dudley Rush. He spoke of the writer blurring the line between reality and fantasy: "After playing all kinds of roles for which Brian Cooke was co-writer, Brian decided he would try to write a series solo. He asked me if I fancied playing the lead in *Keep it in the Family* – I said, 'of course' and he said he would base the character on me. I found that – for once – I could say Dudley's lines as if they were me! The part fitted like a glove, and Brian said, 'Well, yes, I spotted that you were a manic-depressive and that's what I made Dudley.' I don't see the fit, myself, but I loved playing the part, mainly because it presented a warm, joky husband and wife relationship – not like poor Mildred's. It didn't inhibit other casting one bit." Peter Errington thought that Robert Gillespie, in contrast to Yootha, was "a very controlled actor; he would never drink, he would hardly eat during the day, his body was like a machine that would have to be ordered, he was a very dry actor, not a guy that would light up a room, but very reliable and very funny in his own way."

If Yootha did feel some dissatisfaction with the Mildred character, those feelings were clearly put on the back burner. While filming the second series of *George and Mildred*, Brian Murphy recalled that around this time "We encouraged Brian [Cooke] and Johnnie to write for the theatre. We asked them why they didn't do a theatre adaptation of *George and Mildred*. Yootha and I knew about the theatre, and we could help guide them, and they knew about writing, so between us we all got on with it and made a funny farce." - And so they did. Now, Yootha's energies were put into the two-hour *George and Mildred* stage show, which was soon ready, and which she and Brian Murphy began to rehearse. Between rehearsals and the show's tour, there were the usual public appearances at various venues. There were two events in Bournemouth, a luncheon party arranged by the Bournemouth publicity club at the Pavilion Ballroom in the Carlton Hotel, and The Artist Fund Party at Imperial Hotel 'Nite Spot,' with Richard Alton from London's *Evening News*.

Brian recalled at the beginning of the tour "we had a few teething problems, but afterwards it was fine." The plot involved Ethel taking Mildred on a trip to Paris: while they're away, Humphrey persuades George to have a bit of fun in their absence. They invite two girls, Jennifer and Shirley, round to join them. Predictably, Mildred returns early to find them in the act." The cast varied in each season. Reginald Marsh played Humphrey alongside Dilys Laye as Ethel, "we couldn't get Avril Elgar," said Brian Murphy; the actress who played it on television. The understudies were Yootha's friend Harry Littlewood and Susannah Pope.

Brian Murphy remembers that, as Yootha couldn't drive, he would drive them both to venues. He recalled once in a TV commentary that: "Yootha was a collector of teddy bears; she had quite a lot, and she had a load of dresses. I bought a new car, a Ford Granada, on the success of *George and Mildred*, and we had to drive to the next town for a show. Yootha came out with about four suitcases. I said, 'they can go on the back seat as well'; 'no they can't' she said, 'I haven't got my teddy bears yet,' and they all sat on the back seat and in the back window."

Terry Lee Dickson recalled that the *George and Mildred* stage show was a "fairly tiring schedule for them," and that they were in fact "bringing in people that weren't in the habit of going to a theatre." Brian remembered that they were indeed "heady days." The show's first outing was at the Alexandra Theatre in Birmingham on June 13th 1977; a week later it moved to Richmond and from there to a sixteen-week season at the Pier Theatre, Bournemouth, from 27th June to 15th October 1977, playing twice nightly. Brian remembered that the show packed theatres wherever they went, and "People would queue around the block." He also recalled that on stage "we did a lot more clowning and spontaneous things and got away with more than we could on television." Brian remembers that "what was noticeable was the effect when Yootha and I came back to *George and Mildred* on TV after season at Bournemouth, When we started the first shots we were shouting!" – "our facial expressions were much too broad as well. When we saw those first two episodes we were appalled. We realised we would have to adjust carefully our performances."

During the tour, Yootha would do the odd press and radio interview for promotions for the show, which broke all box office records. It played to full capacity over the sixteen weeks they were there, even outselling the neighbouring Val Doonican and Max Bygraves shows. Brian Murphy remembered he and Yootha were "mobbed all away along the pier by fans and holiday makers wanting to shake our hands; we had to set off an hour earlier to get to the theatre on time." He also recounted "we would walk the streets together and people would come up to us and say: "oh what a wonderful show, can we have your autograph?" And if we were with Brian Cooke and Johnnie Mortimer, we would introduce them as the writers of the show. "They weren't really interested though!" he said, commenting that "Brian Cooke, I thought, was a bit of a frustrated performer."

While working in Bournemouth, Yootha no doubt spent some time with her mother, now retired and enjoying life at Elmes Road. A journalist noted that Maude, Yootha's "elderly mother, revelled in the reflected glory." Joy Jameson told me she "knew Yootha adored her mum and remembered she had a lot of time for old people. She told me Yootha almost had a fistfight with someone who was chivvying up a pensioner in a queue. She gave that person what for and told them they'd soon be in the same position." It is sad that I couldn't locate anybody who knew more about Maude or Yootha's father.

The Stage on 18th August 1978 noted that the performance at the Pier Theatre was "tailor-made to suit the television personalities." "Viewed purely as a play, it's a little thin in the story department and there are no prizes for guessing what happens next. But with Brian and Yootha given superb material with which to snipe at each other continually, few give any thought to the plot but just sit back and rock with laughter. Yootha Joyce has the best of the barbs, which she launches at poor Brian, constantly reminding him of his lack of prowess in the love stakes. He defends himself as best he can, scoring points every now and then."

The *George and Mildred* tour continued at a lesser pace throughout 1977 and into 1978, to allow for other work commitments. There were other public appearances too: Yootha attended an event at the London Hilton Hotel, in aid of The Docklands Settlement, in which other celebrities, and Princess Margaret, were present. Looking back on the tours, Brian Murphy recalled it was "OK, not too bad. I do remember having to travel as far as Aberdeen on a snowy day, and we only just got there, but at that point we had a general manager to drive us." During the run in Scotland, Yootha's partner Terry joined the production as stage manager, as they were "both keen to work together." Lyn Harvey was also on the tour, working on the costumes for each show.

CHAPTER 31

In the programme for the *George and Mildred* stage show, Yootha gave an insight into what inspired her: "Give me the chance every serious minded actress jumps at, to expand and develop a character over a period of time, with the constant challenge of retaining audience interest, it really keeps you on your toes," she said.

This is exactly what she was doing with Mildred, but how long could this "period" last? Was she after something else to develop? Was she beginning to get fed up with playing Mildred? Was she trapped? When I asked Denis Norden about this, he said he did not feel she had been 'trapped' as Mildred – rather that "she always enjoyed the role enormously." Glynn Edwards said he thought Yootha "never hated the part of Mildred, but she didn't think it was the greatest role. Like all these TV series, you're offered the fame and a certain amount of fortune, and you jump in and do it, but it wasn't the greatest challenge. Sometimes she would say 'My god the scripts are a bit rubbishy this week', but you would always tend to get better and worse scripts." He added: "it could be a bugbear, like Harry H. Corbett starring as Harold Steptoe". He said: "it was all very nice with the money, but nobody will offer me any other work."

Dudley Sutton said, "She liked the money luv, come on, she liked the money… They used to come back from Spain with a suitcase full of readies, doing a commercial in Spain for cash. Well, that's what she told me!" Perhaps Dudley was right. Yootha went straight into signing contracts for series three of *George and Mildred*, and there seemed to be no rumours of the run ending. People all over the world, Spain, Italy, the Netherlands, were loving it, but at what cost? In November and December, series two broadcasts had huge ratings. On 5th December 1977, it was reported it had been at number one for up to six weeks, with an astounding 19.7 million viewers watching the episode 'The Unkindest Cut Of All'. Professionally, Yootha may have had a dilemma on her hands: on the one hand, there was immense success and wealth, and if she called the thing to a halt, what would she get instead?

Difficulties and pressures would resurface. The respite she needed on holiday in Spain had been affected. Co-star Norman Eshley discovered this for himself, when he went with her to Spain: "I went on holiday with Yootha, and she had a beautiful little place in the mountains which was very quiet, very relaxed and very happy, and I like to swim in the sea, so I said 'let's go down to the beach' and she said, 'no you don't want to do that,' but I said 'yeah let's go on down there' and she said 'OK'; we went down onto the beach, and within two minutes we were surrounded by British people and she couldn't move. We then packed up and went back to the quiet and seclusion of the village. I didn't realise what we were getting into!"

Yootha's life in Spain was losing its sparkle, and she eventually sold the holiday flat in Nerja. Maybe, as one journalist said, this was not so much due to her fear of flying, or being mobbed; but it did come as a relief to the local animal-owning population. She admitted in an interview that she was "known as the fire lady" in Spain, saying: "I have hit more gentlemen hitting donkeys than most people have had hot dinners. I reckon if they are hitting a dumb animal with a stick they're entitled to be hit."

George and Mildred was very popular in Australia. However, a review in *The Canberra Times* on Christmas day 1977, Ian Warden, headlined "Oh Those Unfunny Comedies," makes one think deeper about the show and its element of tragedy. Was it time to call it a day? He continued: "*George and Mildred* is not a side- splitter by any means, but they are rather upstaged and out-acted by their ghastly fascist neighbour and his insufferable son Tristram. But to return to George's impotence. It is a sign of just how much you are enjoying a comedy program if the actual dark, unfunny reality of the subject under jest never occurs to you. *George and Mildred* is never quite funny enough to stop me thinking about how unfunny their marital situation really is. This tragic marriage, this pile of blasted dreams, and the horrible habitual procession of their days together, needs a heavier coat of humour than it has."

As the year drew to a close, it was reported in the Christmas edition of the *TV Times*; in which they featured on the front cover, that Yootha would spend the period "at her flat in London, with her co-star Brian having a traditional Christmas at home with his children, with open house on Boxing Day."
Continuing with their success, Yootha and Brian toured on into 1978, appearing at the King's Theatre Glasgow, and the Leeds Grand, where the takings topped £20,000. The show at the Theatre Royal Nottingham also surpassed all their previous box office records. The Gresh remembers a time when he was called to use his services for an event which was sandwiched between two stage performances, the first in Birmingham on 9th March. He recalls that when they finished the show, "I needed to get them to a hotel in Harrogate for their next appearance in Horsforth, West Yorkshire, the following day. As I had my leg in plaster, I had to hire a driver. They were both exhausted after their performances, so I suggested they get some sleep on the journey: trouble was, I fell asleep too. Waking up, I noticed we had passed our turn-off, as the driver didn't have a clue where Harrogate was. We had to turn back and eventually got to the hotel at 5 a.m. Poor Brian and Yootha only had three hours' sleep before they appeared at the venue. It was an embarrassing moment for The Gresh and I was surprised they ever worked with me again."
The second event was on the 10th March: Yootha and Brian did the official opening of the 'Cucina kitchen and bathroom studio,' in Harrogate's Commercial Street. Was Yootha baggy-eyed and grouchy for the occasion, I wondered? The Gresh told me "Yootha was totally professional with the fans on our PA's. I spent many happy hours with Yootha, and we just got on so well; we made each other laugh. I was so proud to know her. She'd always ask my opinion if a gig came up that I hadn't arranged. She was always pleased as I told her the truth – if I felt a deal way in any way dodgy, I'd tell her to be careful."
He went on to tell me that, looking back, "I got the opinion she was very lonely, and perhaps that's why she was happy making a few bob; being kept busy."
"Yootha was a very special person and we got on so very well. Towards the latter end of the P.A. scene, she would only work through me and sent all requests for her appearances to me. She was an absolute joy to be with."
In the 1990's, when I ran *The Yootha Joyce Memorial Society*, I got many pieces of information from those who had had some experience with her. In 1995, in a letter from Martin Cooksey, a society member, he told me about a mix-up that happened when he was working at the Grand Theatre, Wolverhampton, in March 1978, involving a cleaning lady and the then theatre manager, Humphrey Stanbury. Mr Stanbury had bought his wife a lovely bunch of red roses and left them in the theatre, on the same day that Yootha and Brian arrived to perform

their stage show.

Somebody mistakenly thought they were for Yootha and gave them to her. She thought it was a lovely gesture, and put them in her dressing room. "It all happened too quickly for Humphrey to actually point out they were for his wife" he told me.

After this, on the week of March 28th 1978, they played to the Theatre Royal in Brighton. They were both interviewed, and said they thought that the "*George and Mildred* theme is the same all the world over." Brian Murphy once said that "People used to think we were married: it's flattering! People would say outside our dressing room on the pier theatre, 'they're very good aren't they?'"

During a busy schedule in March, juggling between the tour and rehearsals for the third *George and Mildred* series, Yootha embarked on charity work for the NCDL. Clarissa Baldwin remembers, "Yootha was such a kind person. Her constant good humour and ability to get on with people was a great source of encouragement to the staff on these visits. The media would always be present on these occasions, but a walk around the kennels and a chat to each dog always took priority over a photographic session."

Once, when she was performing in Southsea, she took time out to visit the new NCDL kennels, at nearby Froxfield in Southsea. Petersfield isn't that far away, [about 20 miles or so] but it's doubtful if she went on a trip down memory lane to recapture her time as an evacuee. Perhaps not – after all we know she hated her time there! Clarissa recalled that at the kennels, Yootha was warmly greeted by one of the inmates, a saluki bitch, who was brought into the kennels in a pitiful state suffering from extreme malnutrition. It took several weeks of nursing before she was back to health and a new home could be found. She was christened Georgina by Yootha, after George. Yootha found it difficult "to resist the attraction of those needy dogs."

She attended another charity event the following month, organised by Clive Dunn of *Dad's Army* fame, at Phillips Auction House at Blenheim Street, London where she helped with fundraising for The Stars Organisation for Spastics (SOS), helping to sell eighty lots: a chalk drawing by Eric Morecambe was knocked down to £100!

On 22nd April 1978 Yootha's foal was born, a female thoroughbred. She named it 'Yootha's Choice.' Penny Parry-Williams at Wetherbys.co.uk kindly informed me that Yootha's Choice was registered as a 1978 bay filly – "brown, the colour of a conker," she told me – but that, in fact it "never ran, or had any registered progeny. If the horse had actually raced, we would have records of those races and her performances, but she didn't, presumably because she wasn't good enough or may have been injured. There really isn't any more information to be found out about this particular horse." Glynn remembers that when she grew, he went down with Yootha to see her. "We fed it a lot of carrots, it galloped about the field, and I believe it did quite well but I never followed it, not being a horsy man. But I know that that was a real indulgence of Yootha's, and as Mildred really took off, she had a lot of money, and she quite liked horses as a hobby. But I only met it once. Generally, the horse was the only indulgence I can think of." Dudley Sutton said, "I didn't know she had one." When I told him the

horse never ran, he exclaimed, " Oh, Yootha got taken for a ride probably…
sounds like it."

Yootha went straight back into the studios in spring of 1978, rehearsing for
another *George and Mildred* series. Nicholas Bond Owen remembers that on set
"everybody would be milling around, but nothing would ever start until Yootha
got there. You'd spend about five minutes saying hello to her before you could
even start filming. She'd come up and kiss everyone, hug everyone." Glynn
Edwards recalls that "Yootha's day often started between 4 and 5.30 a.m., when
she started learning her lines. There would follow long hours of rehearsal,
camera checks and recordings in front of a studio audience; sometimes she
wouldn't finish work until 9.30 at night." "When she wasn't working, learning
lines or rehearsing, she would be tearing around doing charity work." He also
said that she would drink brandy to help her unwind after a long day, but he
never at that time thought she was destroying herself with the amounts she was
consuming. As he said: "how can you solve a problem you don't feel exists
yourself?"

Yootha certainly had her contradictions, which no amount of research, and
interviewing those who knew her, are likely to resolve. That's true of any of us,
I suppose, but certainly, even those who knew her well either find her difficult to
pin down, or admit that she couldn't be pinned down. Perhaps Barbara Windsor
got as close as any, when she said it was hard to "get" her. In contrast to the
vibrant effervescent Yootha that appeared on set, Robert Gillespie, who plays
the dry vet in 'The Mating Game' episode, thought that Yootha "seemed an
anxious, vulnerable person, to me." On archive material, just before the
beginning of a shoot, Yootha is heard crying: "Oh! Hold fast my heart!" I asked
him if Yootha ever discussed pre-show nerves with him. He said, "my most
vivid recollection of Yootha is sitting at a table with her, on set at rehearsal, and
she beginning to tell me – a complete stranger, I never knew her at all well –
what a ghastly process sitcom was. Never enough rehearsal time, pressure to
create the illusion that for a 'star' a performance was effortless; a requirement to
engage coolly with the audience before recording and between takes as if no
focused effort or discipline of concentration was required. She wondered if we
really needed an audience, and I put my oar in about experiments with studio
recording (Peter Frazer Jones had tried it): how it had always failed because
however much we performers told ourselves we could create the spontaneity
needed for the specialised gaggery of sitcom writing, in practice we need the
thousand-volt jolt that the live audience gave us – however hateful the
experience was. Yootha often fluffed lines at rehearsal and would immediately
turn to me, or the nearest person, and say: 'Another re-take…' Her anxiety was
unmistakable, and if you were playing the lead, you could only afford one and a
half mistakes – especially when recording for commercial TV. Overtime was
grotesquely expensive, particularly in those days of commercial over-crewing –
the cameramen were always granted their re-takes… the pressure to get through
an episode error-free was immense. So Yootha's attempt to calm herself with
the cotton-wooling effect of alcohol was habitual. Lots of actors tried it to one
degree or another, especially with – say – a brandy at the supper break, just

before the show. For those who could control it, it may have worked well." Phillip Jones was aware of Robert Gillespie's point, and stressed in an interview in 1975 that "situation comedy shows are almost always played with a studio audience. The suggestion that an audience be dispensed with is frequently made for a variety of reasons and could, in fact, be cheaper since the programme could then be recorded like drama productions." But he also insisted that "studio laughter is infectious, helps performers with their timing, and often brings out the best in them. Above all, the ear of the audience at home is attuned to it and expects to hear it. There is no magic formula for success. Comedy is a tough, frustrating area of television. You never quite know. Sometimes the things that you think are sure-fire disappoint you, and the outsiders come romping home." Whether the audience's presence outweighed Yootha's nerves over her timing, we will never know, but it did seem that she was not finding it easy to deal with. Robert Gillespie again: "the director didn't see how petrified she was; she showed absolute terror. She came clean to me at the end of rehearsals saying, 'it doesn't get any better.' And she explained her fears to me. I was touched that this national star was talking to me openly about what a horrible task a live studio audience recording was, I was very moved to share those few moments with her." Even Brian Murphy recalled the moments of terror before a studio audience, "We used to wait backstage together before going on. We paced up and down the set prior to recording. I used to smoke then, and Yootha smoked like an old trooper. Despite our years of experience, it was still very nerve-racking. We paced about so much that I swear we dug a trench in one of the studios with all our walking. She used to say to me, 'what are we doing this for Brian?' I used to reply, 'er, money?,' and she said that was a good excuse, but once we were out there we did enjoy it."

So great was the apparent self-confidence of Yootha's performance though, it seemed that only a select few were aware of nerves, and it certainly doesn't come across to the vast majority of viewers. Zelie Armstrong told me that in her experience: "Most actresses I have dressed suffered the same problem, but once they were in front of the audience and the show was under way they were perfectly fine. Yootha was a consummate professional at all times." Brian Murphy said that television is a "demanding medium" - "The actor on the stage has so much freedom to change their performance from night to night, but you can't do that when a TV show is being taped. The timing has to be exact. It's like being a juggler with three balls in the air. You have one ear and one eye open for the whole studio audience; but you have to control the TV audience more than you do in the theatre. The audience mustn't be allowed to take over and control you."

Jeremy Bulloch, who appeared in the 'Days of Beer and Rosie' episode of *George and Mildred* as George's supposed long-lost son, remembers that he had a great time working with Yootha, and kindly shared with me his moments working with her. He remembers Yootha "never gave me advice but would smile if a scene went well. I tried to watch Brian Murphy to get some idea of the way his son would react when George tells him the unexpected news. Yootha's reactions when she finds out George has a son were superb," he said. "Yootha would walk over to you every now and then and either wink at you or put her arm around you just so you felt 'needed,' I think the word is. I always remember chatting with her about work and what the future held for us all on the next job." Talking of the initial script read-throughs, he said, "Script read-throughs were purely to find out if something didn't work. As the final run-through was finished, we all used to say 'see you tomorrow.' Nerves for me came the night before the recording but on the day I was fine." About Yootha's troubles with her nerves, he said, "All actors must have nerves at some time. I tend to keep quiet and tell the odd joke. I could get away with it with Yootha (I think). I remember her saying to me 'I wish I had a nice son like you' -Maybe that was nerves again? Yootha used to say as the show started, 'here we go.'" He said that he "never knew she was unhappy about being typecast. I was only in the one episode and had a great time in a very strong story." Jeremy told me that he wished he had known her better: "but when you are in just one episode it's difficult, with no time other than to say hello five times."

On the same topic of typecasting, Robert Gillespie said that "the wisdom, in my day, was try to become type-cast, become a commodity and either get into a six-year run in the West End, or an open-ended series on TV. This struck me as deadly, and not why I wanted to act. Because of my lack of height, I realised that I would only be cast in heavy character roles or old men (a ghastly practice of the time) on stage... so it was a happy accident that I began to be cast in situation comedy. The only criterion, in my case, was that I got a reputation for 'never missing a laugh.' Otherwise, I was cast in a huge range of different characters – rewarding and fun."

Andy and Zelie Armstrong also thought that most actresses in Yootha's position would have felt the same. "Yootha was a very talented actress. My personal opinion was that she didn't contradict herself, and was using whatever means available to her so she could be seen outside the 'Mildred' role. Most people only recognised her in that role, so it was difficult to shed the image. Being on chat shows would have helped her address this by being herself."

Perhaps it was beyond her control, something Yootha couldn't come to terms with? Around this time, 'Ropermania' was taking off, with a sudden growth of merchandising, including a board game from Denys Fisher, and Arrow's TV tie-in books. Was it time for Yootha and Brian to stop, and find new directions for their professional careers? Some reviewers expressed their concerns that *George and Mildred* was losing its edge. Roger Bowdler, writing in *The Canberra Times* in June 1978, didn't approve of the tie-in books, describing them as a "pointless exercise" before giving an unfriendly comment on the show. "Television sitcom comedies are created by actors," he said. "The writers hack out weekly variations of what the actors do best. Yootha Joyce has a great look down her nose; Brian Murphy dies a fine indignant self-righteousness and a disarming snigger. The show is created by them and is limited by them." "Consequently reading the old scripts (television novels indeed!) is only enjoyable if you can fondly remember the actors doing the line. I don't know why Arrow books bothered. The series were designed for people who can't read."

"Ropermania" continued at its height in the summer of 1978. The *George and*

Mildred stage show, again at the Bournemouth Pier, had reached a record breaking £62,000 in takings, with the profits going to help restore the Pier itself. The production decamped for a number of weeks to Jersey's Opera House Theatre: this also coincided with the broadcast of the third series. Public interest was at fever pitch, and Yootha and Brian gave many promotional interviews and appeared for various charities. An interview with Shirley Flack for the *TV Times* during the show's run, entitled, 'The Private Lives of Jogging George and the Fire Lady' gives a picture of their thoughts at that time. Flack said: "I had to ask Yootha and Brian if after their long association on stage and TV, they had grown into George and Mildred along the way. They deny it, yet at the same time identify so closely with the characters they play on screen that they cannot help slipping into the identity." However, they did insist to the interviewer that they were "not ideas people," telling her that "any spontaneous thoughts that they may have had to do with the plot were used up back when the series was in its infancy."

Asking Yootha and Brian what they felt about the characters, Flack asked "Do they love them, hate them, resent them? To which Yootha and Brian both agreed, 'yes, it's all of those things mixed up together.' When asked how much of the parts were an extension of themselves, and what characteristics they recognised, Yootha acknowledged bossiness – 'I am bossy, I am often intolerant.'" she said. She went on: "I should like to say goodbye to them by the end of 1979, and so would Brian. It will take us at least a year to get rid of the image; the repeats will always be around. If we go on for very much longer we will never do anything except be George and Mildred, it's flattering, it's security, it's profitable – but it isn't good for an actor or actress, and that matters to us, desperately."

During the season on Jersey, Yootha and Brian shared a house together; by all accounts it was quite fancy. Yootha said: "Mildred would love this. She'd appreciate its poshness, very upper-class and in one of the best parts of Jersey. What's more, it's owned by a 'titled person': it would make her year. She would be round to all the neighbours, (in character of Mildred) 'as I was saying to Lady Kitty, my next door neighbour in Jersey.'" "George would be out there, paddling with his trousers rolled up and a handkerchief on head. Mildred would find that embarrassing, she's always embarrassed by George."

Shirley Flack also revealed that "Murphy is an early riser, and during the Jersey season, had been taking morning jogs along the beach, before returning to the house and cooking his own breakfast." (This activity was eventually turned into a 7" single Brian recorded, entitled *Jogging* and released by Pye Records that year!) Yootha, however, "sleeps late, getting up about 10 o'clock to make a cup of tea, and taking it back to bed. Each makes plans independently for the day and sometimes they may meet for a midday drink."

According to the *TV Times*, their spare time on Jersey was "taken up with their charity work. When time allows, they cover every organisation concerned with the welfare of animals and children." Yootha in particular was interested in the work of the Jersey Wildlife Preservation Trust, founded by writer Gerald Durrell, and now the Durrell Wildlife Conservation Trust. "She had herself signed up as a life member and supporter in September that year, and on one occasion visited the centre with Brian Murphy to help highlight their good work." The trust honorary director, Lee Durrell, told me her visit in 1978 was organized by the then Trust Secretary, Simon Hicks. The trust's zoological director in those days was Jeremy Mallinson: he said he was "most impressed by her very sincere and keen interest in the animal kingdom. It was not a question of a person showing mild interest, she was obviously emotionally attached to the trust. She was a genuine and nice person." "She joined its animal adoption scheme and helped in fund-raising events." Recently, Tim Wright, acting head of conservation training at the trust, told me that there is a plaque bearing her name still visible on one of our enclosures. He kindly allowed me to include it in this book.

CHAPTER 32

In the autumn of 1978, the fourth series of *George and Mildred* was broadcast, and the scripts for the fifth series were delivered. Yootha was still engaged in rounds of public appearances. Also, an opportunity had arisen for the stage show to be taken to Australia and New Zealand: the plans were now being finalised. "It was incredible," Brian said, "there was no time for anything else, we were asked individually to do other types of plays, but we had to decline. We lived and breathed *George and Mildred.*" Brian never said what plays these were, and as Yootha's agent has lost all her records from the time, I doubt we will ever know. The pressures of Mildred would get Yootha down from time to time, but she was always cheery; at least both she and Brian had already mentioned that the characters' end was nigh and they were both keen to do other things. The pressures for Brian Murphy may have been easier to deal with. As he once said: "My wife and children could always restore me to sanity immediately by saying the drains needed unblocking or whatever. Yootha didn't have such stability and that made it harder."
Peter Errington, too, told me that "Brian, unlike Yootha, had a family, and a lot of kids, some of which he had fostered with his first wife Carol, whereas Yootha basically had her friends and her animals." Brian later said that Yootha was a frequent visitor to their home: "We were really close, Yootha was like one of the family."
During the rehearsals and recordings of some scenes for the new *George and Mildred* series, it appeared that the strain was beginning to show on Yootha. Brian Murphy remembered that the characters were "taking up so much of our lives."
Peter Frazer Jones remarked that "Yootha had become painfully thin, and was quite withdrawn, and sometimes, if I wandered down onto the studio floor in the lunch break, I would find her there, sitting quite alone and rather sad."
This sadness was doubtless due to the breakdown of Yootha's relationship with Terry Lee Dickson. She later said: "at long last I can say: we'll thank god that's ended. We would have destroyed each other."

She must have been drinking heavily in secret at this time, to blot out her feelings. Months later, she did talk about her problems in an interview for *Woman's Own*: "no man wishes to be number two darling, and I think that had quite a lot to do with why Terry left. He was earning very good money, so there was no way I was keeping him, but when a woman earns so much more than her man, is famous while he is unknown.... Well it rather rubs, doesn't it? He was a delightful gentleman darling, he did a hell of a lot for me and I think I did a bit for him. But he wasn't mature enough to say 'oh well, who cares what people think?' I would like to warn a lot of ladies: be awfully careful when you are choosing a partner very much younger than yourself. There is no use pretending that you can make all the right decisions at the right time just because you're older. Terry was the biggest mistake of my life. He was too young for me – it's as simple as that. I was a bit silly and he was very immature for his years. God knows how I coped with him and God knows how he coped with me. I'm not saying it can't work. Look at Nyree Dawn Porter – she has a very happy marriage with her younger husband, but then he is very mature and knows how to deal with everything that comes his way. But you've got to know very clearly what you are doing before you take on a much younger man. You've got to be very sure or you'll end up destroying each other. My relationship with Terry should never have happened in a million years – a million years. Another pause, another cigarette, another drink."

"I think that if I had been more or less as old as him our other differences wouldn't have mattered so much, and indeed, since we split he's found someone his own age. I wish them luck but it's a shame really because our relationship worked very well for quite some time." Her voice peters out: "there's nothing more to add apart from the if onlys and I don't believe in those. I demand the most from myself: there is no point in getting bitter, all it does is give you an ulcer" She is unable to crack a smile about Terry just yet."

As Yootha had said in the early stages of her relationship with Terry: "I don't feel I own anybody, and nobody must feel they own me." Joy Jameson told me "I know she would have been shattered at the breakup. How it happened I have no idea but she just told me at some time that Terry had found someone else. Whether that's how it really happened I don't know. I only know what I was told."

Christine Pilgrim's account of this matter is a little different: "Yootha once - but only once - confided her insecurity as far as Terry was concerned. We were sitting in bathing suits by the pool Glynn had dug in our garden in Kew. She wondered whether Terry might think her thighs weren't as tight-skinned as they might be. She was, after all, quite a bit older than he was."

"The split devastated Yootha. And I don't think she was ever ready to find another partner. I can quite see how she would be fearful of getting hurt again. She was very lonely, especially as she felt less and less able to face the curious stares and comments of the general public."

Yootha's friend Adrianne Hamilton thought that "Yootha was such a genuine open loving giving person essentially, that if she didn't get it back, and very often people couldn't, she did feel let down, I think that what she needed would have been an older man to look after her, but that's not what she looked for." "She was such a warm and kind person, that even after she divorced from her husband Glynn, if he was in trouble with his girlfriends, he used to come to Yootha. When his relationships broke up, he'd come and cry on Yootha's shoulder. Yootha would phone us up, we'd invited her, can I bring Glynn, poor darling he's feeling a bit depressed, his girlfriend's let him down or something." Adrianne's husband Mario, who was also Yootha's solicitor, once said: "after her break-up with production manager Terry, she had been very lonely and depressed, and had not been eating properly, according to her friends." Barbara Windsor told me "I'm not sure, but the stability she had with Glynn 'a real big soft cuddly toy' seemed good for her and her life may have gone wrong somewhere after that relationship. But I never knew anything more about her other relationships."

It was clear that Yootha's health was deteriorating, while the ratings for *George and Mildred* where at a high of 20.8 million, for the episode 'The Mating Game.' An American television network bought the rights to do a version of the show with different actors in the roles, which would ultimately be renamed as *The Ropers*, and like *George and Mildred*, was also successful.

In 1979 The *Daily Telegraph* was not so complimentary: "the prolonged Mortimer and Cooke sitcom already has a mass audience – a fact which will have surprised most of those who stumbled on it for the first time last night. - The contortion of the coy euphemism in the dog mating scene was for the studio audience 'hysterically funny'" adding that "others may have pondered on the thought that the days of BBC television were not all bad."

The fifth series of *George and Mildred*, with eight episodes, was still being produced in 1979. The recordings were swiftly followed by the tour of Australia and New Zealand. They flew out in February: the UK press went in force to watch them leaving from Heathrow. Yootha never really liked leaving London, and being away from her dogs: it's unclear who was left in charge of them during the eight-month tour. Perhaps it was Yootha's mother or perhaps actor friend Harry Littlewood, who had begun to stay with her after he separated from his wife. Yootha's route to New Zealand was recorded in a Singapore Airlines schedule she kept with some of her belongings, which included details of her stop-off points and in-flight menu. In those days there would be more stop off points than there are now.

Then it was: London to Frankfurt, Frankfurt to Rome, Rome to Bahrain, Bahrain to Bombay, Bombay to Singapore, Singapore to Perth, Perth to Melbourne – then onto New Zealand, certainly a challenge even to anyone who enjoys flying! Brian recalled that on the flight to New Zealand, and the others that were to follow, "Yootha loathed it." Brian remembered that, though they arrived safely, "our costumes didn't. We were late by one day, and with a total sell-out at the theatre; being a day late, we were missing a day of acclimatising and adjusting to the time differences. The temperature was really hot and humid. We were on stage doing our first show to a lovely audience, and suddenly we stopped, and for a split second we had no idea where we were; we got through it. We were jet-lagged."

The Australasian tour involved lots of promotional interviews on radio and TV and in the newspapers. Yootha and Brian stayed at various locations during the tour. On one occasion they stayed at the White Heron Hotel, Auckland, which had small apartments, overlooking the ocean. In *Bruce: The Autobiography* Bruce Forsyth recalled staying at the same hotel, with both Yootha and Brian, at the same time. It was "one of the longest birthdays of my life," he says, and describes them both as the "most fun loving people, with great senses of humour. When Yootha found out it was my birthday, she organised an impromptu get-together the night before. We sat by the pool at the White Heron under a starlit sky, eating fish and chips – served with champagne – waiting for me to turn 47."

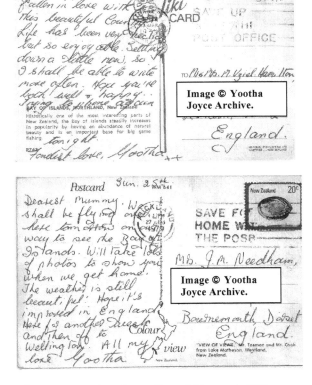

Image © Yootha Joyce Archive.

Image © Yootha Joyce Archive.

The tour moved to Australia and Tasmania "We were playing at different towns each week and it was very punishing," Brian said. "Yootha hated flying and she always used to sit next to me and dig her fingernails into my arm during the take off and landing. She was quite scared. I used to ask her if I could sit by the window, not to look at the view, but to spare my left arm and let my right one get some punishment. I went round with these big gouges in my arm for days afterwards!" he recalled.

Yootha was asked to present an award on one of Australia's famous shows, *The 21st Annual TV Week Logie Awards*, at Melbourne's Hilton Hotel on 16th March. She appeared alongside a star-studded guest list, including Muhammad Ali, Robin Williams and David Hemmings. The event was televised on the Nine Network later that year. They plane-hopped from Australia back to New Zealand, where Yootha took time to send her pal, The Gresh, a postcard, franked from Christchurch 29th March 1979. She gave him an update of her time on the tour.

The Gresh kindly explained the opening phrase for me. "Any questions?" referred to the following: "I was negotiating a deal for Yootha to appear at a huge bingo hall, the management I can't honestly recall. I've looked through my diary and can't confirm it was Mecca, it could well have been Top Rank, as we, the business, did a lot of appearances for that organisation. They wanted Yootha to answer a few questions about her career for their *In Hour* publication. I was waiting for them to send me the questions, but they hadn't been in touch – the deal didn't go ahead, plus I wasn't happy with their offer. But I told Yootha if she wanted to do the deal, I'd step aside. Lovely Yootha said, "No Gresh -- No Yootha - we've enough offers Gresh not to need them!" "I loved her!" He told me.

The months of touring were relentless, with many shows, interviews and personal appearances taken at every opportunity. They visited venues all over Australia (including Tasmania): Townsville, Queensland, the Theatre Royal Sydney, the Princess in Melbourne and the Regal in Subiaco, Perth, Western Australia, and so on, and got rave reviews wherever they went.

In 1979 Rod McNeil was working for Network Ten Television in Sydney. He was a daytime and midday news host, as well as interviewer on the *Celebrity Interview* series. His guests included Bette Midler, Dolly Parton, the Village

People, Harry Belafonte, Iggy Pop, Edith Head, and of course 'Dear Yootha' herself. He told me that he doesn't know how well remembered Yootha is now, in the vast catalogue of TV shows and performers: "I was just talking yesterday here in Pattaya, Thailand, with an events manager who years ago worked on the *Benny Hill* shows, and he recalls how they went about capturing all the antics that went into that show. It was obviously a golden period for a certain style of easy viewing, engaging comic entertainment. I also met Dick Emery in the throes of making a series of *Kelvinator* commercials, where I played his straight man. I had just left ABC in Sydney and had yet to join Channel 10 at Ryde. (While in the newsroom at 10, the opportunity arose to be a part of a series of *Celebrity Interviews*. Kevin Sadlier, the showbiz editor for *The Mirror* in Sydney of old, was also the person behind the *Sunday Veritas* TV page. It was Kevin who brought the concept to 10; a panel of writers and presenters quizzing, usually a visiting celebrity, about their life and career. I was the host with four others I recall.) Kevin was able to arrange visits by some interesting names of the era. Sadly, all too many of them had died within a few years, including a still youthful Harry Chapin, Diana Dors, Hollywood designer Edith Head and Yootha. Others like Pat Boone and even Iggy Pop have lasted rather better". He told me Yootha was "a friendly and forthcoming guest as I recall, but after so long I have no other exact memories of the interview... just that she was a likeable star guest. It is just possible that the TV interview exists. They'd all be old style tapes I imagine but a very useful record if it exists in some form." In addition, Yootha and Brian appeared on *Ten's Townsville News* programme and the famous *Mike Walsh Show* (episode 9139), which also featured Desmond Morris and vocalist Joy Mulligan. The mania that greeted them was reported in *The Canberra Times*, where Yootha stressed "there are millions of George and Mildreds, and they are trying to identify with you every minute of the day." She also said that "it has its good sides, my bank manager is awfully pleased with me, but it gets a bit trying sometimes, you tend to live in a goldfish bowl, everybody looks points pokes and shoves, but loads and loads of nice things come out of it too. People really believe we are married and live as George and Mildred. Brian's real wife: well she can't go to the shops: 'no you're not Mrs Roper,' they say, she can't write out cheques because people think it should be me doing it."
When they were in Townsville, by coincidence Brian Cooke was there too, writing. He told me that he lived on Magnetic Island for several months: "Magnetic Island is so called by Captain Cook (no relation!), who thought it interfered with his navigational equipment (it didn't) It was just across the bay from Townsville, and I invited the whole cast over for a 'Barbie'. Yootha got to meet Sally the boatman, who every morning towed his several rowing boats into the bay at Magnetic, parked himself in a deckchair and read a book. If he liked the look of you, he'd rent you a boat... he and Yootha got on really well." In Perth, Yootha had a little window of leisure to go to the races at The Western Australian Turf Club at the Ascot Racecourse, where she enjoyed a flutter on the Sheraton-Perth Quality Stakes, opting for Hakim Boy and Jungle Royal for a win.

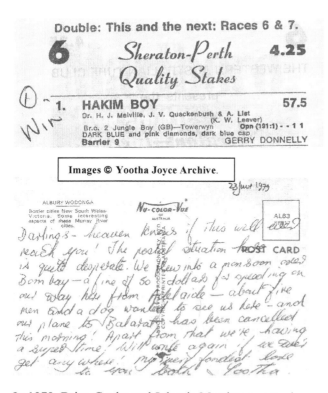

Double: This and the next: Races 6 & 7.

6 𝒮*heraton-*𝒫*erth* **4.25**

𝒬*uality* 𝒮*takes*

1. HAKIM BOY **57.5**

Dr. H. J. Melville, J. V. Quackenbush & A. List
(K. W. Leaver)
Br.c. 2 Jungle Boy (GB)—Towerwyn Opn (191:1) - - 1 1
DARK BLUE and pink diamonds, dark blue cap
Barrier 9 GERRY DONNELLY

Images © Yootha Joyce Archive.

In 1979, Brian Cooke and Johnnie Mortimer were given an award from The Writers Guild, for 'The Best Female Role Created for Television': an award went to Yootha also. But underneath it all this success and hard work, something was wrong with Yootha. Brian Murphy recalled: "She got thinner and thinner. She wouldn't eat properly and she was using up so much nervous energy. She was almost anorexic. I never saw any signs of her being a heavy drinker: the trouble was I think she drank more than she ate. It was a terrible time for both of us, we were absolutely exhausted, we were performing almost every night as well as doing chat shows and radio programmes. And then there was the flying." Glynn Edwards said: "you cannot go on cracking the whip without the machinery giving way. Her health suffered after an arduous tour. She complained of backache and other ailments." According to Brian, Yootha never spoke of her misery and loneliness. Looking back he said he should have spotted the warning signs. He remembers saying to her once on the tour: "'Where are you going Yootha?' 'To the theatre,' she replied. 'Well, you'll get very wet.' I said, 'That's the way to the river! The theatre's the other way.' It was our second week in Melbourne with the stage version of *George and Mildred*, with still several weeks to go. It had taken a national tour of England, two summer seasons and many months of work on the television series for me to realise that Yootha, away from her home, had no sense of direction. Sometimes, she even managed to get lost on her way from her dressing room in a new theatre to the stage. Goodness knows how she would have managed the backstage maze of the National Theatre. Yet dear Yootha, when I first met her, seemed to know exactly where she was headed. Trouble with being an actor, we can sometimes fool our friends and ourselves." (Brian Murphy)

CHAPTER 33

When she returned to the UK in September 1979, Yootha seemed to have changed. She was becoming negative; when interviewed, she remarked: "I am a hard critic"; "I have never been satisfied with my performances on or off stage." She was even admitting her age, something she would never have done in earlier years: "I'm 53 darling, and I don't mind who knows it." Brian recalled that when they got back, "we were asked to go back to Bournemouth, but Yootha didn't want to, she wanted a break before the next series." Could it be that she'd just had enough?

Instead of going on to Bournemouth, then, Yootha stayed at her London flat, but she still worked, doing a series of interviews, public appearances and charity work, as well as guesting on the odd game show. In September, she helped out with the Variety Club in raising funds with BBC Radio 1's *Roadshow* – they held two meals in London and Manchester for the children to celebrate and meet Radio 1 Disc Jockeys, including Jimmy Savile, Tony Blackburn and Dave Lee Travis, and Yootha was photographed with them for the cause.

In October, Yootha also attended a Charity Greyhound Meeting with Joy Jameson at the White City Stadium, for a 'star evening' in aid of 'Old Ben,' the Newsvendors' Benevolent Institution. Joy told me "Curiously, though, I remember her joy when she bought a long mink cape... something she wouldn't have been able to wear for at least the last twenty years. She really WAS great fun... none of this agonising over whether she could do it or not. My perception of her was that she had great confidence." Joy told me that one of her special memories was when Yootha "went off to see the lady with the mink full-length cape and her joy in having it... God I wonder if she ever did think 'I shouldn't have worn fur!' She looked like the Tsarina of all the Russias... truly. She must have been acting herself into the cape... she wore it when she presented a prize to the winner of a race at White City." Sally Thomsett, though, thought Yootha wouldn't have worn it if it was real fur: "it may have looked real but I'm 100% certain that it would have been fake," she said.

Joy remembers, "The only thing I do remember was going with her to the greyhound racing at White City and our being on a table with Ernie and Mrs. Wise, Frankie Howerd, and probably his partner, and both of us were thinking what a miserable lot they were." Yootha was quite superstitious in her choices at the races and "believed in the lucky number 7. She always backed the dogs at greyhound racing events in traps 6 and 1, 5 and 2, or 4 and 3." In October, too, she recorded an episode of the acting charades game *Give Us A Clue*, appearing on the "girls" team with Una Stubbs and Elizabeth Estenson. Richard O'Sullivan joined the "boys" team and at times appeared a little wound up by Dave Lee Travis. Yootha's charades for her team were so well acted that both of them were guessed within about twenty seconds.

During this time, the final series of *George and Mildred* went out for broadcast, and with that, high ratings were guaranteed. However, just before the programmes went on air, Yootha gave a candid interview to Jean Rook, the *Daily Express* columnist, on her feelings about it, and told how her life was going. It was given the title: "Yootha's having trouble with Mildred": Rook quietly but pointedly noticed that "she sips champagne at noon". "Her dog snuggled into her lap, her little black and white cat purred up against her other side," Rook remarked "where Mildred is scarlet and brassy, Miss Joyce is in pale pink and real 22 [not 24?] carat gold." Rook pressed Yootha on the announcement that the fifth series was to be the last. Yootha said, "I suppose I'll miss Mildred, eight years is too long," before she mentioned the problems the character brought her. "When Miss Joyce was at her open door, a road sweeper, at pavement level, bawled down "where's George, is he in bed then?? And then waited like a man who'd said something hilarious, for his laughs" – "it was the first of thousands of times someone would say that to her in one day" Yootha confessed: "it's everywhere you go, every second, mostly I can cope – 'I left him at home you know how he is, ho ho ho, - all that stuff; after eight solid years of it, it's too much. And if it's tough on me, think of poor Brian. Everywhere he goes it's, where's Mildred? Is she getting any? Or 'you can't do it can you?'"

"Brian has teenage boys at school and they shout at them or his wife in the supermarket, 'your old man can't do it can he?' Brian gets uptight and no wonder. These days even he and I don't get on as well together as we did at the start. It's a terrible strain put on us by the public."

"I know it happens to other actors, but George and Mildred are especially hard to live with, much as we have loved the work. Consider it - the middle-aged wife, deeply fond of a middle-aged husband, who can't make love to her, and who gets on her wick. She'd never leave him, she'd be desolate without him, and anyway, what are they going to do apart? But he still drives her berserk. Can't you see, after all these years of doing it, it's hard to take? I'm ashamed of myself for letting Mildred get me down off screen."

"Yootha freely admits to being well loved," confirms Miss Rook, to which Yootha responds: "Lovely things sometimes happen with the fans. I'll never forget the morning I walked straight under a taxi, all my own fault. The driver had a right to play merry hell. But he just leaned out of his cab and said very gently, 'Mildred don't you ever, EVER do that again. We can't afford to lose you'. Miss Rook asked "was Miss Joyce committing suicide?" to which Yootha responds, "No, I was doing the *Telegraph* crossword in the street, I'm a crossword addict. Especially now I'm living alone, and at the moment right off men, I adore the *Telegraph* crossword. Don't worry, I only fold it across and do the crossword, I never read the rest of the paper!" Rook (who of course wrote for the *Express*) finishes the interview: "You can't help admiring that big mouth. It's straight, fresh and bitingly honest. Even though she's sitting there with her foot in it."

As the glory days of the TV sitcom were coming to an end, they embarked on the newly agreed film of *George and Mildred*, to be produced by Chips and Cinema Arts International company (ITC). They started rehearsing in late autumn, and shooting began in early 1980. Though the TV ratings remained very high, even Yootha, Brians Murphy and Cooke and Johnnie Mortimer knew the script ideas were starting to become, as Yootha said, "a little stale." "There was," Yootha admitted, a "deliberate attempt to stop, as the writers are finding less situations for us as characters." The new film script featuring the Ropers was toasted up by a different writer, Dick Sharples. There was also a further promise of a final set of TV scripts in preparation by Cooke and Mortimer, who by now seemed to be focused on devising newer material and formats.

The film's storyline centred on George and Mildred celebrating a wedding anniversary holiday at 'The London Hotel' (actually the Copthorne Tara off Wright's Lane in Kensington). Shooting took place mainly at Elstree film studios in Borehamwood with a new street location used instead of the usual comforting cosiness of the Ropers' home. Gone was the Manor Road location, which was replaced with a new one, at 110 Whitehouse Avenue next to the film studios.

The couple get caught up with a group of mafia types after a case of mistaken identity. The script seemed ill suited to the times; the class differences that gave an edge to the TV programmes were absent, which took away much of the impact, and the characters seemed strangely confined to the previous decade, the 1970s. Both Brian and Yootha seemed creatively and physically burnt out, with only the occasional glimmer of their usual chemistry. Maybe the film should never have been made. Needless to say, the critical response and the box office takings were poor.

Yootha remembered that while she was filming, "Harry Littlewood was my alarm clock. Every morning at 5.30 a.m., he'd give me a little shake. 'Flower' he'd say, 'wake up, flower': I love it, and he literally looks after me." Although Harry was sharing Yootha's flat at the time, she insisted that "The relationship is strictly platonic. He sleeps on the sofa. He's been a good mate for a very long time, he and his wife have gone their separate ways and he's come from Manchester to set up home here in London. Living with Harry suits me well, because he does everything. God, how I hate housework. Harry tidies up and takes things to the cleaners and puts me out my chicken stock cubes for breakfast." she said. Peter Errington also remembered that "Yootha did have a friend in Harry Littlewood, and they kind of looked after each other, they were both similar and I don't think there was a physical relationship between them." The supporting cast for the film included Stratford Johns, Sue Bond, David Barry, Kenneth Cope and old Theatre Workshopper Dudley Sutton, who told me; "I last saw Yootha I think when we did the film version of *George and Mildred* in 1980. I played the part of a biker, and I hadn't seen Yootha for years, and I was very sad to see her... drunk, she was really, and how she was just drowning her sorrows in drink and fantasising about doing good works, and stuff. But her grasp of reality, to be honest, seemed to be quite slender." Nicholas Bond Owen told me: "she was always very professional and never appeared drunk to me. I think it got worse towards the end, when her relationship ended but I didn't know a thing about it until we were due to start rehearsing for the next series, in August." Yootha, it seems, was desperate to rise above the frustrations of the Mildred role, "I've had enough of the role, some day if someone in the street says 'ello Mildred, where's George?' I know I'm going to scream," she said.

In 1980 she said: "A journalist described me once as 'a lady of wit and maturity who, in the Edwardian age, would have had young swains drinking champagne out of her size eight slipper and ordering many an intimate dinner à deux in the red plush private rooms of certain discreet restaurants.' Dudley Sutton saw things differently, saying she was "Deluded, yes, Yootha started seeing herself as a sort of grand lady, a charitable lady, with large hats hanging in front of pillars, serving tea in the garden! She had kind of lost the plot."

David Barry recalled his time on set with Yootha in his book *Flashback - An Actor's Life*. He told how she would disappear into her dressing room and "fuel up on brandy." He remembers that Yootha's dresser would be "summoned to bring a hidden bottle of brandy to the set. But soon we were all openly imbibing Yootha's brandy." He told me that, "When I went to lunch with Brian Murphy, Yootha wouldn't join us, but would go off to her dressing room for a liquid lunch." Tex Fisher, in his book *Man About The House and George and Mildred: the Definitive Companion*: says that "a source close to *George and Mildred* explained how Yootha used to stagger in at 8 o'clock in the morning, legless. It was very sad to think how she could have got so drunk by that time in the morning, but she picked herself up and got on with the show, she was a total professional."

David Barry agreed: although drunk, she was still "very professional."

"In a scene when I was posing as a Frenchman, I let slip in a sentence one cockney word, and she fell about laughing and encouraged me to use it in the film, which I did." He remembers that he did witness her temper too, but "Only once, when they had to pick up a shot from the previous day's shoot, and she had already been dismissed at lunchtime and was called back to the set, which involved going to make-up at lunchtime all over again."

CHAPTER 34

After the filming, Yootha and Brian attended a party at the Savoy; around this time, though, she seemed to become more withdrawn and unhappy. She hardly went out of the flat, even to do her shopping. Her solicitor said that "she bought few of the luxuries she could have afforded, she had no car, and although she had enough money to retire on, she just wanted to carry on working." So she did, in fact, recording another episode of the charades game show *Give Us a Clue*, and agreeing to be interviewed by Tony Bilbow for a half-hour programme for Tyne Tees TV, *Play It Again*, in which actors spoke on camera about their favourite films, how they had shaped their lives and become important to them. Yootha's choices included two in which she starred, *Man*

About the House and *The Pumpkin Eater*; the other three were *All About Eve, Mickey Mouse* and her all time favourite *The Lion in Winter*. She came across as the genuine, honest, friendly woman that most people have spoken of, as well as the bright, well scrubbed glamour puss that we all knew her for. In this show she wore an extra large pick nose collared shirt, a green nylon safari-type suit with flared trousers, desert boots, and she wore her usual gold jewellery.

Occasionally, though, you could see there was a side to her that was becoming a little frustrated with the direction of her career. Talking of her love of film she said, "I don't go to the cinema as much as I used to, as I am usually at home with a script and learning the lines, but I watch films all the time on the TV." She remarked on her frustration as not being seen as anything but Mildred Roper, saying: "I can't do anything else now, people just won't give you the work, I can't be considered as a straight actress any more on television. I think I'll have to wait for a little while before it eases off and then do all sorts of other things; we have another eight more *George and Mildred*'s to do and then we finish." Tony Bilbow, who was an admirer, asked about doing other projects that would stretch her as an actress. She said: "It would be easy to do in the theatre, but the thing is, I just love working in television."

According to her solicitor, this typecasting problem began to make Yootha depressed, as she "wanted to break into more serious acting." Christine Pilgrim thought, "Once Mildred had taken over Yootha's life, she held out little hope that she'd be cast as anything else. She found the character rather two-dimensional, although she did everything she could to round Mildred out. And she succeeded as far as anyone can with a sitcom character. I think she was more frustrated with becoming public property as Mildred. She couldn't go to the supermarket without people addressing her as Mildred. It was as if they owned her. She was part of their lives, so they presumed they could be part of hers. She had no privacy any more. I think that was very wearing for her. She stopped going shopping, or at least did as little of it as possible." There were regular repeats of the problems of being recognised in the street, in which she said "people often come up to me and ask the most embarrassing questions about Mildred's sex life." It was frustrating for her. She said, "I had, before Mildred, established myself firmly as an equally accomplished dramatic actress." "I'd love to play dramas like Gertrude in *Hamlet*, I know I could play it on my head, but when I walked on the stage, people would say, look, it's Mildred, and that's going to happen for years after I stop playing her." She added, "it's worse for Brian, they accuse him of not being a complete husband," "he could no longer go out without being pointed at, laughed at or becoming the butt of jokes about his sexual drive." Perhaps Yootha, like her father Hurst all those years before, didn't want to get trapped on the variety circuit. In the spring, she agreed to make a presentation to Irene Handl in 'The Pye Colour Television Awards / Writers Guild' at the London Hilton: perhaps she hoped she would be offered a distinctly different and challenging role.

Speaking about George in the spring 1980 edition of *Theatre Quarterly*, Brian said: "people ask me whether I'm not fed up with playing George, I'm not," but he did confess: "I don't want to go on playing George forever." Yootha had refused to return with him in the *George and Mildred* stage show; he returned on his own to the theatre at Bournemouth Pier, playing the lead in *Shut Your Eyes and Think of England*. It ran from May 5th – July 19th, He played Arthur Pullen, a bewildered accountant with a city firm who gets caught up in high finance and an Arab takeover.

Later in the summer, Yootha attended the wedding of Fabian Hamilton, the son of her solicitor and his wife. Fabian told me he had fond memories of Yootha Joyce and his family's friendship with her: "She was a lovely person and she came along as a guest at my wedding in 1980, just before she died. I do know my parents adored her." There were the occasional photo opportunities still coming through to promote the *George and Mildred* 'brand,' which must have needled Yootha a bit: at one such gathering, she is pictured on Euston Road at Thames TV's central office, alongside her namesake from the American series *The Ropers*, Audra Lindley. In June, too, a sadder Yootha gave an interview in *Woman's Own*, almost submissive in tone, entitled 'Why my Young Lover Left me.' "I live alone now," she said "and I enjoy it, I'm happy to spend the rest of my life like that; the trouble is I don't know what people mean by love, I don't think it's ever happened to me." "There have been three men in my life, darling. They're all exes because I'm hell to live with. My exes call me demanding." "Both Glynn and Cyril have found happiness, and that's a joy to me." "I don't understand how anybody could envy someone else's happiness – if you love somebody very dearly that's what you want for them, and you hope they feel the same way about you." "Today Cyril and I phone each other up and I see quite a lot of him. We don't want to go to bed together because that's all water under the bridge, darling. We're just good mates. I may be difficult to live with but afterwards, I like to be able to pick up the phone and say hello." Yootha's love of animals and her charity work were still important her, she said, "they eat their dinners out of their individual saucers on my patio, and sleep in individual cardboard boxes, with blankets at the bottom." "I have two cats inside, and one dog. Two wild cats who won't come inside, one is called Treasure, and the other one is called Gentleman Caller. He comes and goes very silently, they both enjoy their lives so they're very happy outside." "If you don't like animals, stay out of my house: we are a hive of industry when it comes to animals, darling, we are everlastingly washing bowls and opening tins." "Yootha takes the bone from Sammy the Westie, who has been happily scrunching it under a table, 'don't do that darling, uncle Harry has vacuumed the carpet and he'll go mad'". "I do a great deal for animals' and children's charities, averaging two charities a week in the summer months."

On the *Play it Again* interview, she had a thoughtful and considered approach to which charities she would support, saying, "I support cancer relief, the hospices, dying with dignity. It's a terrible thing to say, but when you gotta go, you gotta go, but let's go in a nice way. But sorry, not Cancer Research, I have strong feelings about that. I won't support if they straggle up live dogs and cut them open, I can't have that, I'm sorry but I can't. Neither Brian or I" she said. About Brian, she said: "he has been tremendous. He has seen me through all sorts of trouble. He cares about people and he is very well organised." But talking of Mildred, who would appear on the big screen on July 13th, she repeated, "I do get tired of Mildred. I love her and I'm grateful for what she has done for me, sometimes I think if I see Mildred written down one more time I'll scream." But she also said: "I won't give up Mildred so long as the viewers like her."

After the split with Terry, it seems that Yootha wanted to move out of her flat. Joy Jameson told me, "She talked about moving on, but I don't really think she would have done. She loved where she was but I always thought it was a place where she was quite vulnerable – down a few steps, you couldn't be seen, then door open. Who knows! I would have been very afraid there." Dudley Sutton, on the other hand, said: "I'm sure she would have been able to take care of herself if anything happened."

Her appearances on the social scene were becoming fewer. Mario, her solicitor, said that: "Brian Murphy would often phone her up and invite her out to try and cheer her up." Yootha was getting more depressed, it seems: "And of course there was the drinking, but I don't like to criticize because we all have our faults," said Toni Palmer. "She wouldn't drink that much when I knew her, she didn't have a lot of drink in the dressing room or anything, but in the end I think she did wreck her body a bit with it and I think she kept it very secret. When Brian would ring her up and ask whether she would like to go out, she was always busy or going somewhere, but even he didn't know." Peter Errington said, "She certainly liked a fag and a drink, journalists tend to want to know shit, but I know no shit at all about Yootha apart from the fact that she liked a fag, she liked a drink and that's what killed her probably. If she had been drinking, she certainly knew how to control it, I suppose it was part of the culture at the time, everything seemed to develop around that sociability."

Glynn Edwards remembers that "Yootha came to a party at my place just three weeks before she died, and she seemed fine – really as full of fun as always." When I asked him if she was impressed with his new role in *Minder* as barman Dave, he remembers: "Yes, well, she was quite impressed with that, she was riding high as Mildred at the time, but that character hadn't been going on all that long, but of course she didn't see me in it that much, and of course we did talk to each other about our work in more down to earth ways than you would on set." With regard to her health he told me, "she was thinking of going to a health farm to get in shape before recording a new series; she said she wanted to give up smoking and to stop drinking so much brandy." Joy Jameson said, no one thought she was a heavy drinker, and that she never saw her drunk, "She was always full of life and had no apparent sadness in her life. She had plenty of friends and she was a very strong person."

Brian admits he didn't see Yootha for several months after the Australia trip: "I thought she was happily resting, but she was just staying at home getting more and more lonely and miserable. The trouble was she didn't have many close friends and she didn't go out much. I was horrified when I did see Yootha again after the several months away; she had become painfully thin and I should have interfered. I should have tried to help her. Being Yootha, she would have told me to fuck off, but I still should have said something to her and I didn't." "The last few months of her life must have been unbearable."

Career plans for both Yootha and Brian seemed to be taking a new turn: interviewed by Tex Fisher, Brian said, "We all wanted to do other things, I wanted to do some theatre, Yootha wanted to do some Shakespeare and open up a donkey sanctuary." Christine Pilgrim recalled "Yootha adopted lots of retired donkeys. There was a home for them somewhere in the country. She was quite passionate about that cause. And then, of course, there were the doggies. She adored her doggies. In fact she loved animals in general." Brian remembered "She fancied leading quite a different type of life, so we decided to finish *George and Mildred* on a high, "There were even rumours of Yootha working at the BBC on a new comedy role as a high class courtesan." But would this mean playing the funny tart again? One is led to ask what caused her sadness – her frustration about her career, the failure of her relationships or some other inner conflict? Something of all of this no doubt – it's impossible to be certain.

As Yootha became increasingly withdrawn, so she became increasingly ill. Her doctor at the time, Alan Thomas, who had been looking after her since 1976, said "I knew nothing of her drinking problem until two months before her death." The inquest later revealed that Yootha's doctor was called to her flat in early July. Who alerted him is not known: Harry Littlewood, perhaps? Joy Jameson said she hardly saw her eat and that it was the nagging from her friends about this that persuaded her to go into a clinic; "she was due to undergo tests, but she died before she was well enough to have them." While he was at Yootha's flat, the doctor said he noticed "a half-empty bottle of brandy in the kitchen and a glass of brandy by her bed. He had treated her for minor ailments; now he advised her to go into hospital but she was not willing to do so." Joy remembers that Yootha had at last minute "cancelled things, none really important – but interestingly they were personal appearances – being Yootha."

On August 6th, Yootha collapsed after contracting a chronic liver infection: she weighed just under seven stone. She agreed to enter a Harley Street clinic: when she was admitted she was disturbed and distressed when she was told she could no longer drink, and a psychiatrist specialising in alcohol problems was called as "she was suffering from hepatitis." Joy thought that Yootha had initially gone into hospital with what she thought was "chest infection, as she had a dreadful cough. She was always coughing and I did nag her to get it looked at in case it was anything nasty. It wouldn't have surprised me if they had come back with a cancer diagnosis. She was underweight and getting feeble (that's not the word I want, but you know, you wonder if she had to be careful because she certainly wasn't herself). I truly believed they would sort her out in time. You certainly don't expect someone to go in with something you think is curable."

Toni Palmer said: "Nowadays, I'm sure there would be a different programme of withdrawal, hopefully. The trouble with drinking is, if you don't want to stop, nothing can make you, I mean Lionel Bart drank himself to death, and he drank and drank and drank for years and then one day he found somebody to help him and I'm not sure, but I think one of his mentors was Dudley Sutton. Lionel went to 'Alcoholics Anonymous', and he stopped completely; he didn't drink for ten years. I used to go out with Lionel to posh places that we couldn't afford to go

to, but Lionel could, but he never had anything to drink. He used to order a bottle of champagne for us, and have nothing himself, but suddenly something happened and he went back on it and he was dead. They told him, they said: 'if you ever drink again then your liver will just disintegrate.'"
Glynn Edwards recalled, "I got a call saying Yootha had been taken into hospital. She was in for 10 days and never came out again. The awful thing was she refused to have any visitors. She didn't want to see anyone. It was sad because she had a birthday while she was in there and I thought what a lovely surprise it would be to arrive with a bunch of flowers. But she wouldn't see me."
Peter Frazer Jones, the producer of *George and Mildred*, said: "I knew she had gone into hospital, but it was all kept very secret, what the problem was, and I sent her the scripts for the new series which apparently she never read, because by then she was too ill." Norman Eshley said, "I had no idea what was going on at all, and when it did come, bloody hell, it really was a hell of a shock."
I have no idea of how Yootha's mother found out what was happening: she was increasingly frail and living in Bournemouth. Nor could anyone tell me who looked after her animals. Some of the press behaved in a disgusting fashion: Joy Jameson told me that: "There were disgraceful things. Journalists trying to get in the hospital to photograph her in the room... then journalists trawling round all the off-licences in her neighbourhood. It was shameful."
It was reported on 22nd August that doctors at the clinic thought she was on the mend. Two days earlier, on her 53rd birthday, Brian Murphy recalled, "she was sitting up in bed, surrounded by hundreds of flowers and cards from fans and the press and it looked like she was improving. *The Sun* reported "On her birthday she received 800 cards and telegrams at the hospital. That bucked her up immensely." On Sunday 24th , he went over to the hospital. "I had gone to visit my own dear mum and I was on the way back home, when I decided to pay Yootha a visit instead. She went into a coma as I was there. It
was a great shock. But she had a relapse and slipped away literally while I was sitting there. It was so very sad." Sitting at her bedside, he was "stunned, I don't think any of us knew how seriously ill she was until the last couple of weeks. I hadn't seen her for a while because I was doing a summer season." "It wasn't until I saw her fairly recently that I knew how ill she was. We were due to star in a new series of our show today, I think it's probably the first show that Yootha ever missed."
A statement released by the clinic simply said: "she died here at one o'clock".

**Test shots
for television**

Yootha on set in Bath.

Signing autographs outside flat in Sussex Gardens

Publicity shot early 1970's

Pop Promoter Cyril Smith.

Yootha relaxing in
a kaftan at her flat

Walking Tallulah and Sammy.

**With Milo O'Shea
1971**

**Checking her lines as
Mildred on location at
Alma Square London
1974**

Christmas Celebrity Squares 1975. Image © Rex Features.

Signing autographs at a
public appearance

At a charity event with ?,
Danny La Rue, Keith
Harris and Norman
Collier.

One of many events
with co-star Brian

At an awards ceremony at the
Grosvernor Hotel 1977. With
William Franklyn amongst
others.

154

Yootha & Brian

**Yootha lending a hand for a
charity event for guide dogs.**

Yootha and Brian at the Pier Theatre Bournemouth for their amazing summer season in 1977

Terry Lee Dickson 1977

Charity work with
Brian Murphy.

With Kismet the cat,
rescued from a dustbin.

At the Durrell Wildlife centre
in Jersey with Dennis Moseley

Wednesday.
POST CARD
Darlings - at last
catching up on all
the sincere thank-yous
that I should have
done last week! It
was so lovely to see
you both. Sorry I was
a bit 'twitchy' but the
memories came flooding
back! All gone now!
My fondest love to you
both Yootha

Mr.& Mrs. M. Uziell-Hamilton,

Yootha's postcard from
Jersey 1978. © Yootha
Joyce Archive.

N. W. 2.

Riding Double Header with Brian Murphy. Image © Rex Features.

Yootha at home

PART THREE

CHAPTER 35

The press was shocked with the news of Yootha's death, with most papers, including *The Sun* and *The Daily Star*, reporting the news on their front pages the next day. The *Daily Express* carried a front-page story, headlining: "TV's Yootha Joyce dies at 53," quoting a sad Brian Murphy who said, "it's a great loss, I've lost a friend, poor old George has lost a wife, and the viewers have lost a very funny lady."

The Stage focused on her comic abilities in their obituary, remarking "It is often said that there are few good women comediennes in Britain but if true, certainly Yootha Joyce was one of the few; caustic but warm-hearted, she knew how to make the most of an ironic line." Brian Murphy recalled that he was invited onto the ITN news programmes to talk about Yootha: "The recording went fine, but then when it was broadcast that evening, the weirdest thing happened. They led up to the interview saying 'We have Brian Murphy in the studio to discuss the sad demise of Yootha Joyce.' But after the link when my interview was to be played, it all went quiet. We had lost sound, nationwide. Everybody had lost sound on their televisions all across the country for my interview, but afterwards the rest of the news went without a hitch. When my bit was replayed later on in the evening, it was perfect. The sound was restored and was clear as a bell. It was so odd. There were no known technical problems and we could only assume that it was Yootha's influence, looking down on us. To this day I still think that."

Joy Jameson said "I couldn't believe it," "news of Yootha's death came as a dreadful shock to me. It was a Bank Holiday. I was at my cottage. I'd just heard my daughter had not passed her A levels, and then that news, it was truly devastating."

Terry Lee Dickson, working as a production manager for a show in Glasgow at the time, was "extremely upset by her death," "she was a great lady, it is a terrible loss to me and to show business, we were very close and had many happy times together. I will be attending Miss Joyce's funeral."

The actors, writers and crew on the *George and Mildred* programmes were all told about Yootha. Johnnie Mortimer called her "a great lady – one of the greatest I ever worked with." Nicholas Bond Owen said: "it was a terrible shock to us all."

A spokesman for Thames TV said: "Her death came as a blow to all her friends. We all feel a sense of grief at the loss of a fine and very popular actress." Sally Thomsett said "I was terribly terribly shocked. I knew she was ill, but I never guessed she would die."

Others who had worked with her shared their grief at the news too, Barbara Windsor told me "I was really shocked to hear of Yootha's death. She was so young; I tried to make some sense of it by thinking of how the pressures of the business could have affected her. Theatre and TV producers alike would often tell you that even off stage and away from TV cameras, the minute you open the door and step outside, you're always on show for the general public." David

Barry thought, "she was so professional and nice, I was very upset to hear the news," with Jeremy Bulloch adding, "She had so much to give and should have had more time to show the public what a great actress she was."

The Gresh, who had such happy memories of working with Yootha, told me he was phoned by some TV presenters at the time of Yootha's death, who wanted to go down the "wrong road" about her with him, "there were times that even though we were broadcasting live, I'd just say 'goodbye' and put the phone down."

The charities she had worked for showed their intense gratitude for what she had done for them, tinged, of course, with a great sadness at the loss of a great champion. Clarissa Baldwin said, "I remember some very happy times with Yootha; not only was she an excellent actress, she was also a warm and generous person. The day she died she was due to open a new rescue centre for us in Norfolk. I knew she was in hospital, but sadly had no idea of the seriousness of her condition." At the Durrell Trust, too, there was shock: Yootha had been particularly interested in an exciting new gorilla development, which was due to be opened in the spring.

The day after her death an episode of *Give us a Clue* in which Yootha appeared was scheduled; it had been recorded early on in the spring,. After much deliberation, Thames TV decided to show it. I remember watching it with a strange feeling of sadness. The same was true when I went to see the newly released *George and Mildred* film. She left her mark on this kiddie.

The coroner who first reported her death, Dr Paul Knapman, stated that she had "fallen into a coma brought on by a severe turn of hepatitis." At a preliminary inquest hearing in Battersea, on the 28th August, the cause of death was given as "alcoholism portal cirrhosis of the liver," with an expert saying this could "only have been caused by alcohol." A full inquest was to be held on 15th September at Westminster.

When news of Yootha's death hit Australia, Rodney MacNeil, the television interviewer who had worked with her, told me "we very surprised to read that she had had a supposed problem with alcohol; not unknown in the acting profession but totally unobserved by those of us on the TV panel that day."

Yootha's funeral took place on 3rd September at Golders Green Crematorium: her ashes were scattered on the crocus lawn; plot 3P. The press and television news teams covered the event. Among the mourners at the funeral were those close to Yootha, Glynn Edwards and his son Tom, Brian Murphy, Sheila Fearn, Nicholas Bond Owen, Roy Kinnear, Jenny Hanley and Tessa Wyatt. Among the flowers and tributes was one from Bruce Forsyth and his then wife Anthea Redfern, who sent a wreath with the message "to a very special lady."

With any death, there are feelings of numbness and shock, but for someone so full of life and still relatively young passing so suddenly, it was particularly hard to take in. The circumstances of her death, too, and her ability to hide her drinking and other sadnesses came as a shock for her ex-husband Glynn, who couldn't believe reports that she drank one or two bottles of brandy a day: "at the most she would have half a bottle, which she drank with water. Sometimes she would have wine," he said. "Then when she died of it, it was a terrible shock, and an awful tragedy. I don't want the same to happen to me." It was later reported that Glynn was "secretly terrified of meeting an early death," "and so cut back on the booze." "Sometimes when I see other people with glasses in their hand, I really fancy a drink, but I know I'd never just have one, so I grit my teeth and ignore it." Glynn believed that Yootha's relationship with Terry left her "heartbroken" and believed "that's why she drank herself into an early grave. Yootha should have got married again – it would have saved her life. It would have helped if there'd been somebody to see what she was doing. She had lots of boyfriends after me, but nothing lasted."

On the reports of Yootha's dependency on alcohol, Joy Jameson said "I had not an inkling, and I say this now with my hand on my heart." She added "There was definitely not a word from any employers. There had never been a word about Yootha and drinking from Thames TV or ANYONE she'd worked with. Employers would love to speak to agents about ANY problem. They think it gives them clout when next negotiating, and very often it does! I suppose I am one of the people she tried to hide it from... but I'm not daft... I have had three actors (very famous!) who did have drink problems: I guess it's par for the course in our business."

I asked Joy how Yootha's mother coped with her death. She told me "How her mum coped with the news is not known to me. However, it would be clearly tough for a mother to lose her child before her own demise. I know Yootha adored her mum," she said. "If she had been my daughter and I'd known more about what was going on I think I would have had something to say about her treatment at the clinic. You do not take people off alcohol and cigarettes – just like that. The shock to the system must be horrendous. I've always thought that, but she had quite a few people around her and it wasn't my place to kick up a fuss. There are various reasons why I believe if she'd gone into hospital with any problem associated with drink she'd be with us now. If you have someone with an alcohol problem why didn't they gradually take her off alcohol? What a shock to the system too to be deprived of cigarettes... that was what we were worrying about. Today, if that was the problem she'd have been in the Priory Clinic and it would have been sorted. Not that it would have helped anyone to say so...Yootha had passed away. I sometimes wonder if I had not been so concerned with MY family problems if I wouldn't have given that clinic hell." It does seem that Yootha refused treatment early on; later, her problem became so advanced that it may have been too difficult to remedy.

Yootha's solicitor Mario had to organise Yootha's estate on her death: she had left over a hundred thousand pounds. He said at the time that he was "absolutely shattered upon hearing the news of Yootha's drinking, and said "she was a victim of her own success." He found that she became "increasingly depressed by the fear of being typecast as Mildred Roper, the bossy wife, but no one suspected she was a heavy drinker; she was always clear-headed and knew her lines when she took to stage or film set. She was a professional." He also said, "although I couldn't disbelieve the evidence of her alcoholism, I had cleared her flat and had found none of the tell-tale signs of a heavy drinker. I found one unopened bottle of brandy and the normal bottles found in every home. There

were no hidden stores of alcohol or off-licence receipts."
The main inquest was held on 16th September; its main findings were that
Yootha "drank upwards of half a bottle of brandy a day for at least ten years,
and died a chronic alcoholic." The doctor at the clinic, Dr Ian Murray Lyon,
noted that when Miss Joyce had been admitted to the Harley Street clinic, he had
discovered that she had been drinking half a bottle of spirits a day for ten years,
and recently very much more." The pathologist, Dr Rufus Crompton, also
revealed that "Miss Joyce's liver was twice the normal size, and her heart and
lungs had also suffered because of her drinking. Her condition could have only
been brought on by chronic drinking for a long period. She had many symptoms
showing ten years of regular excessive drinking."

Peter Errington told me he thought: "Yootha was very depressed. Thinking
about it now, you have amazing amazing highs in the business and then of
course the tragic lows: the thing with Yootha is that she was on a very
comfortable – shall we say high – before she died, but her body could only take
so much I suppose."
Brian Murphy remembered, "It was very sad, and it took me a long time to get
over it. There was a huge postbag of letters and cards that got sent into the
office, and the public were very kind, they were genuinely distraught as they
actually regarded us as man and wife. One letter suggested we carry on with
George as a widow, but the writers thought it was too early, and I did as well,
but it may have worked in time."

Murray Melvin, talking of Yootha's drinking, said "She had made a lot of
money in her career so had the wherewithal to destroy herself. Brian tried
desperately to get her off it, but when she was in hospital all she wanted was the
bottle. I never knew about it and I wonder whether anybody has gotten to the
bottom of why she died. She had great success, but there was a destructiveness
within her somewhere: with some people there seems to be some gene which
destroys! And of course a lot of alcohol problems are hereditary; you never
know what triggers it though; where did it all go wrong?" Somewhat in contrast,
Christine Pilgrim thought: "Yootha's loneliness after the split with Terry might
have led to self-destruction. It certainly led to her drinking more heavily. But I
don't think she was always self-destructive. In fact, I think she was quite
resilient in the early days."

Talking a few years later Brian said "if only I had realised she had a problem
and done something to help her. I was one of her closest friends – but I didn't do
enough. Although we were close Yootha never really confided in me. Looking
back I should have realised there was a problem, but I didn't. She relied on
booze to cope with her failed marriage to Glynn, followed by a doomed love
affair with Terry. And she hid away to hide from her incredible fame. But she
put up a brave front to hide the suffering from her close personal friends."

CHAPTER 36

Since Yootha's death her appearances have never been off the television screen. However, apart from a few guest appearances on some shows such as *Give us a Clue* and the Max Bygraves show, *Max*, she has only appeared as the brilliant Mildred Roper; of course, the programmes still reached large audiences, but I think it is a great shame that programme schedulers have ignored a great deal of her work history. The studio space had been booked for recording *George and Mildred*'s final series in December 1980. Instead, Brian Murphy and Roy Kinnear starred in a new series, *The Incredible Mr Tanner*, about an escapologist. According to Brian Murphy, it was sad making the series, as Yootha's presence was still keenly felt. The show also went against *Hi De Hi* in the ratings, and was short lived.

A great deal has been said about Yootha's final appearance in *Max*, which wasn't broadcast until some time later, in January 1981. Most of the reporting seems to be inaccurate. It has often been said that she sang the Carpenters' song *'For All We Know,'* a "fact" duly noted on *Wikipedia*, and reported in *The New York Times*. This is untrue; she actually sang the Fred Coots and Sam Lewis song *'For All We Know (We May Never Meet Again)'* with the final line "Tomorrow may never come for all we know," which gave the number an extra poignancy.

Kenneth Williams remembered the broadcast of the *Max* show in his diaries, recording, on Wednesday 14th January 1981: "it looked like she was crying, at the end of the number she got up and said to Max, thanks that was good of you and she walked off the stage, [she actually said to Max, "I love you, I really really love you"] one had the feeling she never intended to return, we know from the inquest she had a drink problem, but all I know is that I worked with her and found her totally professional and very loveable, she showed no sign of either the drink problem or the turmoil that caused it." Years later, on 9th April 1988, not long before his own death, he added "can't get Yootha Joyce out of my head – and the time she sang *'For All We Know,'* there was almost a break in the voice when she got to tomorrow may never come, but she carried on. She died shortly after. A lady who made so many people happy and a lady who never complained."

Barbara Windsor said to me that with Kenneth "there were never any false praises, and if he mentioned her, he must have been impressed."

Joy Jameson told me she thought "this 'contractual' duty to appear on programmes like these was 'horrible'. You know the thing: to be seen as not dead – you have to do them." It is strange, though, that Yootha was to sing in this performance, the very thing that her family said she was not very good at! When asked by Bygraves if she could sing, she replied "well, I'm no Kate Bush."

Yootha was glamorous as usual on this show, but what was concerning was a rasping chest and some clear weight loss. What was worrying too was the insistence on being associated with the part of Mildred in a small routine written by Eric Davidson, the very role that was holding her back.

Joy told me that she thought Yootha would have "been a good Mrs. Danvers in Daphne Du Maurier's *Rebecca* but she was too popular in comedy roles. Until *George and Mildred* ended: did it really end? I can never remember a time that I was told it had ended. Maybe if Yootha had not died so young it would have continued? We were still having meetings about the series. She would never have turned anything down that was 'different'. You must remember that she was very busy from *Man About the House* onwards into *George and Mildred*. Then there were the summer seasons; I can remember Bournemouth and Jersey. Huge theatres, and standing room only. Of course she would have liked to have played lots of different roles after Mildred, but there just wasn't the time between the end of Mildred and her death. Truly... because she was a 'name', all the management wanted her to tour... why wasn't she keen on that? Being away from central London... leaving the dog? I don't know."

Talking to Dudley Sutton about Yootha's troubles finding other work, he said; "Television is a dangerous game for really creative actors. I am going to include myself in there, having come out through Joan Littlewood. But I found when I was doing the series *Lovejoy*... creatively, I found it to be extremely frustrating. But in terms of coping with this myself, I think I had already sorted out my own drink problem by then, which Yootha found extremely amusing, in a patronising way, as drunks tend to do. But being stuck in *George and Mildred*, well that's you done for! I didn't work in television for four years after *Lovejoy* finished. If it was America, I would have been working on another show, but that doesn't happen here in the UK."

Joan Littlewood once told me that in her opinion, "it was the endless repetition of *George and Mildred* which killed Yootha." When I mentioned this to Barbara Windsor she said: "Oh yes I'm sure Yootha's success wouldn't have sat well with Joan, Joan would have hated that." Indeed when Brian Murphy featured on his own *This is Your Life* programme for the BBC in the 1990s, Joan's contribution to him began with "what are you doing there?"

Joan told me that she thought at Theatre Workshop "Both Brian and Yootha were beautiful artists in a unique company – unfortunately the exhilaration of working creatively could not compensate forever financial hardship and reluctantly, Brian, Yootha AND Harry H. Corbett accepted TV work – They did not foresee the years of repetitive work they were letting themselves in for. In my opinion it was this repetition which was responsible for Yootha's decline and death."

She also told me, "With us, she would have created character after character - and did – but TV can mean money and publicity and both can kill."

When I enquired about preparing a piece on Yootha's success for an issue for the *Yootha Joyce Memorial Society* magazine, Brian Murphy told me that: "The price of success can be very high, and while it lasts, we can be misled into believing that success was all that we had strived for and easily forget integrity and humanity.

Recognition and popularity bring a loss of privacy and independence, which also means a loss of one's individuality – ironically, the very things that may make an actor unique. We shall never know, and I myself, having been a close friend as well as a working partner, feel this ignorance deeply, what unhappiness Yootha suffered during her last months – maybe she had just lost her way again?"

When I asked Dudley how he dealt with his own success in *Lovejoy*, he told me, "I don't have it! When Harry H. Corbett did *Steptoe*, he virtually destroyed his career. It's similar to what happened to Yootha, because he was a very fine classical actor, and once he'd done *Steptoe*, he couldn't walk on to the stage in London because people were saying, 'there's Steptoe,' and that's the fault of the business. People like Harry and Arthur Lowe, who was in line for the lead as George Smiley in *Tinker, Tailor, Soldier, Spy*, and who I thought would have been a hell of a lot better than Alec Guinness, didn't get the part because he was 'too well known for comedy,' so the chance for a challenging role was denied him. When I was working myself on television in the 1960s, I had worked with Norman Wisdom and Cilla Black, and the BBC just wouldn't let you do what I called 'senior English,' so the things I really love, like Shakespeare, Chekhov, Shaw and Wilde, well, they're simply not offered. I am hardly offered anything on television now except 'cardigan jobs' in old folks homes! You're meant to just sit there and dribble. I'm sure Yootha would have experienced this crap too. But I've told my agent I'm not doing television until they come up with something a bit more grown up. They're bastards you know, they really are. The people I've always worked best with are the outsiders, like Joan Littlewood, Ken Russell, Derek Jarman and Sam Wanamaker."

When I asked Yootha's co-star Nicholas Bond Owen: "Apart from featuring as Charley Bates in *Oliver Twist*, did you find a life of proving your versatility as an actor too demanding?" he replied: "No, not really, I was actually cast in more roles later on in my career that were cockney or working-class characters than upper class, I found that when I was getting older it was harder to compete for adult roles as I was so lucky as a young boy that most people knew me, and my experience in *George and Mildred* enabled me to get a huge amount of commercials off the back of my character, but once I grew up a bit and got uglier it seemed to get harder to get work and I had to work twice as hard to get new roles. It reached the stage where acting became a chore. I loved doing *George and Mildred* and Brian and Yootha were smashing, for me it meant working virtually every weekend and I missed a lot of school. I'd still like to get back into television one day, but as a writer rather than a performer. I dropped the name 'Bond' and also the glasses, my eyes are better now. In fact I only needed them until I was ten, but they we kept them in the show as a prop. I do watch *George and Mildred* from time to time; they're politically incorrect at times but great fun, though I do cringe whenever I see Tristram."

CHAPTER 37

Memories of Yootha and her legacy are still with us now, many years after her death. Some of her performances, including all those on *Man about the House* and *George and Mildred*, are available on DVD to anyone, fans included, who wants to see how versatile she was. For those that haven't appeared, it's clearly a case of forwarding requests for their releases from those who hold the rights. Ultimately though, Yootha was famous as Mildred Roper, and we can't doubt that Mildred was her greatest achievement. Even as I write, repeats of the shows Mildred featured in continue to be shown on ITV 3. Sally Thomsett, for instance, thinks that *Man About The House* is still funny today. There have also been many versions of *Man About The House*, including versions in Sweden, Russia and Poland. There have been dubbed versions around the world, including Spain and Italy, where curiously, they replaced the famous "Prune Brandy" with "Cherry Brandy," which seems to miss the British sense of toilet humour entirely! In 2001 ITV broadcast a half-hour documentary with some reminiscences of those who knew her and worked with her.

Yootha's Mildred role has had such an impact that it has reached further into different artistic genres, as well as being taken up by new generations of fans. Famously, "The Smiths" used an image of Yootha on their 1986 record cover *Ask*. In David Bret's book *Morrissey: Scandal & Passion*, he said that "some thought that by using Joyce on the cover of the single *Ask /Cemetery Gates*. That Morrissey was offering a veiled warning to Johnny Marr to curb his own drinking."

The Australian poet Jude Aquilina was inspired by Yootha to write a poem on her too. She generously allowed me to reproduce it here. When I asked her for some insight into the thinking behind the poem, she said: "I wanted to capture the timelessness of the faces and people in front bars – in those no-frills local drinking-holes, where salt of the earth characters talk, laugh, bet, listen to music and, of course, drink alcohol. I think these characters span over centuries and continue to grace the bars of the UK and Australia. I chose Sid James because of his wonderfully wrinkled face, and his twinkling smile – a face you see in pubs, under a haze of cigarette smoke, telling a yarn to a group of merry listeners. I could have just as well chosen Bob Hawke, our past Prime Minister! The Buddhas are the beer-gutted ones; while the Jesus look-alikes have long hair and beards (and, these days, tattoos and orange vests). In the poem, the face of Yootha Joyce represents those thin, pretty, blonde women you often see enjoying a night at the pub. They smile and chat to everyone – always friendly and well groomed, yet perhaps existing on a diet more liquid than solid. To me, Yootha had this look, compounded by her role as Mildred, so she seemed like the perfect addition to the poem."

Jude Aquilina

"In the Queen's Arms"

Every town's front bar has its
Sid James, Yootha Joyce, a Jesus lookalike
and a couple of Buddhas
From the white hats of bowlers
to the blue singlets and bikie jackets
characters recycle each generation
knocking back a nip, a pony or a pint
of whatever the era ferments

Music swirls from a jukebox
local fiddlers, pipers
get stompers and songsters going.
Storytellers cite comic tragedies
self-heroes battle and disappear.
Each Friday night in that bitter happy hour
punters float in a stream of ale,
clear spirits, betting slips.

Sometimes, a violin and tin whistle
transform stone walls
into mirrors of past:
beaten copper plaques
of semi-stoic men with mugs,
a laughing skirt at their side
Jesus, Yootha, Sid and Buddhas
all smiling from behind.

I was also amazed to see Mildred's fashion sense appearing in *Vogue*, no less. Designer Katie Briggs kindly allowed me to use some of the sketches and images from her "Yootha" collection and told me: "I grew up watching *George and Mildred*. My parents were teenagers in the 70's, and introduced me to the many great sitcoms of the time. When I decided to study fashion, I found myself looking to this fun and flamboyant decade for inspiration. I chose interiors of the 1970's as the concept for my final collection at university, and Yootha Joyce became my muse. Her fabulous ensembles were the inspiration behind the feel and style of my collection: pastel colours, jumpsuits, vibrant patterns, extreme femininity and absolute power! I greatly admire the character Yootha portrayed, and I knew that I wanted the girls who would be wearing my clothes to reflect Mildred's gutsy attitude and incredible wit. My collection, 'Yootha', was selected to be shown at Graduate Fashion Week, and was then short-listed for the Gold Award. Thank you, Yootha!"

When I told Zelie Armstrong, who worked in the costume department at Thames TV about the "Yootha" collection, she said: "The fashion industry draws on many influences and it isn't surprising that the garish styles created for Mildred are a source of inspiration. I think it is testament to both Lyn Harvey and Yootha that they are remembered for this work and I think Yootha would have considered it hilarious to see the designs used for fashion today, many of which she found extreme."

So although Yootha left us many years back, her presence is still around. How will she be remembered? A comedienne? An actress? A celebrity? A fashion icon? Whatever the case, she was without doubt an original, a lovely lady. Those who knew her recall someone honest, loyal, well-liked, a woman interested in everyone, at times frosty, but firm, generous and caring. To her agent Joy Jameson, "Yootha was always good fun. I doubt if she had a mean bone in her body. I'm going to stop this because it's making me cry. You've made me recollect the good times." Brian Murphy said, I'm sure we would be doing sell out shows now if Yootha were still alive." Barbara Windsor told me "Every time I walk past her little basement flat in Paddington, I give a little wave, even now." But, as she rightly pointed out about Yootha, "you could never quite get her." After all this time, I wonder if I managed to "get her" either; but for that matter, do we find it that easy to "get" ourselves?

Interviews and publicity, on tour 1979.

New Zealand Tour, 1979.

Yootha's flat in Sussex Gardens, as it is today.

Australia Tour 1979.

**Yootha, summer
1980.**

Yootha Joyce 1927-1980.

Image courtesy The
Durrell Wildlife Trust.

'Yootha' collection by
Katie Briggs. Images
Courtesy Katie Briggs

APPENDIX A

Yootha Joyce: Theatre (Known) *Denotes Theatre Workshop
1979
George & Mildred. Australasian Tour. Johnnie Mortimer & Brian Cooke
Role - Mildred Roper
1977-78
George & Mildred. UK Tour. Johnnie Mortimer & Brian Cooke
Role - Mildred Roper
1976-77
Cinderella. [ad. Bryan Blackburn]
Role - Mildred
1975
Boeing, Boeing. Marc Camoletti [ad. Beverly Cross]
Role - Bertha (The Maid)
1972
The Londoners. Stephen Lewis *
Role - Bridgie Judd
1967
The Man in the Glass Booth. Robert Shaw
Role - Mrs Rosen
1964
Signpost To Murder. Monte Douglas
Role - Sally Thomas
1962
Fings Aint Wot They Used T'be. Frank Norman/Lionel Bart
Role - (As Assistant Director – Manchester)
1961
Fings Aint Wot They Used T'be. * [West End Transfer]
Role 1. - Murtle
Role 2. - The Brass Upstairs
Role 3. - Policewoman
1960
Fings Aint Wot They Used T'be. * [West End Transfer]
Role 1. - Murtle
Role 2. - The Brass Upstairs
Role 3. - Policewoman
The Hostage. Brendan Behan * [West End Transfer]
Role - Collette
1959
Fings Aint Wot They Used T'be. * [Cast recording on CD. Hallmark (2011)]
Role 1. - Murtle
Role 2. - The Brass Upstairs
Role 3. - Policewoman
The Hostage. *
Role - Collette
The Dutch Courtesan. John Marston *
Role - Mistress Mulligrub
1958
Celestina. Fernando de Rojas *
Role - Lucrezia
The Respectful Prostitute Jean-Paul Sartre*
Role - Lizzie
A Christmas Carol. Charles Dickens *
Role 1. - Ghost Of Christmas Past
Role 2. - Mrs Trossit
1957
Playboy Of The Western World. J. M. Synge *
Role - Susan Brady
Duchess Of Malfi. John Webster *
Role - Julia
By Candlelight. Harry Graham
Role - Unknown
1956
Good Soldier Schweik. Jaroslav Hašek. *
Role - Unknown? (Small part)
Captain Brassbound's Conversion. George B. Shaw *
Role - (As Box Office Manager)
Treasure Island. Robert. L. Stevenson *
Role - (As Box Office Manager)
1955
Murder at the Vicarage. Agatha Christie

Role - Anne Protheroe
Call Of The Flesh. Rex Howard Arundel
Role - Stella Loman
1953
Wide Boy. Ian Stuart
Role - Clara
Charlie's Uncle. Author Unknown
Role - Sylvia
The Gift. Author Unknown
Role - Unknown
The Deep Blue Sea. Terence Rattigan.
Role - Unknown
The Happy Prisoner. Author Unknown
Role - Farm Girl
Our Family. Author Unknown
Role - Unknown
Widows Are Dangerous. Author Unknown
Role - Unknown
Autumn Crocus. Dodie Smith
Role - Unknown
Music For Murder. Author Unknown
Role - Priscilla
Born Yesterday. Garson Kanin
Role - Billie
The Outsider. Dorothy Brandon
Role - The Crippled Girl.
Smilin' Through. A.L. Martin
Role - Unknown
Worm's Eye View. R.F. Delderfield
Role - Unknown
Maiden Ladies. E.V. Hoile & G. Paxton.
Role - Unknown
Murder Mistaken. Janet Green
Role - Unknown
Wild Horses. Ben Travers
Role - Iris
Relative Values. Noel Coward
Role Unknown
Waters Of The Moon. N.C. Hunter
Role - Unknown
My Wife's Lodger. Dominic Roche
Role - Unknown
Having A Wonderful Time. Author Unknown
Role - Unknown
Glad Tidings. R.F. Denderfield
Role - Unknown
1952
The Young In Heart. Derek Benfield
Role - Teenager
Heaven And Charing Cross. Author Unknown
Role - Unknown
The Happy Marriage. John Clements
Role - Unknown
1951
Peace Comes to Peckham. R.F Delderfield
Role - Grace
Nothing But The Truth. James Montgomery
Role - Unknown
The Light of Heart. Emlyn Williams
Role - Unknown
Mountain Air. Author Unknown
Role -Unknown
Night Must Fall. Emlyn Williams
Role - Unknown
Grand National Night. Campell & Dorothy Christie
Role - Babs
A Lady Mislaid. Kenneth Horne
Role - Unknown
The Perfect Woman. Wallace Geoffrey
Role - Unknown
The Seventh Veil. S & M Box
Role - Unknown

Mother Of Men. Ada G. Abbott
Role - Unknown
1949
Hay Fever. Noel Coward
Role - Unknown
1948
Humoresque. Fanny Hurst
Role - Peony Barker
1946-48?
ENSA tours, (No Records)
The Merchant of Venice. William Shakespeare
Role - Portia? (Unknown)
1946
You Cant Take It With You. Moss Hart & George Kaufman.
Role. - Essie
She Stoops To Conquer. Oliver Goldsmith
Role. - Kate Hardcastle
1945
Pride and Prejudice. Jane Austin
Role - Lydia Bennet
Henry V. William Shakespeare
Role 1.- Archbishop of Canterbury
Role 2.- Private John Bates
This Happy Breed. Noel Coward
Role - Sylvia
Escape Me Never. Margaret Kennedy
Role - Girl
Autumn Crocus. Dodie Smith
Role - The Young Lady Living in Sin, (also credited as A.S.M.)
Cymbeline. William Shakespeare
Role 1. - Lord
Role 2. - Imogen
Heartbreak House . George Bernard Shaw
Role. - Lady Utterwood

APPENDIX B
Yootha Joyce, Film, TV and Radio (Known)
1981
Max (TV)
Role - Herself
1980
George & Mildred (F)
Role - Mildred Roper
Give Us a Clue (TV)
- Episode (1980)
Role - Herself
-Episode (1980)
Role - Herself
1979
Give Us a Clue (TV)
- 2 Episodes (1979)
Role - Herself
Radio 1 Roadshow (Radio)
Role - Herself
The 21st Annual TV Week Logie Awards (TV) [Australia]
Role - Herself
Ten Celebrity Interviews (TV) [Australia]
Role - Herself
Ten Townsville News (TV) [Australia]
Role - Herself
The Mike Walsh Show (TV) [Australia]
- Episode 9139
Role - Herself
1977
Star Turn (TV)
Role - Herself
1976-1979
George & Mildred (TV) (38 Episodes)
Series 1 Episodes

- 06/09/76   Moving On
- 13/09/76   The Bad Penny
- 20/09/76   ... And Women Must Weep
- 27/09/76   Baby Talk
- 04/10/76   Your Money or Your Life
- 11/10/76   Where My Caravan Has Rested
- 18/10/76   The Little Dog Laughed
- 25/10/76   Best Foot Forward
- 01/11/76   My Husband Next Door
- 08/11/76   Family Planning
Series 2 Episodes
- 14/11/77   Jumble Pie
- 21/11/77   All Around the Clock
- 28/11/77   The Travelling Man
- 05/12/77   The Unkindest Cut of All
- 12/12/77   The Right Way to Travel
- 19/12/77   The Dorothy Letters
- 26/12/77   No Business Like Show Business
Series 3 Episodes
- 07/09/78   Opportunity Knocks
- 14/09/78   And So to Bed
- 21/09/78   I Believe in Yesterday
- 28/09/78   The Four Letter Word
- 05/10/78   The Delivery Man
- 02/10/78   Life with Father
Series 4 Episodes
- 16/11/78   Just the Job
- 23/11/78   Days of Beer and Rosie
- 30/11/78   You Must Have Showers
- 07/12/78   All Work and No Pay
- 14/12/78   Nappy Days
- 21/12/78   The Mating Game
- 27/12/78   On the Second Day of Christmas
Series 5 Episodes
- 24/10/79   Finders Keepers?
- 30/10/79   In Sickness & in Health
- 06/11/79   The Last Straw
- 13/11/79   A Driving Ambition
- 27/11/79   A Military Pickle
- 04/12/79   Fishy Business
- 18/12/79   I Gotta Horse
- 25/12/79   The Twenty Six Year Itch
Role - Mildred Roper
1976
The Wednesday Special: Pub Entertainer of the Year
Role - Herself (Judge)
Whodunit? (TV)
- A Bad Habit
Role - Herself
Looks Familiar (TV)
Role - Herself
Nobody Does It Like Marti [Caine] (TV
Series 1 Episode 6
Role - Herself
The David Nixon Show (TV)
- Series 7 Episode 5
Role - Herself - Guest
Those Wonderful TV Times (TV)
- Series 3 Episode 1
Role - Herself
The TV Times Top Ten Awards (TV)
Role – Herself
1973-1976
Man About the House (TV) (39 Episodes)
Series 1 Episodes
- 15/08/73   Three's a Crowd
- 22/08/73   And Mother Makes Four
- 29/08/73   Some Enchanted Evening
- 05/09/73   And Then There Were Two
- 12/09/73   It's Only Money
- 19/09/73   Match of the Day
- 26/09/73   No Children, No Dogs

- 25/12/73 SPECIAL SKETCH (see All Star Comedy Carnival (1973)
Series 2 Episodes
- 09/01/74   While the Cat's Away
- 16/01/74   Colour Me Yellow
- 23/01/74   In Praise of Older Men
- 30/01/74   Did You Ever Meet Rommel?
- 06/02/74   Two Foot Blue, Eyes of Blue
- 13/02/74   Carry Me Back to Old Southampton
Series 3 Episodes
- 09/10/74   Cuckoo in the Nest
- 16/10/74   Come into My Parlour
- 23/10/74   I Won't Dance, Don't Ask Me
- 30/10/74   Of Mice and Women
- 06/11/74   Somebody Out There Likes Me
- 13/11/74   We Shall Not Be Moved
- 20/11/74   Three of a Kind
Series 4 Episodes
- 06/03/75   Home and Away
- 13/03/75   One for the Road
- 20/03/75   All in the Game
- 27/03/75   Never Give Your Real Name
- 03/04/75   The Tender Trap
- 10/04/75   My Son, My Son
Series 5 Episodes
- 04/09/75   The Last Picture Show
- 11/09/75   Right Said George
- 18/09/75   A Little Knowledge
- 25/09/75   Love and Let Love
- 02/10/75   How Does Your Garden Grow?
- 09/10/75   Come Fly with Me
Series 6 Episodes
- 25/02/76   The Party's Over
- 03/03/76   One More for the Pot
- 10/03/76   The Generation Game
- 17/03/76   The Sunshine Boys
- 24/03/76   Mum Always Liked You Best
- 31/03/76   Fire Down Below
- 07/04/76   Another Bride Another Groom
Role - Mildred Roper
1975
(Christmas) Celebrity Squares (TV)
Role - Herself
1974
Man About the House (F)
Role - Mildred Roper
The Dick Emery Show (TV)
 - Series 4 Episode 12
Role - Vicars Wife
1973
All Star Comedy Carnival (TV)
Role - Mildred Roper
This Is Your Life: (TV)
 - George Sewell
Role - Herself
Frankenstein: The True Story (TV)
Role - Hospital Matron; Mrs McGregor
Steptoe and Son Ride Again (F)
Role - Freda - Lennie's Wife
On the Buses (TV)
 - The Allowance
Role - Jessie
7 of 1 (TV)
 - Open All Hours
Role - Mrs Scully
Never Mind the Quality: Feel the Width (F)
Role - Mrs Finch
1963-1973
Comedy Playhouse (TV)
 - Home from Home (1973)
Role - Lil Wilson
 - Me Mammy (1968)
Role - Miss. Argyle

- A Clerical Error (1963)
Role - Rita
- Impasse (1963)
Role - Mrs. Spooner
1972
Tarbuck's Luck (TV)
Unknown Episode?
Role - Herself
Tales From The Lazy Acre (TV)
- The Last Great Pint Drinking Tournament
Role - Mrs Gaynor (English Landlady)
The Fenn Street Gang (TV)
- The Woman for Dennis
Role - Glenda
Jason King (TV)
- If It's Got to Go, It's Got to Go
Role - Sister Dryker
Burke & Hare (F)
Role - Mrs. Hare
Nearest and Dearest (F)
Role - Mrs. Rhoda Rowbottom
1968-1971
Me Mammy (TV) (21 Episodes)
Pilot (See *Comedy Playhouse*) (Deleted)
Series 1 (Deleted) Episodes
- 15/09/69 The Day We Blessed the Bench
- 22/09/69 The Day Verilia Went to Pieces
- 29/09/69 The Night Me Mammy Snuffed It
- 13/10/69 The Day the Saints Went Marching Out
- 20/10/69 The First Time I Saw Paris
- 27/10/69 The Day Concepta Got Engaged
Series 2 (Deleted) Episodes
- 07/08/70 The Night Miss Argyll Got Canonised
- 14/08/70 Me Mammys Tomb
- 21/08/70 The Night We Saw Old Nick
- 28/08/70 The Last of the Red Hot Mammies
- 04/09/70 The Night Edna Entered a Convent
- 11/09/70 The Night I Left the Church
- 18/09/70 The Morning After Finnegans Wake
Series 3 Episodes
- 23/04/71 The Day We Went Dutch
- 30/04/71 The Night the Banshee Brought Me Home
- 07/05/71 The Day I Got Engaged
- 14/05/71 The Day I Went Commercial.
- 21/05/71 The Sacred Chemise of Miss Argyll.
- 28/05/71 The Mammy Murder Case
- 11/06/71 How To Be a Mammy In Law (Postponed from 4/6/71)
Role - Miss Argyll
1971
The Night Digger (F)
Role - Mrs. Palafox
All the Right Noises (F)
Role - Mrs. Bird - Landlady
1970
Conceptions of Murder (TV)
- Peter and Maria
Role - Maria Kurten
Fragment of Fear (F)
Role - Miss Ward-Cadbury
The Misfit (TV)
- On Reading the Small Print
Role - Pamela
Manhunt (TV)
- Fare Forward, Voyagers
Role - Denise
1964 -1969
Dixon of Dock Green (TV)
- Reluctant Witness (1969)
Role - Mrs. Harper
- You Can't Buy a Miracle (1966)
Role - Joyce Watson
- Forsaking All Others (1965)

Role - Landlady
 - The Night Man (1964)
Role - Mabel Davies
 - Child Hunt (1964)
Role - Mrs. Gates
1969
W. Somerset Maugham (TV)
 - Lord Mountdrago
Role - Elvira
ITV Sunday Night Theatre (TV)
 - A Measure of Malice
Role - Erica Seydoux
BBC Play of the Month (TV)
 - Maigret at Bay
Role - Mademoiselle Motte
1962-1969
Armchair Theatre (TV)
 - Go on... It'll Do You Good (1969)
Role - Alice
 - The Fishing Match (1962)
Role - Cissy
Twenty Nine (TV)
Role - The Prostitute
1968
ITV Playhouse (TV)
 - Your Name's Not God, It's Edgar
Role 1. -Phoebe
Role 2. -Mrs. Bewley
City 68' (TV)
 - Love Thy Neighbour
Role - Hilda
Luther (TV)
Role - Katharina Luther
1967
Harry Worth (TV)
- Four's a Crush
Role - Ingrid
Market In Honey Lane (TV)
- The Birds And The Business
Role - Unknown
1965-1967
The Wednesday Play (TV)
 - An Officer of the Court (1967)
Role - Miriam Green (a bird)
 - Little Master Mind (1966)
Role - Miriam Green
 - The Portsmouth Defence (1966)
Role - Miriam Green
 - The Confidence Course (1965)
Role - Rosalind Arnold
1967
Charlie Bubbles (F)
Role - Woman in Cafe
Our Mother's House (F)
Role - Mrs. Quayle
Stranger in the House (F)
Role - Shooting Range Girl
The Avengers (TV)
 - Something Nasty in the Nursery
Role - Miss Lister
Thirty-Minute Theatre (TV)
 - Teeth
Role - Agnes
Turn Out The Lights (TV)
 - A Big Hand for a Little Lady
Role - Monica Nolan
1966
George And The Dragon (TV)
 - Merry Christmas
Role - Irma
A Man for All Seasons (F)
Role - Averil Machin

The Saint (TV)
- The Russian Prisoner
Role - Milanov
Love Story (TV)
- The Public Duck
Role - Mrs. Barker
Kaleidoscope (F)
Role - Museum Receptionist
No Hiding Place (TV)
- Ask Me If I Killed Her
Role - Hilda Myers
1965
Theatre 625 (TV)
- Portraits from the North: The Nutter
Role - Miss Binnington
- Try for White (1965)
Role - Jane Matthews.
1963-1965
Steptoe And Son (TV/Radio)
- A Box in Town (1965)
Role - Avis
- The Bonds That Bind Us (1964) (Radio version only)
Role - Madge
- The Bath (1963)
Role – Delia
1965
Six of the Best (TV)
- Charlie's Place
Role - Doris
The Wednesday Thriller (TV)
- The Babysitter
Role - Mrs. Seam
Cluff (TV)
- The Convict
Role - Flo Darby
Catch Us If You Can (F)
Role - Nan
Fanatic (F)
Role - Anna
Frankie Howerd (TV)
- Episode 6
Role - Drunk Woman
1962-1964
Z Cars (TV)
- First Foot (1964)
Role - Grace
- The Main Chance (1963)
Role - Mrs. Gilroy
- Full Remission (1962)
Role - Clara Smales
1964
BBC 2 Play (Unknown Play Series Title) (TV)
- A Traveling Woman
Role - Ruth Cowley
Redcap (TV)
- A Town Called Love
Role - Magda
Diary of a Young Man (TV)
- Money
Role - Mrs. Baggerdagger
ITV Play of the Week (TV)
- Gina (1964)
Role - Vera Maine
- I Can Walk Where I Like Can't I? (1964)
Role - The Woman
- A Tricycle Made For Two (1964
Role 1. - Marylyn
Role 2. - Cecily Tarrant
Role 3. - Jane Willows
The Pumpkin Eater (F)
Role - Woman At Hairdressers
1962-1963

Benny Hill (TV)
 - Mr. Apollo (1963)
Role - Elvira Crudd
 - Cry of Innocence (1962)
Role - Bella
1963
A Place to Go (F)
Role - Bit Role (uncredited)
Corrigan Blake (TV)
 - The Removal Men
Role - Abigail
Sparrows Can't Sing (F)
Role - Barmaid
1962
Brothers in Law (TV)
 - Separation Order
Role - Mrs. Trench

SELECT BIBLIOGRAPHY

Books;
Aquilina, Jude. *On a Moon Spiced Night.* (Wakefield Press. 2004.) p.6.
Barry, David. *Flashback - An Actor's Life.* (Authors Online Publishing. 2006.)
Bret, David. *Morrissey: Scandal & Passion.* (Robson Books. 2004.) p.80-81.
Cooke, Brian. *Writing Comedy for Television.* (Methuen Publishing. 1983.) p16-17.
Clunn, Harold P. *The Face of London,* (London. 1956.)
Fisher, Tex. *Man About the House - George and Mildred: The Definitive Companion.* (Deckchair Publishing. 2010.)
Forsyth, Bruce. *Bruce: The Autobiography.* (Pan Books. 2012.)
Gresham, Carl. *The Gresh – A Lifetime in Show-Biz.* (Bank House Books. 2009.)
Jeffery, David. *Petersfield at War:* (http://www.suttonpublishing.co.uk. 1980.)
Littlewood, Joan. *Joan's Book: Joan Littlewood's Peculiar History as She Tells It.* (Bloomsbury Methuen Drama, an imprint of Bloomsbury Publishing Plc. 2003.) p.514.
Meades, Jonathan. *This is Their Lives,* (Salamander Books. 1980.) p.71
Meikle, Denis. *A History of Horrors: The Rise and Fall of the House of Hammer,* (Scarecrow Press Inc. 2009.)
Phoenix, Pat. *All My Burning Bridges.* (Arlington Books. 1974.) p.99
Williams, Kenneth. Russell Davies Ed. *The Kenneth Williams Diaries.* (Harper Collins. 1994.) p.626 & 799.
Williams, Kenneth. Russell Davies Ed. *The Kenneth Williams Letters.* (Harper Collins. 1994.) p.201
Windsor Barbara. *All of Me: My Extraordinary Life.* (Headline Publishing. 2001.)
Windsor Barbara. *Barbara, The Laughter and Tears of a Cockney Sparrow.* (Century Publishing. 1990.) p.43.

Newspapers/Magazines;
Blitz Magazine. p.27-30. 05/1985 (Issue 31). Morrissey. Interview With Pat Phoenix.
The Canberra Times. (Reviews) Various dates;-
1) 25/12/1977. p.22. Television by Ian Warden - Oh Those Unfunny Comedies.
2) 18/06/1978. p.24. Anon. George and Mildred, released by Roger Bowdler.
3) 23/12/1979. p.11. Timestyle Article.
4) 26/08/1980. p.15 & p.5.Anon.
The Croydon Advertiser. 27/07/1945. p.2. Anon. 'Escape Me Never', Drama at the Croydon Grand Theatre.
Evening News 28/3/72. p.? First Night Review – Colin Frame. (The Londoners)
The Evening Standard. 27/8/80. Anon. Letters, Yootha Joyce.
Daily Express;-
1) 12/10/79. p? Rook Jean. Yootha's Having Trouble with Mildred.
2) 25/08/80. p.1. The Tragedy of TV's Mildred.
The Independent. 23/09/2002. p.16.Anon. Obituary; Joan Littlewood. *Keighley News.* 29/04/1961. p.12Anon.

Motion Picture Herald. p.201. 1967. Volume 237.

Daily Mirror. 25/8/80. p.14. Anon. Farewell to Yootha -The Lady Who Made Millions Laugh

National Canine Defence League. Newsletters;-
1)1972 (Autumn). 2)1975 (Spring). 3)1976 (Spring). 4)1977 (Autumn) 5)1978 (Autumn). 6)1980 (Autumn).

The Observer (Reviews) Various dates;-
1)p.? 3/3/1957. Anon. 2) p.? 22/2/59. The Inside Story by Michael Croft.
3) 3/05/1959. Anon. The Dutch Courtesan.

Plays and Players (Reviews) Various dates;-
1)4/58. Celestina. Peter Roberts. 2) 12/58.Anon. 3)06/59.Anon.

The Stage [& Television Today] (Reviews) - various dates;-
1) p.7. 28/10/48. 2) p.9. 18/6/49. 3) p.12. 14/06/51. 4) p.12. 31/1/52. 5) p.12. 29/1/53.
6) p.16. 11/5/53. 7) p.12. 28/5/53. 8) p.12. 25/6/53. 9) p.12. 2/7/53. 10) p.12. 6/8/53.
11) p.12. 3/9/53. 12) p.12. 8/10/53. 13) p.12. 26/11/53. 14) p.12. 27.2.57. 15) p.17.
30/4/59. 16) p.17. 21/1/60. 17) p.12. 28/6/62. 18) p.12. 30/7/64. 19) p.15. 22/4/65. 20)
p.12. 9/12/65. 21) p.12. 18/12/65. 22) p.12. 12/12/68. 23) p.12. 10/7/69. 24) p.11.
11/09/69. 25) p.? 30/08/1973. 26) p.9. 20/3/75. 27) p.18. 23/9/76. 28) p.25. 16/12/76.
29) p.23. 13/1/77. 30) p.28. 18/08/77. 31) p. ? 1980. Obituary.

Daily Star, 25.8.80. p.9 Anon. Star Comment.

The Sun, 18/3/88. I Still Blame Myself for Yootha's Death. by Tessa Cunningham.

Sydney Morning Herald p.108. 1/9/63 -TV Merry Go Round.

Daily Telegraph, (Reviews) Various dates;-
1)17/01/1957. Anon. The Theatre Workshop, Playboy of the Western World. 2)p?
17/12/58. Review. 3) 25/3/72 John Barber, Littlewood's Matey Cockney Musical. (The Londoners). 4)22/12/78. Review (*George & Mildred*).
5)*Daily Telegraph Magazine*, p.9. 21/08/70. No, 305. You Know Who They Are, But Who Are They?

Theatre Magazine, p.19. 3/8/67. Lary Spurling (Man In The Glass Booth).

Theatre Quarterly, p.23,24,25 & 26. (spring 1980). No. 37. Brian Murphy; Acting in Television Comedy - From Theatre Workshop to Chart Topping Weekly Sitcom. Clive Barker & Simon Trussler.

Theatre World (Reviews) Various dates;-
1) 08/1959. p.19.Whispers From The Wings, By 'Looker On'. 2) 03/1960. p.14. Anon.

The Times, (Reviews) Various dates;-
1)17/1/57. The Theatre Workshop, Playboy of the Western World.
2)23/2/57. Theatre Royal Stratford E, The Duchess of Malfi' by John Webster.
3)30/04/58. Two Studies of the Deep South. 4)25/04/1959. A Lesson for the Social Realists. 5)p.? 25/04/59. 6)15/08/59. Soho Square Dance at Stratford East.
7)(Review *The Londoners*) ?/?/72. 8)Alan Coren. (Review *Man About The House*) ?/8/73. 9)Alan Coren. (Review *George & Mildred*) 7/9/76.
10)*The Times* 16/9/80. Actress Drank Half a Bottle of Brandy a Day Inquest Told. 11) 30/8/80. Anon. Miss Yootha Joyce.

Titbits,
1) p.12-13 8/4/76. No. 4699. 2) p.28. 19/1/80. Why Peter Keeps It In His Pocket by Peter Robson.

TV Times. ;-
1) p.4,5,6&7. 28/10/1976. (Granada Edition).Coleman Alix. Yootha Joyce - I Never

Cried in Bed and I Never Will.   2) 07/12/1978. p.17-18. Anon. George and Mildred On Tour, The Private Lives of Jogging George and The Fire Lady.   3) 1975. (Granada Edition) Inside TV. Man About the House is Dead, Long Live George & Mildred'. Antony Davis.
4)*TV Times Extra*, 1972. Anon. Roger Moore - The Early Days.
Womans Own. p.10-15 28/6/1980 Why My Young Lover Left Me.
Weekend. Centre Pages. 24/09/1975. Yootha's Problem - The Men Who Misunderstand Her.

Television;
Harty. ITV London Weekend Television. 20/10/1976. [Recording Date]
The Unforgettable Yootha Joyce. ITV North One Media 3/10/2001. [Broadcast Date]
Play It Again; Yootha Joyce. ITV. Tyne Tees Television. 6/5/1980 [Recording Date]

Websites;
http://www.arthurlloyd.co.uk/Hastings.htm. Date Accessed 12/12/2013.
http://www.arthurlloyd.co.uk/Croydon.htm. Date Accessed 12/12/2013.
http://hawkley.ctie.org.uk/Evacuee_history/evacuee's_story.htm. Date Accessed. 10/03/2013.
http://www.janenightwork.com/recollections/the-rada/. Date Accessed 01/01/2014.
http://sounds.bl.uk. Harris Kate. Jean Gaffin, Interview Transcript; Interviewer: 25/04/2007. British Library. Date Accessed 29/09/2013.
http://sounds.bl.uk. Theatre Archive Project. Jean Gaffin on Joan Littlewood. British Library. Date Accessed 29/09/2013.
http://www.thefreelibrary.com/Culture%3A+The+life+of+BRIAN%3B+Brian+Murphy+talks+to+Alison+Jones+about...-a071556327. Date Accessed 12.02.2013.
http://www.writersguild.org.uk/news-a-features/theatre/153-life-with-theatre-workshop.html

FURTHER READING

Barlas, Chris. *Man About the House*. Tv Tie In Publication. (Sphere books. 1977.)
Miles, Barry. *London Calling: A Counter Cultural History of London since 1945*. (Atlantic Books. 2011.)
Bowdler, Roger. *George and Mildred*. Tv Tie In Publication. (Severn House Publishing. 1977.)
Cooke, Brian & Mortimer, Johnnie. *While the Cat's Away* (Stage Show) (Previously titled *George & Mildred*). (Samuel French. 1989.)
The Herald. 15/10/02. Murray Melvin On Joan Littlewood, Neil Cooper.
O'Sullivan, Richard. *Man About the Kitchen*. 1980.
Corbett, Susannah. *Harry H. Corbett – The Front Legs of the Cow*. (The History Press. 2012.)

Galton, Ray, Simpson, Alan & Stevens, Christopher. *The Masters of Sitcom: From Hancock to Steptoe.* (Michael O'Mara books. 2011.)

Melvin, Murray. *The Art of Theatre Workshop.* (Oberon Books. 2006.)

Norman, Frank & Bart, Lionel. *Fings Ain't Wot They Used T'be.* (Samuel French. 1960.)

Newlove, Jean. *Yum Di Dee Dah.* (CreateSpace Publishing. 2013.)

Steafel, Sheila;-

1)*Bastards.* (Fantom Films Publishing. 2012.)

2)*When Harry Met Sheila.* (Apex Publishing. 2010.)

Spinetti, Victor & Rankin, Peter. *Up Front.* (Portico. 2008.)

White, Leonard. *Armchair Theatre: The Lost Years.* (Kelly Publications. 2003.)

Lookin Magazine. 10/1975- 07/1976.

TV Times, Genower Peter. Alfred Lynch; A Man For All Seasons, 1970 P.44-45.

The Scotsman. 30/12/2004. Anon. Raising a Glass to Minder - and Endless Repeats.

The Guardian;-

1)12/08/2013. Anon. The Artwork of the Smiths - In Pictures.

2) 9/1/04. Obituary Alfred Lynch, By Antony Page.

Daily Mail 25/8/80. p.3.TV's Mildred Dies At 53.

News of the World. p.11. 31/8/80. Waterman Ivan. Alan Lake; How Mr Dors Fought the Sad Yootha Trap.

The Stage [& Television Today];-

1)27/10/1977. Anon. Yootha Joyce and Brian Murphy at Imperial Club Party.

2)3/3/1977. Anon. Yootha Joyce.

Shooting Stars Productions. BBC Television. *Omnibus; Joan's Lovely War.* 19/4/1994. [Broadcast Date]

The Sun, 16/9/80.

RELATED WEBSITES AND FURTHER LINKS

http://www.adherents.com/people/pb/Tallulah_Bankhead.html

http://www.angelfire.com/ab7history_doorstep/about.html

http://archive.spectator.co.uk/article/4th-august-1967/19/theatre

http://www.artsthread.com/p/katiebriggs/gallery/my-galleries/Katie%20-Briggs

http://www.ashton-under-lyne.com/history/lilyhulme04.htm

http://www.borehamwoodtimes.co.uk/news/4415013.Whatever_happened_to_Sheila_Fearn_/

http://bufvc.ac.uk/tvandradio/tvtip/index.php/about

http://www.carlgresham.com/html/gresh_biography.html

https:www.christinepilgrim.com

http://www.comedy.co.uk/news/story/00000316/frankie_howerd_1948_show_missing_believed_wiped/

http://www.corsetiere.net/Spirella/Corsetiere/Fitter.htm

http://www.criticsatlarge.ca/2010/02/catch-us-if-you-can-appraisal-of-having.html

http://www.cwgc.org/find/casualty/63995/REVITT,%20ARTHUR%20THOMAS

www.davidbarryauthor.co.uk

http://math.boisestate.edu/gas/whowaswho/index.htm. 'Who Was Who in The D'oyle Carte Opera Company (1875-1982) Date Accessed 31/3/2014.

http://pinafore.www3.50megs.com/artistidx.html. Date Accessed 31/3/2014.
http://collections.vam.ac.uk/item/O35187/costume-design-tingey-cynthia/. Date Accessed 4.08.2013.
http://www.croydononline.org/history/the_war_years/wwii.asp. Date Accessed 22/04/2014.
http://www.dogstrust.org.uk
http://www.dorsetmagazine.co.uk/outabout/places/the_end_of_the_pier_show_in_bourne mouth_1_1634967
www.durrell.org
http://www.entertainment-focus.com/featured-slider/robert-gillespie-interview-beginnings/
http://www.entertainment-focus.com/theatre-review/oedipus-retold-review/
http://es.wikipedia.org/wiki/George_y_Mildred
http://www.evacuees.org.uk/education.html
http://www.ft.com/cms/s/2/16bf4106-0bd9-11e3-8f77-00144feabdc0.html.
https:www.galtonandsimpson.com/
http://www.jamesbooth.org/his_work_theater_table.htm
http://www.jeanettefarrier.com/about.html
http://www.jeannewlove.com/
http://www.independent.co.uk/arts-entertainment/whats-an-actor-worth-1157486.html
http://www.independent.co.uk/news/people/obituary-johnnie-mortimer-1549424.html
http://www.itnsource.com/en/shotlist//ITN/1976/11/03/FS031176008/?s=Yootha+Joyce+&st=0&pn=1
http://www.iwm.org.uk/history/evacuation#
http://www.lacasadelosroper.com/es
https://www.minder.org/#
https://mobile.twitter.com/msyoothajoyce
http://www.motorcycle-uk.com/lmm/beginning.html
http://www.oxforddnb.com/templates/article.jsp?articleid=74665&back=
http://www.petersfieldmuseum.co.uk/education/loan-evacuees-suitcase.php
http://www.petersfieldpost.co.uk/news/evacuees-reunite-again-1-698113
http://rodmcneiltv.wordpress.com/about/
http://www.roger-moore.com/old/Roger/sirrogermoore/november2007.htm
http://www.shadyoldlady.com/location.php?loc=2209
https://sites.google.com/site/yoothajoycearchive/
https:www.sheilasteafel.co.uk/
http://sparksinelectricaljelly.blogspot.co.uk/2011/02/sparrows-cant-sing-portrait-of-queenie.html?spref=tw
http://www.sporthorse-data.com/d?i=10598024
http://springboardarts.blogspot.co.uk/2012_08_01_archive.html
http://www.startrader.co.uk/wed_play/wed_ep_07.htm
http:wwwstratfordeast.com/
http://www.stuff.co.nz/manawatu-standard/features/5834314/Welcome-to-the-world-of-Bruce-Warwick
http://www.tcm.com/this-month/article/176226%7C0/Die-Die-My-Darling-.html
http://www.theatrevoice.com/2156/interview-murray-melvin-the-veteran-actor-and-member-of-joa/
http://www.theclaphamgrand.com/Club/index.php
http://twgpp.org/information.php?id=2827922
http://www.valendale.myby.co.uk/entertainment.html
http://www.whosdatedwho.com/tpx_687109/george-and-mildred/crew
http://wipednews.com/tag/yootha-joyce/

Coming Soon.... Dear Yootha... The life of Yootha Joyce (The Play)

Printed in Poland
by Amazon Fulfillment
Poland Sp. z o.o., Wrocław